BEYOND THE PILLARS OF
HERCULES

Other books in

THE GREAT EXPLORERS SERIES

published by Tandem Books

conceived by
Vilhjalmur Stefansson

general editor
Evelyn Stefansson Nef

Beyond the Pillars of Hercules

The classical world seen through
the eyes of its discoverers

RHYS CARPENTER

14 Gloucester Road, London SW7 4RD

Originally published in the United States as *Beyond the Pillars of Hercules* by Delacorte Press, 1966

First published in Great Britain by
Universal-Tandem Publishing Co. Ltd, 1973

Acknowledgment is made to Methuen & Co. Ltd, London,
for permission to quote from
The Ancient Explorers
by M. Cary and E. H. Warmington

Maps by Veronica Laing

LIST OF MAPS

MAN DISCOVERS
HIS EARTH

The following statement was found among Vilhjalmur Stefansson's papers after his death. Despite its lack of a final paragraph, it forms such an appropriate introduction to the Great Explorers Series *that I cannot help thinking it was so intended.*

EVELYN STEFANSSON NEF
Washington, D.C.
November, 1944

THE Great Age of Discovery is, in many books, the name for a group of centuries that began in the thirteenth with Marco Polo and Henry the Navigator, included Columbus, Cabot and Magellan, and closed with the death of James Cook in 1779. But calling this a great age is no more than a self-centered characterization by Europeans of their own awakening to a vivid knowledge of the rest of the world. Some, a degree more broadminded, would start the history of discovery with the voyage to Britain and Iceland by Pytheas about 330 B.C. and end it with the attainment of a pole of the earth by Robert E. Peary on April 6, 1909.

But (with the exception of things like reaching the spot farthest from the equator or climbing highest above sea level) the famous "discoveries" of history will mostly turn out to be rediscoveries, and thus second-rate. The British were there ahead of Pytheas when the Greeks "discovered" Britain; the Eskimos were in Labrador ahead of the Norse Leif; the Indians were in the West Indies ahead of the Latin Columbus; the Maoris were in New Zealand ahead of the Dutch Tasman.

The true discoverers of every land were those who stepped upon shores where human foot had never trod. Theirs was the great romance. It began at man's cradle in the tropics a million or two million years ago; only the last few paragraphs of its last chapter exist as written history found in hieroglyphics, ideographs, runes or script. But the story of the Great Romance can nevertheless be read, for it has survived through indubitable characters that we decipher by the light of sciences like paleontology, archeology, anthropology, physiology, comparative linguistics, and the dozen or score of other disciplines that can be brought to bear on the problems of the history and nature of man.

The supreme romance of human achievement is how man discovered his earth, how he groped his way farther and farther from the place of his origin till he reached the outermost shore of the farthest land.

Man never discovered the tropics, for that is where he originated. If any creature ever was, man is completely a warm-weather product. By nature completely tropical, he cannot live except under tropical conditions. He is not furred like a rabbit or feathered like a grouse; what hair he has on his body is not well distributed to keep him warm. So, of necessity, his movements were confined to his native lands of perpetual summer until he found out at last how to carry an artificial tropic climate around with him. This he eventually managed, through garments that conserved the warmth created by the heating mechanism of his body.

Man's ability to move afield from his natal region, to become an explorer and colonist of new lands, was increased by a secondary discovery, that through the use of fire within a shelter he could devise stationary asylums of tropical warmth where he was safe from the inclemency of a nontropical winter.

When our ancestors became carnivorous, which is supposed to have happened a million years ago, an inexorable need began to draw them into new districts. For it is in the nature of things that a group of hunters will thin out the game of a region or destroy it entirely, whereupon they are encouraged if not forced to move into parts that have not been depleted.

At first such migrations by ancient man were free of climatic restraint, for people could move east and west and still remain in the tropics. This was no tiny concentration camp; the tropics is a belt more than 3,000 miles wide from north to south and more than 11,000 miles long from east to west. For man's first home is supposed to have been in the Old World tropics, meaning that these early hunter-explorers had all of central and most of northern Africa through which to seek new gamelands, as well as southern Asia. Within these millions of square miles our ancestors were free to wander unclad and unhoused.

Both north and south of primitive man's tropic paradise were border lands deceptively promising in the warmth of summer but cruel to naked man in the chill of winter. These belts of alternating friendliness and hostility must have caused trouble to hapless groups that strayed too far during the temperate-zone summer. When winter came, these adventurers retreated or died; the rest, who had luck on their side, spread east and west till the Old World tropics had been explored and populated.

But tropical lands are not, on the whole, good hunting grounds; they are likely to be forested if they are rainy or deserts if they are dry. From the hunter's point of view a dense forest is practically a desert. Most game animals are grass eaters and so are found in glades, in sparse forests, in reedy marshes and in such prairie areas as are fortunately intermediate in climate between the rain forest and the rainless desert. It is the temperate zone and the Arctic that, along with some tropical uplands, contain the great prairies with their vast herds of grazing animals.

The belly is a nagging taskmaster, and necessity is the mother of invention. Those two sayings explain to us what we know must have happened. Man, physically weak in comparison with the lion, tiger and many of the rest of his hunting competitors, would not have survived except that he was an inventor. Necessity told him he simply had to devise a way of following the game into the lands of chill winter.

Early man's progress through invention was no doubt mainly by trial and error. If there were philosophers in those times, they must have reasoned as we do: "Man cannot live except under conditions of perpetual summer; but he must eat, and there is more food on the winter-chilled prairies than in the overwarm forests; besides, we have already thinned out the game in our tropical homelands and must leave them, at least some of us. But we need continual warmth; so we must discover a way to carry the tropics around with us wherever we desire to go."

And so it became possible for each man to carry around a personal climate, through the invention of garments that conserve body heat.

Protected by clothes, fortified by skill in building or discovering shelters and in using fire, man was launched upon his great adventure, the conquest of hostile nontropical countries. Southward the early hunters could not move far, since there is relatively little Old World land beyond Capricorn, merely the southern tip of Africa and perhaps southern Australia, if that continent was then attainable. But northward from the Tropic of Cancer vast regions awaited the migrant—northern Africa, all of Europe, most of Asia. To invade these grasslands and forests, our forebears had to devise ways and means for staying alive through lengthening and more chilly winters. This they managed, chiefly by the gradual improvement of clothes and houses.

Winter proved in the temperate zones pioneer man's only new and serious problem. As he moved north or south he adjusted himself to increasingly nontropical and therefore hostile conditions by wearing more and more clothes during the longer and colder winters into which he had to follow the game. But at last he approached diminishing returns: a northward boundary line beyond which furred beasts and feathered birds prospered but where unfurred and unfeathered man found conditions more and more distressing because his clothes became increasingly heavy, bulky and stiff.

At this stage of his world conquest, man made increasing use of his stationary tropics device, the house; he constructed better ones, used more fuel in them, and resorted more frequently and for longer periods to their protection. By accumulating food during the summer and storing it for winter use near the house, he gained advantages similar to those of beasts that hibernate.

Behind primitive man on his northern invasion there was little game because it had been killed off. Before were lands well stocked with grazing animals, because man, a far more devastating hunter than the tiger or the wolf, had never been there to wreak his destruction. There would be no end to this enticement; for new game country would always be ahead of the people as they moved north. The depleted lands were always behind because the hunters themselves had gathered the crop.

This was the general rule; but there must have been exceptions, the chief of which probably were in relation to fishing. There is little doubt that man became a fisher almost or quite as early as he became a hunter, although his fishing methods may not have improved so rapidly. Fishing grounds are hard to deplete. Even in modern times, with the tremendous destruction wrought by our modern gadgets, the fisheries of waters like the North Sea and the Baltic keep replenishing themselves in a way that is not possible on land after a similar carnivorous destruction, such as that, for instance, which swept the bison from our North American prairies and which is now sweeping the eland from the plains of Africa and the caribou from the prairies of the Far North.

So it must have happened from time to time in the northward march of early man that he found districts that there was no reason to abandon on the score of depleted food supply, places comparable to the Oregon-Alaska section of the coast of North America, which has a steady output of salmon after a hundred years of such modern destruction as primitive man could never wreak. There was probably no section quite so large and productive as our northwestern salmon country to detain early man as he gradually moved northward through Europe and Asia, but still the lesson is applicable.

Today our marvelous commerce is so taken for granted that we find it a little hard to realize that the northward compulsion that we have described must have applied not merely to the earliest men when they were hunters and gatherers but must also have continued to apply 100,000 years later when herding and agriculture had been developed. For a striking difference of the last hundred or so years from all the times that went before is that now, for the first time, it is almost universally possible to live in one place on food that comes from another. Formerly, men had nothing to eat except what they and their near neighbors produced locally.

It is commonplace nowadays that, if you are a movie star in Hollywood, a banker on Wall Street, or in some other way the possessor of a large income, you can dine at any time of year on any sort of food from any country you like—caviar from the Soviet Union, figs from the not so Near East, potatoes from Idaho, oranges from Florida, whale steak from the Antarctic. This ability results not merely from our steamship lines, railways, highways and airways, but also from a ramified system of exchange: foreign and domestic trade. As recently as two thousand years ago there were only a few cities, like Rome, that could depend in considerable part on food from remote countries. Most cities and every village had to draw mainly upon surrounding farmlands and local fisheries, and this held true until there were railways as well as steamers.

The difficult thing about man's territorial conquest was always the move that took him north. We have pointed to the obvious truth that, in the earliest times, the explorers and settlers could move freely east and west within the tropics, because they required neither houses nor clothes. They needed both in order to leave the tropics at all. But once they had made a northing of say a thousand miles, they could move freely east and west from that vantage point. For the houses and clothes that were a sufficient protection during winter in Greece would also be sufficient westward into Italy and Spain or eastward through Turkey and down past the southern end of the Caspian. When a culture had been developed anywhere that was good enough to face a winter of two or three months and a temperature well below freezing, then the possessor was equipped to live in the style to which he was accustomed in any other land of similar winters. So far as climate went, he was free to move east or west to any distance; but, if he wanted to continue northward into new country, he would have to improve his clothes, houses, and general technique of fighting or evading cold.

It seems to us likely that primitive man made his progress northward over the land, and forward in culture, without any great amount of such philosophical speculations as are today more or less forced upon us when we try to picture what his intellectual and physical progress must have been. The hunter who knew that the game lands to the south of him were no longer well stocked while those to the north offered relative abundance was probably not at the same time conscious that he was being enticed into a locality of colder and longer winters. But whether he expected it or not, he did meet with slightly more severe winters as he moved to the considerably better game lands. The process must have been costly in suffering and in life.

But it is our byword for nature that she is prodigal; she kills a thousand that one may survive. Many of the pioneer hunters suffered greatly and many died. But there was progress northward in latitude, and there was progress upward in culture, at least in the utilization of clothes, houses, and fuel.

But the time must have come at last, or at any rate it would have come in some districts, when the best clothes the hunter could devise were no longer good enough to enable him to move about freely during the midwinter period. Then he must have developed the art of preserving food. He would accumulate supplies during autumn, storing them near the house for winter. So provided, he would no longer have to call upon the portable tropics within his clothing for protracted midwinter hunting but could take asylum in the stationary tropics of his house, thus securing some of the advantages of beasts that hibernate.

Semihibernation by going into winter quarters, like the armies of Cornwallis and Washington, has its disadvantages, but with these we are likely to be overimpressed, for we think nowadays, and have thought for 10,000 or more years, chiefly in terms of agriculture. It is the farmer rather than the hunter who goes into winter quarters and derives from his house the benefits of hibernation. It is the plowman who can most easily store up food, especially grain. And he stores up hay to feed his barnyard cattle. The plow does not serve if he tries in winter to cultivate the soil; and, since he cannot then reap or sow, he is naturally led toward the winter-quarters style of life.

Not so with the hunter. The game animals are well furred and many of them prosper as well in winter with snow on the ground as in summer when it is hot with mud and mosquitoes. The beasts move around freely at all seasons and the hunter is strongly motivated to do likewise. For 40,000 years, if not for a longer period, man has had such good clothing that he has been able to move about practically as freely as the game animals during the coldest winters on earth, those of northern Siberia.

As to speed or slowness in human learning, the guiding principle seems to be that advance is rapid when a people have once embarked upon a cultural advance along a certain definite line, but that advance in a new line is slow. An example of speed when once well started is the geometric progression we have observed among ourselves the last few years in the advances of physics, whereas in the realm of sociology we have advanced hardly at all. We of today are in a frame of mind to do anything anybody tells us, if he speaks as a chemist, physicist, or engineer; we are stubborn, balky and even likely to retrogress if somebody wants us to move ahead along sociological lines.

But it was sociological progress that hunting man needed when he was being restrained at the edge of the forest by a woodland culture but tempted in the direction of the prairie by the abundance of food.

VILHJALMUR STEFANSSON

INTRODUCTION

SEVERAL thousand years ago a nameless Mycenean artist made a golden cup that still glistens in that amazing storehouse of meaningful riches, the National Museum in Athens, Greece. I had read about the cup and seen pictures of it, but when I looked at it for the first time last summer, it caught me unawares and I found myself involuntarily exclaiming aloud with pure pleasure. This communication from the deep past by an unknown person, whom I suddenly "knew" because of the emotional response he had evoked, is largely what this book and others in the Great Explorers Series is about. Our concern is not with the differences between our own and other cultures, but rather with the thin, strong cord of human sameness that connects us with all our ancestors of whatever age: the quality that speaks to us sharply and immediately from lines of poetry that, millennia after they were composed, remind us of half-known but newly recognizable truths; or the white line of the Parthenon's Doric columns, striking as a blow at first sight; or the universal connection that rules that we laugh where Aristophanes' audiences have always laughed and weep where Euripides designed that we should; the power that finds us equally speechless with admiration before a huge archaic Greek sculpture or a tiny ancient Eskimo ivory carving, both of which we recognize as related and modern, *our* modern, although the two works are separated by thousands of geographical miles and years of time.

It was Vilhjalmur Stefansson, with whom I worked for more than twenty years, who first taught me the importance of going back to firsthand sources. Stef had collected what, back in the

1940's, was the largest polar library in the world. It was staffed by as many as twenty researchers. We were in the business of supplying polar information to industry, government and individuals; therefore the library was designed as an everyday working tool rather than a collector's hobby. Stef believed religiously in gathering and quoting, wherever possible, original sources in preference to all others, and he preached the gospel to his staff. He insisted that, however old, certain kinds of information were interesting and useful a decade, century or millennium after they were written and that the chances were good that any original was more accurate than later reports. He had a horror of writers who mirrored their prejudices by "improving" a narrative, often cutting out just those nuggets of information most needed by a researcher to give life to the past. To prove his thesis, he published *Great Adventures and Explorations,* a book composed largely of carefully selected quotations, which was a great success. This present series is a natural, expanded outgrowth of that original idea. We planned it together but he did not live to see the first completed manuscript.

It is a painful commentary on the workings of the human mind to discover that, in some cases, the little we know about some of our explorers—Pytheas, whom we encounter in this volume, is a good example—is due to their having been considered terrible liars by their contemporaries. The strange, new facts they recited on returning from an expedition often excited the ridicule and disbelief of orthodox geographers and writers of their time. Most of what we know about Pytheas is derived from the derisive passages preserved in the works of his critics, while his own books were lost. Centuries can pass before another explorer retraces the path of his predecessor and returns to pronounce the "lies" to be truth. What was thought fiction may turn out later to be the certain proof that an explorer did exactly what he said he did, since it is unlikely that anyone could improvise facts at once so strange and so accurate.

Some 2,000 years after Pytheas, Stefansson encountered much the same kind of difficulty when he returned from an expedition to announce that, contrary to common belief, animal life *did* exist in the Arctic Sea and that he had survived for months on the moving sea ice by hunting that life, in the form of seals and polar bears. As a result of this "preposterous statement," some called him a charlatan and a liar. Years later Ivan Papanin's 1936 North Pole expedition confirmed Stef's findings, as did Admiral Calvert's more recent trans-Arctic voyage in the U.S.S. *Skate*, the nuclear-powered submarine. Stef was philosophical about the matter, saying: "Man finds it easier to change the face of nature than to change his own mind."

However painful, during the last few decades man has been forced to change his mind often and radically about the age and behavior of his ancestors. To the relatively new science of archeology, modern genius has given strange, extremely accurate methods of dating ancient finds involving the use of radioactive carbon 14, argon, thermoluminescence, and other equally mysterious and seemingly magical techniques. Remarkable intellectual feats have matched the technical achievements, the most moving perhaps being the deciphering of Linear B script from ancient Crete by the brilliant young architect *amateur* Michael Ventris. Leakey's discoveries in Africa have played havoc with our past ideas of how long man and his close ancestors have occupied the earth, making obsolete innumerable published chronologies. Last year, what appears to be the first genuine discovery of physical evidence that the Norsemen were in North America was made by the Helge Ingstads, a Norwegian husband-and-wife team. Here, too, a surprise was provided by sixteen-year-old Tony Beardsley. Taken along as a handyman, he found the sole artifact. From all these happenings we must conclude not only that man has been on the earth longer than we thought, but that on the whole he has always been far more sophisticated than we gave him credit for being.

Beyond the Pillars of Heracles, more than any of the eight volumes of the Great Explorers Series that will follow it, is concerned with prehistory, especially archeology. It deals with the seeds of history so early in time that surviving materials, whether carved in stone or written on clay tablets or skin, are sparse in number and detail. The task of the editor in this case is Herculean (to use a classical idiom), for he must deal not with the sets of solid fact available for more recent happenings but with an enormously wide range of speculations, however informed. We are singularly fortunate that the first-born of the series bears the name of the distinguished Bryn Mawr professor Dr. Rhys Carpenter, who brings a formidable constellation of talents to his difficult task. He is a classicist, an archeologist, a linguist who translates the narratives he quotes. He has been the Director of the American School of Classical Studies in Athens, and he is a recognized authority on Greek art. But from our point of view his most valuable asset, rare among high-ranking scholars, is the ability to write about learned matters with clarity, enthusiasm and style.

It is the hope of the editor and the purpose of the Great Explorers Series to increase the respect and admiration we feel for our ancestors and provide enjoyable avenues of communication with them.

EVELYN STEFANSSON NEF

BEYOND
THE PILLARS
OF HERCULES

THE ROLL OF HONOR

DIOGENES IGNOTUS

EUDOXUS OF CYZICUS

EUTHYMENES OF MASSALIA

HANNO OF CARTHAGE

HIMILCO OF CARTHAGE

KOLAIOS OF SAMOS

THE FIVE NASAMONIANS OF AUJILA

NEARCHOS OF CRETE

PYTHEAS OF MASSALIA

and

All the Nameless Explorers
Whom Written History Has Ignored
and Man's Memory Forgotten

❦ I ❦

THE NAMELESS
ADVENTURERS

BECAUSE human beings of one sort or another have inhabited the earth during many hundreds of thousands of years, they must have spread far and wide across the continents in the course of that enormous stretch of time. It follows that there can be no such thing as unexplored land—unless it be what the polar ice covers or the ocean hides among its most distant reaches. Exploring, therefore, must be understood as the activity of searching out other peoples' territory—except where this chances to lie within the polar ice or in uninhabited atolls of the ocean or atop the highest mountain ranges or, lastly, in the heart of the most arid deserts. And even these deserts can hardly be termed totally unexplored, in view of the fact that, like the Sahara and inner Arabia, they have not always been desert nor yet deserted. There is incontrovertible evidence that some 10,000 years ago most of the Sahara was green pastureland with flowing streams that fed and watered herds of tended cattle. It cannot be asserted that there is any nook or corner of the huge Sahara that has not at some time or another been occupied by men. To say that enormous areas of the Sahara remained unexplored until the nineteenth century merely means that these regions had not until then been visited and examined by any European traveler. To ask what men first explored Africa or the steppes of Asia or the forestlands of Europe is to pose a question that, by its very nature, admits no rational answer.

There is another preliminary consideration that should be clarified. The Roman poets were fond of pointing out that the memory of great men and their deeds survived only because they, the poets, celebrated them in their poems and thus immortalized them. In this conceit—as is the way with literary men—the poets were taking rather too much credit to themselves. Nevertheless it is true that, except where an event has been recorded in writing and the written record has survived, human memory must lose contact with the past achievements of the race. On this account, of all of the explorations on this great planetary globe of ours, more than two-thirds of which is immersed in seawater and not a little is held fast in ice, nothing certain can be known today save what was once recorded in some form of written speech and, having been recorded, can still be read and understood. It is therefore an obvious truism to say that most of the company of the Great Explorers in times long past (yet not only those of remoter days!) resemble the Unknown Soldier of our contemporary wars in that we cannot discover their names nor have any certain knowledge of what they did.

Archeology and ethnology can sometimes succeed in tracing, by inference, the movement of people from one region to another, long ago. But this sort of exploration, whether by peaceful migration or militant invasion, is not the theme of the present volume, which undertakes to rehearse the achievements of those individuals in antiquity whose explorations were of sufficient magnitude and daring to earn them the title of "Great," and which, through one chance or another, can still today be traced on the map and intelligibly set forth in print.

Because of the restrictions thus imposed, this initial volume in the Great Explorers Series must confine itself to the comparatively small portion of the world that was literate in antiquity and was concerned to put itself on record in such matters as voyages of exploration by sea or land. Ages passed before it occurred to men that invisible speech, which dissipates itself even as it is uttered, may be transmuted into visible and enduring form by means of conventional graphic signs. Thus defined, the device of writing will be seen to be by no means a self-evident and inevitable invention, but a recondite and highly ingenious discovery, whose occurrence marked an epochal

moment in civilized progress. Actually, the art of writing has
no greater age than five thousand years or so and has been
widely diffused for less than three thousand. Originating at
much the same period in lower Mesopotamia and in Egypt—
though whether independently or through cultural contact is
not at present known—it developed into two widely divergent
systems, the wedge-shaped abstract patterns of Mesopotamian
cuneiform and the concrete pictorial images of Egyptian hieroglyphic. Fortunately, both systems can be read and their sense
understood by present-day scholars. But unfortunately for the
purposes of the present volume, neither cuneiform nor hieroglyphic writing has much of importance to say about voyages of
exploration. Quite possibly, none of any great scope was ever
undertaken.

Both Mesopotamia and Egypt were riverlands, shut in by
formidable desert and arid mountain country discouraging to
penetrate and unattractive to explore. In consequence, political
intercourse and commerce moved upstream and downstream
without much interest in lateral extension into the adjacent
regions beyond the arable domain. Yet, human nature being
what it always has been, curiosity or social compulsion must
have led or driven many men at many times into the surrounding desert and mountains. But scarcely any record remains of
their activity, despite the fact that the Egyptians were much
addicted to making written records of themselves.

Something, however, has survived to prove that the nearly
lifeless lands shutting in the Nile valley were not left wholly
unvisited in antiquity. The eastern mountains with their
barrier of high, wild uplands between the Red Sea and the
Nile were penetrated from the earliest dynastic period by pros-
pecting parties searching for gold and precious stones, notably
emeralds and turquoise (also discovered in abundance in the
Sinai Peninsula), and by workmen quarrying hard volcanic rock
for statuary and sarcophagi and other perdurable uses, especially the incredibly resistant porphyry of the waterless "Mountain of Smoke," on which the Romans later relied for their
supply. In addition, there were developed caravan routes for
traffic between the Red Sea coast and the Nile valley. Along the
track of these, in the heart of the abruptly Alpine wastelands,
hieroglyphic inscriptions cut in rocky walls keep company with

Greek, Coptic, Arabic, Himyaritic, and Sinaitic characters to testify to the five thousand years of coming and going through this inhospitable wilderness. But if we ask who it was that first explored and opened up these passageways between the river and the sea, no answer can be given.

Westward of the Nile, across the plateau of its enclosing cliffs of sandstone and limestone, there stretches a seemingly endless waste of gravel, rock, and sand. In the midst of this there exist occasional depressions wherein subsurface water rises through breaks in the sandstone bed to create the desert islands of fertility called oases. Although these lie widely separated from one another and are rarely less than one hundred miles distant from the Nile valley, these comfortable spots in an otherwise comfortless land were known to the ancient Egyptians from early times. But again, if we ask who first discovered their existence, no answer can be given. Indeed, it may be that the question itself is wrongly framed, because the oases may have been inhabited before the Nile valley, when the Saharan zone was still a vast grazing ground and the Nile trough was impenetrable marshy jungle. In that case it was the "desert" dwellers who discovered the Nile rather than the Nile dwellers who wandered out to explore the desert.

But, however much or little known to them, the arid world on either side of their well-watered valley remained repellent to the Egyptians, who (except in the spreading fan of the Delta) lived on the long narrow ribbon of the Nile in what has aptly been termed a "one-dimensional existence" of length without breadth. If one moved at all, one went upstream or downstream, with the river for road and a ship for vehicle. A meteorological accident made communication easy.

In Egyptian hieroglyphic writing the word for journeying upriver on the Nile used a symbol depicting a ship with upright mast and raised sail, whereas the word for travel downstream was written with a sailless boat afloat upon the sign for water. The distinction between the two hieroglyphic symbols was founded on everyday experience. The trade wind, which across most of the Mediterranean Sea blows only during the summer months, prevails during the rest of the year over the northern end of the Red Sea and the whole length of the Nile valley from Cairo to Aswan. Though differing greatly in size, both these basins extending southward between parallel ranges of much loftier land act as funnels to draw the great air current of the trade wind on its low-level return toward the equatorial zone. On the less confined Red Sea, meteorological conditions are not entirely stable; but up the enclosed valley of the Nile south of the Delta, a north wind, blowing steadily but without undue violence, may be counted on through most of the year. With sail hoisted and wind on the stern quarter or directly astern, a sailing vessel could proceed uninterruptedly upstream against the current. But this current, running with even greater constancy northward, would serve to carry the same vessel downstream without use of oar or paddle, once the sail was lowered and stored away. In view of this wonderfully convenient disposition for facilitating travel along their sole line of communication, it is easy to comprehend why the ancient Egyptians believed that Hapi, the god of the Nile, had them under his special protection. Besides, it was Hapi who flooded their fields to keep them fertile.

Nature had thus dictated to the Egyptians the directions that exploration could profitably take. Northward beyond the Delta the open Mediterranean deterred them with its emptiness. There is no evidence that Egyptian ships ever ventured far out upon it. They at most confined themselves with following its shoreline westward as far as Cyrenaica, with its often hostile Libyan tribes, and eastward to Palestine and Syria, where they encountered more competent mariners than themselves, the seaboard Phoenicians. The landways out of Egypt were unalluring and perilous for want of food and water. Save for those along the Mediterranean coast, which led to the Libyans and to Palestine (and these too were waterless desert tracks), the landways led nowhere. If one went east out of the Nile valley, the final journey's end was always the same Red Sea; if one turned westward, there was only the boundless emptiness of the Sahara. Under these restricting conditions, exploration for the Egyptian had to be by water rather than by land. To the Egyptian mind, travel was a shipborne enterprise.

In consequence, there were only two routes open for profitable exploration of the outside world. Both of these led south into the tropics. And both were attractive in that they assured the explorer of safe return to his native land by never breaking his line of communication. If he followed the Nile upstream into Ethiopia or the Sudan, no matter to what distance, the Nile would always lead him home again. Or if he took to the Red Sea and cruised south along its western shore, he could journey onward for more than a thousand miles, and the coast would always be there to guide him back to the port from which he had set out. Necessarily these routes, being by water all the way, were available only to those who could build ships and knew how to work them. Those who elected to keep to the Nile needed lighter rivercraft that could be dismantled and conveyed around rapids and other obstacles. Those who essayed the less gentle waters of the Red Sea required much more strongly constructed and better-rigged oceangoing ships. But these restrictions on Egyptian exploration do not define the period in which such expeditions were undertaken. As far back as the Egyptian records run, the Nile folk knew how to build boats, barges, and ships of various types for moving themselves, their cattle, and their commerce upon their river. As early as the reign of Snofru (ca. 2720 B.C.), immediate ancestor of the builders of the great pyramids, there is mention of building seagoing wooden ships, with a length of 150 feet, capable of making the voyage to Lebanon or of navigating the Red Sea. Already from the latter part of the sixth dynasty, around the year 2300 B.C., there are records of trips to the Upper Nile above the cataracts, as well as to Palestine and Syria and to a land whose name is written *Pwnt* (popularly known as "Punt" among modern historians), which was located near the southern end of the Red Sea or beyond it on the Somali coast.

The original occasions on which these various regions were first visited by Egyptian navigators over hitherto unvoyaged routes, opening up knowledge of lands previously denied to their countrymen, escapes us utterly. No personal names attach to exploits of exploration far or near; and only purely hypothetical dates may be suggested for the anonymous explorers who were the forerunners of Egyptian commerce with the outside world. No doubt such explorers existed; and perhaps their accomplishments were such as to merit them the title of Great Explorers and put them in the company of those with whom the present volume is concerned. But we shall never know who they were or where they went or what they did. At best, we can only guess at the scope of their unrecorded voyages by noting how these voyages were repeated later by others whose names have chanced to be preserved. For sake of the light that these "secondary explorers" may shed on their dimly discernible predecessors, it should be of interest to reproduce here in translation the Egyptian records that relate to them.

Among several notices of expeditions into the Nile lands south of the First Cataract the most extensive document is one carved on the facade of the rock-cut tomb of an Egyptian nobleman named Harkhuf, who was (according to his own account) a high official in the king's service and had been engaged in upriver expeditions beyond the First Cataract into Nubian territory. On two occasions he went without any show of armed force "to open up the way" and establish trade relations with various Nubian tribes. From a third journey he returned with a caravan of three hundred asses laden with such wares as incense, ebony, panther skins, ivory and "every good product," along with assurances of native friendship and cooperation. Finally, under a succeeding king, he made still another journey into Nubia and on this occasion brought back with him, in addition to the expected products of the south, "a dancing dwarf from the land of ghosts." Notice of the safe arrival of this strange trophy at Aswan aroused such excited interest in his royal master that a correspondence ensued between captain and king, which Harkhuf caused to be inscribed in full on the facade of his tomb.

Wrote the king's scribe to Harkhuf:

> I have noted the content of your letter which you have sent to the king to make known your safe return from the land of Yam with your armed force. . . . In this letter you say that you have brought a dancing dwarf of the god from the land of spirits, like the dwarf that the divine treasurer *Ba-wr-dd* brought from *Pwnt* in the time of King Issi.[1] You say, "Never before has the like of him been brought by anyone else who has visited Yam."

Apparently much intrigued by the news of the "dancing dwarf," the king sent the following instructions to Elephantine

---

[1] One of the last kings of the preceding dynasty, who reigned shortly after 2500 B.C.

(Aswan) commanding Harkhuf to bring him at once to the royal court at Memphis (near Cairo):

> Come north to the court immediately and bring with you this dwarf that you have brought alive, healthy, and in good state from the land of spirits, for the god's dances, to rejoice the heart of the king, lord of Upper and Lower Egypt, *Nofr-ka-Ra*, living forever. When he enters into your ship, set excellent people to be beside him on either hand, and take care that he does not fall into the water. When he is asleep at night, set excellent people to sleep beside him under the canopy, and do you yourself make ten inspections every night. My Majesty desires to see this dwarf more than all the gifts of Sinai and of *Pwnt*. If you arrive at court with this dwarf alive, healthy, and in good condition, my Majesty will do more for you than was done for the divine treasurer *Ba-wr-dd* in the time of Issi, such is my Majesty's desire to behold this dwarf.

For King Pyopi the dwarf may have been the object of his greatest interest; but for us who can never behold this creature and are chiefly concerned with Egyptian exploration, the real matter of importance is the mention of the land of *Pwnt*. To this there will be further reference a little later on.

From the tenor of Harkhuf's reports it seems that his Nubian explorations were conducted on foot, whereas the five-hundred-mile trip from the Cataract to the royal city of Memphis was of course made by ship. River ships, equipped with cabins and capable of carrying a considerable load of goods, crew, and passengers, had long been navigating the Nile. More than four hundred years before Harkhuf's time, under the first of the pyramid builders, construction of ships of surprising size is already on record. On the great document known as the Palermo Stone the following entries appear under the dateline of one of the years of Snofru's reign, to be set about 2720 B.C.:

> Construction of 150-foot *dw'-t'-wy* ships of *mr* wood.

and for the following year again:

> Construction of a 150-foot *dw'-t'-wy* ship of cedar wood and two 150-foot ships of *mr* wood.

The mention of cedar wood is significant, and still more so the entry under the preceding year of

> Arrival of forty ships laden with cedar wood.

Such a cargo must have originated in Syrian Lebanon, where alone there were cedar trees growing on the mountains, and its transportation to Egypt must have been over the open water of the Mediterranean, past Palestine, to a mouth of the Nile. But it should be observed that the record does not state that the forty ships that brought the cedar wood were *Egyptian* ships; and it is an open question whether in Snofru's day any Egyptian fleet ever plied the Mediterranean Sea. It is entirely possible that (as is known to have happened in later times) delivery of the cedar was left to the Phoenicians, who felled them on the high, steep slopes behind their seaboard towns. But on either explanation, the large number of ships in the fleet is remarkable for such early times.

Whether or not the Egyptians built ships that were seaworthy enough to exchange the placid water of the Nile for the often turbulent Mediterranean, there can be no doubt that they navigated the somewhat less stormy, but by no means windless and waveless, Red Sea and ventured on coasting voyages along its western shore that may have taken them the better part of a thousand miles from their port of sail. This is the conclusion that must be drawn from the reference to *Pwnt* in Harkhuf's mention of a dwarf imported from that land "in the time of Issi." There is further evidence from Harkhuf's own period in an inscription carved on either side of the doorway of a tomb next to his own, hewn like his in the rocky bank across the Nile from modern Aswan, opposite the island anciently known as Elephantine. Pyopi-nakht, who was here laid away, was a nobleman of rank and distinction, serving the king whose surname he bore, Pyopi Nofr-ka-Ra, the last great figure of the sixth dynasty. On the facade of his place of burial, Pyopi-nakht, "royal companion, ritual priest, leader of caravans, bringing the products of foreign lands to his lord," recounted his exploits: how he had traveled upstream beyond the Cataract into Nubian territory in order to pacify, or if necessary subdue by force of arms, its dissident tribes and semisavage peoples—all this to the great contentment of his sovereign and his own eminent satisfaction, as appears from his report on the expedition when

> the Majesty of my king sent me to hack up the Wawat and the Irchet. I did so, slaying a great number of chieftains' children and excellent commanders of soldiery. I brought many back to

the king's court alive as prisoners, myself a hero at the head of a mighty army. The heart of my lord the king was satisfied with me for every commission on which he sent me forth.

On another occasion he brought back, seemingly as hostages for good behavior,

> two chieftains of these lands together with chiefs' children and two captains of companies: also bulls and live goats.

Such punitive expeditions into the Nubian desert hardly rank as exploration. But a commission that led Pyopi-nakht in quite another direction hints at much more extensive voyaging down the Red Sea. Somewhere along that sea's western shore, perhaps at the port that was later given the Greek name of Berenice by the Ptolemies and was situated on the same latitude as Pyopi-nakht's Elephantine, an important naval officer of the king had been murdered by raiding "Beduins," and Pyopi-nakht was instructed to recover his body and bring it back for proper burial. He recounts the incident in some such words as these:

> Now the Majesty of my lord the king sent me to the country of the Easterners to convey the body of his royal companion, the captain of ships, the caravan leader, Anankht. He was building a ship there for a voyage to *Pwnt* when Easterners from among the Desert-wanderers slew him, together with a company of soldiers under his command.

Here again, as in the case of Harkhuf and the dwarf, it is the mention of the land of *Pwnt* that gives this entry its importance. As subsequent references to this same, somewhat mysterious country seem to prove, "Punt" lay south of the great desert belt that stretches from the Persian Gulf across Arabia and Africa to the Atlantic Ocean. Such a location for Punt follows from its reputed tropical fertility and the character of the products brought back by the Egyptian ships that found their way to it. But whether Punt should be identified with Eritrea at the extreme southern end of the Red Sea or with the southern shore of the Gulf of Aden beyond, or with Aden itself in Arabia Felix, or even with the Somali coast of Africa fronting the Indian Ocean, has been much discussed and inconclusively debated. Whichever of these locations is favored, the fact that a commander serving King Pepi II (or Phiops or Pyopi, as the reader chooses to call him) was preparing to sail thither from

Berenice, or some such Red Sea port, suggests that there must have been Egyptian expeditions by sea at least as far as the Strait of Bab el Mandeb at the southernmost tip of the Arabian peninsula by the middle of the third millennium B.C. But what Egyptian first explored this passageway to the great ocean will presumably never be known. But of Punt itself there is much more to say.

Its products, notably incense and myrrh, had been reaching Egypt from the time of the pyramid builders, though not necessarily by direct contact between Egyptians and Puntites. The earliest instance of an Egyptian emissary's actual visit to Punt seems to be the one to which Harkhuf referred when he noted that one of King Issi's officials, "the divine treasurer *Ba-wr-dd,*" had brought back to Egypt a dwarf from Punt. There are other notices of expeditions to the land during the period of the Middle Kingdom, shortly before and after the year 2000 B.C. But as Professor James Breasted, in listing them, observed, "None of these sources contain more than the meagerest references to the fact of the expedition." Then, in spectacular recompense for this niggardly information about the land, the people, and the products of Punt, there follows a carved pictorial account, with inscribed commentary, of a sea voyage to Punt in the ninth year of the reign of Queen Hatshepsut. Professor Breasted speaks of this as not merely the only early source of information about the land, but as "undoubtedly the most interesting series of reliefs" surviving from ancient Egypt, "as beautiful in execution as they are important in content." The sole complaint that can be brought against their vivid chronicle is the regrettable damage deliberately done to the carved likenesses of the queen by the brother who hated her memory, and the obliteration of some of the pictured scenes by the ill will of time and fortune.

The great figure of the opening years of the fifteenth century B.C. and the only woman ever to rule the Egypt of the pharaohs with the full title and dignity of kingship, Queen Hatshepsut entertained grandiose ideas for immortalizing herself and the achievements of her reign. She restored the temples desolated by the barbaric Semitic invasion of the "Chieftains of the Beduin," the *hkw-Shasw,* whom we know as the Hyksos. At Thebes she made additions to the great temple of Amun and erected there two enormous shafts of granite from Aswan, one of which still stands as the tallest obelisk in Egypt. But her greatest achievement was the construction of a huge mortuary temple at Deir el-Bahri across the Nile from modern Luxor, which may rank as the supreme attainment of the ancient Egyptian architects. Here, along the farther side of a great courtyard terrace, double rows of square pillars formed colonnades, and on the blank rear walls of these there were carved reliefs celebrating, in the right-hand colonnade, the divine procreation and birth of the queen and her consecration to the kingdom and, in the left, a shipborne expedition to the land of Punt accomplished at her command. This latter, the most interesting pictorial narrative surviving from preclassical antiquity, is securely documented by its accompanying hieroglyphic inscriptions detailing the successive stages and incidents of the journey. All this is too long for full inclusion here.[2] A summary survey of its scenes will make clear its scope and character:

SCENE 1: Departure of the fleet; two ships are still in mooring, three others are already under sail.

From the Inscriptions:

May Hathor, mistress of Punt, send favorable wind!

The sailing on the sea, beginning the goodly course toward God's Country in peaceful journey to the land of Punt.

SCENE 2: Arrival of the fleet in Punt, laden with merchandise for trading. The chieftain of Punt advances toward the Egyptians, followed by his spectacularly obese wife and three children. In the background, huts built on poles, among trees. Water (the sea?) in the foreground.

From the inscriptions:

The king's emissary in God's Country with his army behind him in presence of the headmen of Punt.

The coming of the headmen of Punt, doing obeisance with head bent low.

These say, "Wherefore are you come hither to this land that your people know not? Are you descended from the sky, or are you come by ship that sails upon the sea?"

---

[2] Those interested in more extensive acquaintance will find everything fully set forth in the second volume of Professor James H. Breasted's monumental collection *Ancient Records of Egypt* (5 vols., New York: Russell and Russell, Inc., 1963).

SCENE 3: Barter of Egyptian merchandise for products of Punt.
From the inscriptions:

Pitching of the tents of the king's emissary and his army on the
myrrh-tree terraces of Punt beside the sea.

SCENE 4: Loading the ships for the return journey. Two ships
are shown laden with cargo of incense trees in tubs, sacks of
incense, precious woods, ivory, and apes, with still more sacks
and trees being carried up the gangplank.
From the inscriptions:

Mind your feet, men! The load is passing heavy!
The loading of the ships heavily with marvelous things of the land
of Punt.

(The various items in the cargo are listed and include ebony,
ivory, cinnamon, several kinds of incense, monkeys, dogs, and
panther skins.)

Never was the like of this brought for any king since the beginning.

SCENE 5: The Return Journey. Three ships under full sail
are completely laden with cargo.
From the inscriptions:

The sailing, the peaceful arrival voyaging to Thebes.

SCENES 6–9: Presentation of the merchandise and the gifts of
the people of Punt to the Queen.
Dedication of gifts to the god Amun.
Measuring and weighing the merchandise brought back.
SCENE 10: The Queen before the god Amun.
Inscription: a long and fulsome text, in which particular in-
terest attaches to the mention of an oracle of Amun to the
effect that

the way to Punt shall be explored, the highways to the myrrh-
tree terraces shall be entered on

and the categoric statement put into Amun's mouth in a dec-
laration to the Queen:

I have given thee all of Punt, even as far as the region of the
gods of God's Country. No one before has trod the myrrh-tree
terraces. The people knew them not. They were but heard of
from mouth to mouth by hearsay of their ancestors.

The marvelous things brought from there under thy fathers, the kings of Lower Egypt, were passed from one to another in return for many payments. But I shall make thy armies to tread the terraces; I shall lead them on water and on land to explore the waters of inaccessible ways. For I have been to the terraces of myrrh. A glorious region is God's Country: the place it is of my delight!

In this pageant of pictured scenes and written words there are two matters of importance for the history of exploration. The first of these is the explicit assurance (which may not be founded on fact) that Hatshepsut's expedition to Punt was the first ever to reach that land, all previous communication having been through intermediaries in a succession of "many payments" from trader to trader. In that event, Queen Hatshepsut's expedition would have been in truth a voyage of exploration into the farthest confines of the Red Sea. However, the claim may have been an idle boast to heighten the queen's self-esteem. As already noted, some eight centuries earlier the "king's companion" Harkhuf recovered the body of an official who had been murdered on the Red Sea coast while "building a ship for Punt"—which certainly suggests that the sea passage to that land was already known. Later, but still long before Hatshepsut, there are four separate records of officials or nobles who assert that they had been to Punt.

The second matter of interest in the Deir el-Bahri chronicle of Hatshepsut's expedition may be somewhat more debatable, but seems to lead to a more certain conclusion. It hinges on an observation that cannot well be gainsaid and that has often been discussed among Egyptologists. Although the queen's fleet is not shown leaving Thebes on the Nile for the voyage to Punt, but is labeled as "sailing on the sea, taking the head of the way toward God's Country," it is nevertheless depicted and described as "journeying to Thebes" on its return to Egypt. The ships seem to be the same that were pictured landing and loading in Punt; and there is nowhere mention or representation of any transportation of the fleet's cargo overland from the Red Sea to the Nile. Yet the conveying of "thirty-one growing myrrh-trees" in tubs, to say nothing of all the other load of "marvelous things of Punt," on pack animals over desert mountain paths for the five-day caravan trek from El Qoseir on the Red Sea to Coptos on the Nile, with reshipment thence by river to Thebes, would have been a task of such magnitude that its successful accomplishment would not have been passed over in silence in the inscribed commentary nor omitted altogether from the pictured scenes. Besides, had the ships landed their cargoes at a Red Sea port for transport overland to Coptos, we should have expected to see these goods conveyed to Thebes in riverbarges and not in oceangoing sailing ships.

The unavoidable conclusion seems to be that Queen Hatshepsut's fleet was built at some Red Sea station—perhaps the one from which Harkhuf recovered the body of the murdered "captain of ships, the caravan leader" who was slain while "building a ship for a voyage to Punt"—and that this same fleet on its return from Punt somehow succeeded in passing from the Red Sea to the Nile and thus reached Thebes with all its cargo intact. This is not so fantastic a supposition as might be judged on first hearing. The whole matter hinges on the crucial question of who first opened up the Nile-Suez canal.

That such a canal existed and was in use for shipping in late classical times admits of no doubt whatever.

A century ago, when the modern Suez ship canal was being dug between the Mediterranean and the Red Sea, one of the difficulties encountered was that of supplying drinking water for the 25,000 native workmen on the project. For a time, the Canal Company was obliged to bring water daily on camelback from a considerable distance and at consequent expense. Then it was realized that fresh water could be channeled directly from the Nile across the intervening desert by the simple expedient of digging out the sanded and disused bed of an ancient canal connecting a branch of the Nile with an old lagoon of the Red Sea. It was learned that this canal had last been in effective operation about a thousand years before, in the time of the Arab conquest of Egypt. Before that, the Roman emperors (notably Trajan) and before these the Greek Ptolemies (notably the second Ptolemy, Philadelphus) had kept it in repair, so that ships could travel from the docks of Alexandria to the Indian Ocean by way of the Nile, the canal, and the Red Sea. But this surprising anticipation of our own Suez Canal, maintained in service through the centuries, was not the work of Greek engineers. As will be more fully explained in a later chapter, the Persian king Darius put it into active use about the year 500 B.C., almost precisely a hundred years after the Egyptian pharaoh Necho had made the attempt and failed. But it would be a mistake to conclude that the canal was Necho's original conception. He, too, was reviving a project fallen into disuse, a project whose original execution may already have been a thousand years older than he.

The truth of the matter is, that Nature herself had prepared the way for such a canal by opening a watercourse, the Wadi el-Tumîlât, through the low desert hills between the eastern edge of the Delta and the "Crocodile Lake" on the course of the present Suez Canal, about halfway between Port Said and Suez. Yet it was a human mind that thought of widening and deepening this natural passage through the desert and continuing it southward from the Crocodile Lake through the low rocky barrier separating it from the ancient "Bitter Lakes" and the once not so distant head of the Gulf of Suez. But it is not an easy matter to discover whose mind it was or whose the power responsible for carrying out this scheme for joining the Red Sea to the Nile. No surviving document names the king in whose reign ships first made the voyage from the great river to the even greater eastern water. There is, however, a piece of negative evidence seeming to show that no such canal was yet in existence in the year 2000 B.C.

Among the kings of the eleventh dynasty, in what is known as the Egyptian Middle Kingdom, one of the Mentuhoteps had for chief minister a noble whose name is spelled *Hnw* and whom we shall for convenience call Henu. This dignitary commemorated his services to his royal master in a long hieroglyphic inscription carved on the rock walls of the eastern desert valley through which the caravan route led from Upper Egypt to the Red Sea. Therein Henu recorded how King Mentuhotep

> sent me to dispatch a ship to Punt to bring him fresh myrrh. . . . I set forth from Coptos, and with me was an army of the South . . . that cleared the way before me, overthrowing those that were hostile to his Majesty.
>
> I went with three thousand men. I made the road to be even as a river, and the desert even as a sown field. To each man I gave a leather bottle, a carrying pole, two jars of water, and twenty loaves of bread. The asses were laden with sandals for

their feet. I dug two wells in the wasteland and three more in Idahet. I reached the Red Sea. I built then this ship. I dispatched it laden with everything [for trading in Punt].

So, on my return from the sea, I carried out his Majesty's command and brought him all the gifts found in the regions of God's Country.[3] I returned through the valley of Hammâmat.[4]

It is clear from this inscription that in the eleventh dynasty, and therefore until about the year 2000 B.C., traffic with Punt involved overland portage of the goods and merchandise (the "gifts" to the pharaoh) from a Red Sea port to the Nile in Upper Egypt. This does not completely exclude the possibility that the much longer all-water passage via Suez and the canal to the Delta was available in that period; but it strongly suggests that the canal was not yet in existence.

The Mentuhoteps were succeeded by a dynasty of much more powerful and energetic kings who made the Middle Kingdom one of the most prosperous and cultured periods in all Egyptian history. These rulers of the twelfth dynasty gave unusual attention to hydraulic works, especially for irrigating the great basin of the "Lake Land" known today as the Fayum. The most illustrious of this series of kings, Sen-wsrt III, became immortalized as the legendary Sesostris of the Greek historians. Accordingly, a certain amount of consideration must be paid to the account in Strabo's *Geography* where he speaks of the Nile–Red Sea canal and gives a brief summary of the history of its construction. The passage in question reads:

There is also [in the Delta] a canal that gives on the Red Sea and the Arabian Gulf near the city of Arsinoë.[5] It flows through the Bitter Lakes, as they are called, which were indeed bitter in former time but changed their nature through mixture with the river when the aforementioned canal was cut. Today they abound in fish and are full of waterfowl. The canal was originally cut by Sesostris before the time of the Trojan War, though some say by the son of Psammetichos,[6] who only began the work and then died, and later by Darius the First, who fell heir to the project. But he too, persuaded by an erroneous

---

[3] Punt.

[4] That is, overland by the same road through the desert by which he had made his way to the sea.

[5] Situated north of Suez; this, therefore, is our Nile–Red Sea canal.

[6] Necho, *ca.* 600 B.C.

opinion that the Red Sea lay higher than the land of Egypt and that therefore, if the intervening neck of country were completely cut through, Egypt would be overwhelmed by the sea, abandoned the work just as it was nearing completion. However, the Ptolemaic kings completed the cutting and closed the channel so that at their discretion they could sail out into the exterior sea and sail back in again.[7]

It should be noted that in an earlier book of the *Geography* Strabo gave a different version of the history of the canal's construction, asserting that it was Sesostris and not, as above, Darius who "abandoned the undertaking because he supposed the level of the sea was too high." But such confusion on Strabo's part suggests that he knew nothing very certain either about Darius or about Sesostris. Still, there is a chance that Strabo's references to Sesostris in connection with the construction of the canal reflect some actual Egyptian record or tradition dating back to the far-distant but still illustrious twelfth dynasty. In that case, the New Kingdom's dynamic eighteenth dynasty might well have put the once existent canal back into operation, even as it repaired so much else of the damage and neglect incident to the incursion of the Hyksos; and Queen Hatshepsut's ships might then have made use of its waterway to the Nile on their return from their voyage to Punt about the year 1486 B.C.

The only specific description of the canal as it existed in classical times to be found in any ancient author occurs—like so much else on which the present volume relies for its material! —in the pages of Herodotus. The following precise and probably entirely accurate account is included in his second book, devoted to Egypt:

> Now Necho was son of Psammetichos and became king over Egypt. It was he who was the first to attempt the canal leading to the Red Sea, the same that Darius the Persian was the next to dig. Its length is a voyage of four days; and it was dug wide enough for two warships to be rowed abreast. Water is led into it from the Nile, taking off a little below the city of Bubastis at the desert town of Patumos; and it extends to the Red Sea. First there was dug the sector on the Arabian side of the Egyptian plain, extending above the lowland by the Memphis hills where the quarries are. Accordingly, the canal was led

---

[7] Strabo, *Geography*, XVII.1.25.

along the skirts of these hills from west to east and was then directed into the natural cutting, bearing at first east and then south of the hills to the Arabian Gulf. Now, the shortest and most direct passage from the northern to the southern sea runs overland from Mt. Casius, by which Egypt is separated from Syria. This is a distance of exactly a thousand stades to the Arabian Gulf.[8] This would be the shortest route; but by the canal the distance is much greater because of its winding course. One hundred and twenty thousand Egyptians lost their lives digging the canal under King Necho. Yet Necho stopped in the midst of the enterprise, being deterred by an oracle to the effect that he was working for the benefit of the "barbarian"—as the Egyptians call anyone who does not speak the same language as themselves. Desisting from the canal, Necho turned his attention to military matters and had warships built, both on the Northern Sea and in the Arabian Gulf of the Red Sea. The slips for hauling these ashore are still to be seen.[9]

King Necho's activity in building warships for service on the Mediterranean can scarcely have been a unique or even an unusual performance, in view of much earlier accounts of Egyptian sea fights with foreign ships in the mouths of the Nile. But there is no evidence that any Egyptian navy ever cruised very far on Mediterranean waters. It will be recalled that among the notices reproduced earlier in the present chapter, as far back in time as the pyramid builders there were references to large ships built of cedar wood or carrying cedar wood for cargo. It was pointed out that this cedar wood must have been brought from Mount Lebanon, the region that throughout ancient times supplied the Near Eastern world with its cedar for building ships and for roofing palaces and temples; but in this same connection it was remarked that King Snofru's importation of cedar wood did not necessarily prove that this was brought to Egypt in his own ships, since the Phoenicians who dwelt along the Lebanese coast must have felled and hewn the trees and dragged them down to the sea, and these same Phoenicians may equally well have towed or transported them to the Nile. Some 1,700 years later, when Solomon set about building his temple, he asked King Hiram of Tyre for "cedar trees out of

[8] About 120 miles; the actual distance from Port Said to Suez through the modern canal is 105 miles.
[9] Herodotus, *History*, II.158–9.

Lebanon" and according to the account about this matter in the First Book of Kings (V. 8–9) Hiram complied with Solomon's request, saying:

> I will do thy desire for timber of cedar and timber of fir. My servants shall bring them down from Lebanon into the sea; and I will convey them by sea in floats unto the place that thou shalt appoint, and will cause them to be discharged there.

On any interpretation of Snofru's much earlier importation of cedar, there must have been Phoenicians involved in the affair; and this seems to be their first appearance on the scene of history.

They had not always been a Mediterranean shoreland people. Of much the same racial stock and speech as the other Semites of Canaan and northern Syria, the Phoenicians were markedly distinct from these in their addiction to the sea. Perhaps this trait had been developed because of the character of the long narrow strip of shoreland which they inhabited and which with its steep sharp valleys and gorges running down to the sea made all communication difficult except for those who took the Mediterranean for their highway. But it is also possible that knowledge and liking of the sea had been inbred into this particular branch of the Semitic stock from a much earlier period. For, according to Herodotus (VII.89), the Phoenicians had a tradition that in other times they dwelt "by the Ery-thraean Sea" [10] and migrated thence to the Mediterranean's eastern shore on the skirts of the Lebanon range, where "they betook themselves to distant sea voyages for the conveying of Egyptian and Assyrian merchandise." Herodotus sets no date for this transference from the southern to the midland sea; but he elsewhere says that on his visit to Tyre he was told by the priests that their temple was founded when the city was first settled and that this event occurred 2,300 years before his day. If by any chance the priests' tradition about their town and temple was sound, Tyre would have been first occupied about the year 2750 B.C. and in that case would have only lately come into existence when Egyptian Snofru sent to the land for cedar trees. And if their other tradition was correct, that they had migrated from the Erythraean Sea and we may interpret this

[10] Usually interpreted as that part of the Indian Ocean now known as the Arabian Sea and the Persian Gulf. It was also called the Red Sea in antiquity.

to mean the Red Sea and not the Persian Gulf or the Indian Ocean, an old acquaintance with salt-sea navigation would have been theirs and it would be easier to understand how it happened that, centuries later, the king of Tyre stationed ships at Ezion-geber at the head of the Red Sea's Gulf of Aqaba and knew how to send a fleet down the Rea Sea to Ophir to bring back gold and *almug* trees for King Solomon, as is related in the First Book of Kings and again in the Second Book of Chronicles.

Succeeding chapters in the present volume will have much to say about the Phoenicians and their far-western colonies at Carthage and in Sicily, Sardinia, and southern Spain. But here it must suffice to state that there is no sound evidence for thinking that in the days of Snofru or of Solomon the Phoenician ships ever sailed the open Mediterranean far beyond their homeland shore. Instead, they confined their voyages to Sicilian Tarsus, north of them, and to Palestine and Egypt to their south, clinging to the coast in both directions; and in addition they may have maintained their old connection with the Gulf of Aqaba and the Red Sea. Until other new civilizations developed beyond them in the west, the Phoenician merchants were interested only in trafficking with the established lands of wealth and power centered in Egypt, Babylonia, and Assyria. Compared with the magnificence of Memphis or Thebes on the Nile or the prosperity of the Mesopotamian towns between the Tigris and Euphrates, the more western Mediterranean countries of four thousand years ago were backward and commercially unprofitable regions, offering little or nothing to the Phoenician merchant to recompense him for the thousand-mile coasting voyage to the Greek mainland, to say nothing of the two-thousand-mile trip to Sardinia and the three-thousand-mile trip to Atlantic Spain. When contact by sea was established between Phoenicia and the Aegean world, it was Aegean ships that found the way east rather than Phoenician ships that sought the West.

The spread of civilization through the Greek island world was a delayed event—if by "civilization" we mean conditions of a material, social, and intellectual kind such as already prevailed north of the Persian Gulf in Sumer five thousand years ago and only a little later could have been found on the Egyptian Nile. Indeed, if we search only another thousand years or so behind the rise of Sumer and pharaonic Egypt into the fifth millennium B.C., it would appear that the closely clustered islands of the Aegean basin, lying between Asiatic Turkey and European Greece, were uninhabited by human beings and had been so for a great many centuries. This surprising state—if really it was thus—could have been due only to man's poverty of invention and want of technical experience in shipbuilding and his lack of daring in trusting himself on the sea. At least, it has been maintained in competent quarters that it was not until some six thousand years before our time that men on rafts or in rudimentary types of ships first ventured out from the Asiatic coast to take possession of the Aegean islands, one after another, as occasion offered or chance determined.

Although it is not strictly true that the Greek islands are so numerous and so closely set that from any one of them there is always some other island visible on the skyline, nevertheless this exaggerated claim comes near enough to the actual truth to give a fair impression of that fascinating domain of deeply drowned mountains whose peaks and highest ridges alone protrude above the sea to shape an archipelago of habitable isles. Today's tourist travelers talk of "exploring" this attractive realm, whose every stopping place offers some new sight or scene or custom peculiar to itself. But though they may write their impressions of their explorations by sailing yacht or island steamer, neither they nor we can ever in imagination recapture the feelings of those forgotten men of five or six thousand years ago, who truly and for the first time explored the Aegean Sea as they worked their way from island to island, discovering that there were always other islands awaiting them beyond.

These were not Greeks, either by race or by language, who first explored and settled this island world, but people out of Asia Minor, bringing with them a neolithic mode of life dependent on farming and herding. Having installed themselves in their scattered dwelling places throughout the Aegean Sea with their domesticated animals and their supplies of sown cereals and fruit-bearing shrubs and trees, these neolithic islanders perpetuated their simple economy and unambitious culture without much growth or change, until in the course of the third millennium B.C. a knowledge of metallurgy reached them, with its consequent echoes of heightened activity in trade and commerce. Thereafter a new and truly remarkable level of civilization and material prosperity was attained—if not everywhere among the islands, most certainly in the largest island of all, Crete, lying across the mouth of the Aegean like a breakwater against the wide-open African Sea. Here on Crete, where wild and difficult mountains shut off the west, while elsewhere behind lesser heights lay fertile inland basins, and arable land led down to a deeply indented coast, a truly wonderful flowering of early Mediterranean civilization broke into full blossom.

Perhaps as remarkable as the splendor of the Minoan Age itself, while it endured, is the almost total oblivion into which it lapsed after its political dissolution. Knossos with its amenities of courtly life and all its material wealth and far-reaching power left so little mark on recorded history that only semimythical legends, recounted by the Greeks of the classical age, preserved even a shadow of its vanished glory until, to the modern world's astonishment and intense interest, archeological excavation uncovered the vestiges of its henceforth unforgettable greatness.

This is not the place for a description of the intricately planned and sumptuously fitted royal palace at Knossos, with its vividly drawn and brightly colored wall paintings. Neither is there any pertinent reason for sketching the sites of the lesser palace buildings at Phaistos and Hagia Triadha and Malliá or the ruined traces of half a hundred towns on the island of Crete. What is cogent to the interests of the present volume is the classical Greek tradition that the navies of King Minos of Crete once dominated the eastern Mediterranean, and the confirmatory evidence on the extent of Minoan navigation afforded by some of the Egyptian tombs from the eighteenth dynasty in the time of Queen Hatshepsut and her immediate successors.

Rekh-mi-Re, vizier to King Thothmes III, was laid away in a rock-cut tomb in the hill behind the Ramesseum across the Nile from the capital city of Thebes. A straight corridor running into the hillside is preceded by a transverse vestibule, on the walls of which there are still distinguishable colored drawings showing Rekh-mi-Re engaged in various activities. Among these he is seen receiving "tribute and gifts" from emissaries of foreign nations. Syria, Nubia, the "Southlands," and Punt are represented, and also a people labeled *Kftiu*. The Nubians bring a panther, a giraffe, and apes among their offerings; the Syrians, horses and cars, an elephant, and a bear. The *Kftiu* bring no animals, but have piled up quantities of metalware bearing unmistakable resemblance to some of the gold and silver vessels discovered by the celebrated archeologist Heinrich Schliemann in the graves of the kings at Mycenae. It is a current opinion among scholars that these Mycenaean treasures were loot or gift or purchase from Minoan Crete. Consequently, the similar vessels shown in Rekh-mi-Re's tomb should be of Cretan manufacture and their bearers, the *Kftiu,* should be Minoan ambassadors or merchants from Crete. Their costumes might be identified either as Cretan or as Mycenaean Greek; but the date of the tomb, which can hardly have been constructed later than 1440 B.C., makes the identification as Minoan Cretan the more probable of the two.

Above the procession of the *Kftiu* there is a long hieroglyphic inscription, which begins:

> Peaceable arrival of the chieftains of the *Kftiu* and of the lands in the heart of the Great Green Sea, in obeisance, in head-bowing before the might of His Majesty the King, as they hear of his power over all lands, their gifts on their backs.

H. R. Hall has given a vivid description of the scene to which this hieroglyphic commentary refers:

> Confidently the tall Minoans or Mycenaeans march along the walls, wearing their high Cretan boots, their typically "Mycenaean" waistcloths, and their long black hair hanging to their waists or knotted on their heads, just as we see them on the walls of their own home, Knossos, where the famous fresco of the Cupbearer, discovered by Sir Arthur Evans, might be a replica of one of these contemporary Egyptian figures. . . . Confidently they advance to the foot of the throne, led by their "Great Chief," a young man with fair face and small European mouth—markedly small it appeared to the large-mouthed Egyptian who sketched him for the picture—and followed by a darker and older man whose Roman nose and heavy jowl remind us strongly of an Italian type. Another, a young man, follows, who bears a sword in his hand as well as a great vase on his shoulder; and as he walks he looks back with open mouth to make some loud remark to the next man, much as a young Gothic ambassador might have guffawed in the presence of a Roman Caesar. All

is represented to the life. These Minoans were no servile Semites or cowed negroes.[11]

We shall never come nearer to comprehending the type and character of the Minoan seafarers, whom we may plausibly take to be the first Great Explorers of the Mediterranean world.

A similar (though not so well-preserved) scene exists on the wall of the nearby tomb of Sen-n-Mut, who was Queen Hatshepsut's chief architect and confidant and probably belonged to much the same generation as Rekh-mi-Re.

In view of evidence such as these two tombs offer, it cannot be doubted that Cretan ships journeyed to Egypt in the early fifteenth century B.C. and even voyaged up the Nile to the royal capital at Thebes. Nor would it be reasonable to doubt that it was the Cretans who explored the sea passage to Egypt, rather than the Egyptians who sought out the way to Crete. In all likelihood, the Minoan shipmasters first made acquaintance with the nearer shore of Asia Minor and thence, working their way eastward along the Turkish coast, made contact with Syria and the closely adjoining island of Cyprus. There, in the ports of those lands, knowledge must have come to them about the rich kingdom on the Nile lying yet farther ahead and easily to be reached if one but followed the shoreline south past Palestine.

What other lands these Minoan seamen may have visited, what other routes across the Mediterranean they may have opened up for trade or plunder, remains unclear. They could not possibly have failed to become familiar with all the Aegean mainland and islands or have missed the narrow passage through the Dardanelles into the Sea of Marmora (although there is nothing to show that they ever penetrated the Bosporus' swift channel to the Black Sea). Westward beyond the Greek mainland the Minoan ships must have steered along the continental coast at least as far as the Adriatic and must have sighted, as they sailed through its narrow mouth, the low-lying white headlands of Apulian Otranto, announcing the easy crossing to southern Italy. How much farther they may have explored the Italian waters is mere conjecture, unless some measure of belief is accorded the classic Greek legend that Daedalus, the great craftsman of Crete, had fled to Sicily and that King Minos, in

[11] H. R. Hall, *Ancient History of the Near East* (London: Methuen & Co., 8th Ed., 1932), p. 293.

pursuit of him, had met his death there. We have no means of discovering what basis—if any—such a semimythical tradition may have had; and there is scant archeological evidence to support the theory that Minoan trade ever penetrated very far into the western Mediterranean.

But when Minoan Crete sank from power, and control of the Aegean passed to the Greek chieftains of the nearby mainland, already long established in such centers as Mycenae, Tiryns, and Sparta, a new era of seafaring seems to have ensued. Vases of Mycenaean manufacture, clearly distinguishable from Minoan by the specialist in such matters, have been turned up—usually in fragments—on every eastern Mediterranean shoreland. Judging by such ceramic evidence, the Mycenaean Greeks must be given first rank among all the possible, probable, or problematical nautical explorers in preclassical antiquity. If only they had been as competent in writing and as inclined to record their own achievements as their remote descendants in the Greek classical era, the history of ancient exploration with its roster of Great Explorers would have opened a thousand years earlier. As it is, only silence, hardly interrupted by archeological conjecture, hangs over the centuries until long after Minoan and Mycenaean ships alike had moldered and disappeared and in the wake of four hundred years of cultural retrogression and collapse there had returned energy and ambition to the remnants of the Greek-speaking race. Only then, with the advent of the great new era of classical Greece, are the shadows lifted from the Mediterranean world.

When seafaring begins once more in the Aegean and ships travel east and west to seek what they may find, it is the eighth century before Christ, and Greeks, who have lost all traditional knowledge of Egypt and are barely aware of the older civilizations east of them, are looking out on the great waters west of them as an Odyssean world of fairy tale. With present ignorance and half-forgotten legend hemming them in, these Greeks took again to building ships that were strong enough to take them oversea, where all the wide Mediterranean and the Atlantic world beyond were waiting to be explored.

II

THE GREEKS EXPLORE
THE WEST

THE Mediterranean is actually made up of two distinct seas, interconnected by the Tunisian Strait but differing markedly in character. The Western Sea, considerably less extensive than its eastern complement, lies several degrees farther north, so that its southern shoreline along northwest Africa, if projected eastward, would define the *northern* margin of the main body of water in the Eastern Sea. Another trait of difference is the mountain girdle ringing the Western Sea in contrast to the low, dreary desert coast that bounds the Eastern Sea on the south. And though there are mountains shutting in the eastern basin in its farther sector, especially where southern Asia Minor hems it in, these mountains abruptly give way to the intrusive waters of the island-studded Aegean, homeland of the Greeks; and thereafter, to the west of the Greek mainland, a long narrow arm of sea stretches northwest to separate Yugoslavia from Italy—a body of water so nearly enclosed by land as to constitute virtually a separate sea, the Adriatic. In addition, there is annexed to the Aegean basin a very much smaller sea, the Marmora, to be reached from the Mediterranean only through the swift-flowing sea-river known to the Greeks as the Hellespont and to us as the Dardanelles; while out of the Marmora Sea, in turn, through the even swifter-running salt-river of the Bosporus, there is unexpectedly sudden access to another huge inland sea, fed by the Danube and the rivers of southern Russia. This is the sea called Euxine by the Greeks, or more simply "The Sea" (*Pontus*), and by us not too appositely named

"Black." It has its own un-Mediterranean characteristics to set it apart from the rest of this three-thousand-mile-long sequence of conected and everywhere navigable water, all so locked in by three continents that one might expect it to be, like our own land-enclosed Great Lakes, fresh instead of salt. And so it would be, were it not for the comparatively tiny eight- to nine-mile break in its continental girdle at the Gibraltar Strait, through which the Atlantic ceaselessly pours its salt flood to make good the enormous evaporation of the inland sea. This loss of volume through evaporation so greatly exceeds all that heaven's rain and earth's rivers supply that the Mediterranean would soon sink to a deep dead sea if the Atlantic did not constantly keep it at its own planetary ocean level.

This brief description will give some idea of the geographic complexity of the Mediterranean, a complexity hard to keep in mind unless one has studied its map or, better, journeyed over it. But its very intricacy lends it charm and interest and makes of it a marvelous domain for exploration.

It was in the Aegean branch of this maze of interlocking waterways that the Greek race taught itself how to build ships and how to handle them through wind and wave over seas that, while tideless in comparison with Atlantic waters, were crossed by endlessly moving currents.

Not that the classical Greeks were the first or the only race to venture out on the deceptively gentle Mediterranean. As the previous chapter has already narrated, fully a thousand years before them the Minoan ships of Crete had been finding their way eastward to Cyprus and the Syrian coast and thence to Egypt on the Nile. And long before these Cretan traffickers, Phoenician ships had been traveling the Asiatic coast from well-wooded Lebanon past the desert barrier that separates Palestine from the Nile Delta, bringing timber of cedar trees to the all but treeless Nile valley. But (contrary to general belief and repeated assertions) there is no indication that in these early days Phoenician coasting cargo vessels ever ventured farther west than the nearby stretches of the Asia Minor coast or entered into competition with the hardy and enterprising Minoan fleet.

Elsewhere in the Mediterranean, the Dalmatian waters of the Adriatic Sea were as though designed by nature to become a training ground for sailors. Long and extremely narrow islands that are crests of submerged mountain ranges running parallel to the mainland make canal-like passageways extending hundreds of miles. These channels may be wavelessly calm for days on end; but at other times and often with unexpected suddenness they are swept by tremendous gusts traveling along them. In such a region men must take to the sea in order to live upon the islands, but must acquire sound seamanship if they would live there long. Theirs would be a world full of hiding places for quick concealment, with coves and tiny beaches from which to make sudden sallies—a pirates' paradise. No wonder that in classical Greek and well into Roman times the Liburnian pirate craft along this coast were feared and their haunts avoided! Today the mariner tradition is still alive there. It has been said that the best seamen in the Italian merchant marine come from longtime Italian Dalmatia and the Quarnero.

The Mediterranean's Western Sea is not thus shaped by nature to breed and train mariners. Its African shore is especially unsuited for navigation in small ships dependent upon sail and oars. Although it lies north of the desert belt and does not suffer from the shallow water and sandy shoals of the Eastern Sea's African coast, it sets throughout its length a lee shore to the summer trade wind and is swept by a steady eastward current flowing from the Atlantic. There is little properly sheltered harborage. In consequence, this is not a mariners' land and its inhabitants were never noted in antiquity for knowledge of the sea or the skillful handling of ships. Neither is the portion of Spain that lies opposite to this African coast much better endowed by natural advantages to tempt its dwellers to take to the sea.

Northward along Spain's Mediterranean shore the harbors become more frequent and some, most notably that of Cartagena, are very good; but not until the Balearic Islands, lying well out to sea from the mainland below the Gulf of Valencia and strung out for nearly two hundred miles northeastward, is there found a natural setting for a seafaring populace. Beyond Minorca, the last of these islands, there is only open water, east and north and south, with another two hundred miles of empty sea intervening before, on due-east course, the very much larger island of Sardinia is sighted. This is the great gap on the open-water crossing between Spain and Italy. Otherwise there is always land on the horizon, since the westernmost Balearic is visible from the Spanish capes, and at the other end of the crossing Sardinia almost joins with Corsica, while off Corsica's northern head the iron-mined isle of Elba forms a stepping-stone to the Italian mainland.

The archeologist—the only one qualified to probe into the prehistory of the western Mediterranean—sees evidence enough to persuade him not only that the Iberians inhabiting the eastern coast of Spain had crossed to the Balearic Islands during the third millennium before Christ, but that there was direct seaborne communication between these islands and Sardinia at least a thousand years before any Greek ship ventured into these western waters.

This summary sketch will set a geographic background for the time when written history begins for the western Mediterranean and the earliest Greek explorers arrived upon the scene with intent to search out its hitherto unfamiliar lands with their unknown races of men.

Perhaps Odysseus, the beguiling hero of Homer's epic, should be termed the first Greek explorer of these western seas. To be sure, his adventures are fairy tales of impossible encounters with one-eyed monster cannibals and giants and enchantresses; but the places in which these adventures are set do not seem to be equally imaginary. Like the companion epic of the Greek battle for Troy, the *Iliad,* in which all the geographic setting is actual, whatever may be the historicity of the narrated events, the *Odyssey* makes its story credible by pretending to set its scenes in the actual world of the Mediterranean.

Most ingeniously, Odysseus is made to sail out of the familiar south Aegean into the wonderland of fairy tale by being caught in tempest in the open sea between Crete and the southern tip of mainland Greece. "For nine days," he says, "I was driven by deadly winds across the fishy deep." Apparently it was the unrelenting gale of the midsummer trade wind, blowing from the northeast in those waters, that carried his ships before it. The "nine days" should not be taken literally, because a poetic convention made nine the number for any prolonged effort, leading to fulfillment in ten, the number for final accomplishment. (Critics who insist on finding true history in the ancient epics have been very naive in failing to grasp this poetic convention, holding that the siege of Troy took ten years to accomplish, that the Greek army took ten years to assemble, that Odysseus took ten years to return home from Troy to his native Ithaca. There are dozens of similar instances of this inactual way of speaking). If one locates the sea passage between Greece and Crete on a modern map and draws a straight line thence from northeast to southwest, he will see that Odysseus should have brought up on the northern African coast somewhat east of the present city of Tripoli. Here, at the present day, there is a headland of dense groves of date palms, like an oasis amid an arid desert. Those who live in such a climatic environment and tend the "honey-sweet fruit" of the Tripoli dates lead an idle and, for most of the year, an easy existence. In Homer's poetic turn of speech, this was a land of lotus-eaters "who live on a flowery food . . . and whoso ate the honey-sweet fruit no longer cared to come back [to the ships] to report thereof, but wished to stay among the lotus-eaters, nibbling lotus and forgetting the journey home."

Farther to the west, where Tripoli gives place to Tunisia, the well-wooded and wonderfully fertile island of Jerba, close to the mainland, is the island on which Odysseus' ships ran ashore on a moonless night. At the present time it is densely inhabited; but when Odysseus came upon it there were only "numberless wild goats" on it, for it lay "unsown and unploughed, empty of men," because the savage mainland dwellers, whom Homer transformed from "round-faced" into "one-eyed" ogres, had "no red-painted ships nor yet shipwrights to build them boats" with which to cross to Jerba.

The terrible experience in the Cyclops' cave is familiar to everyone. Thereafter, as adventure follows close on adventure, the geographical setting becomes ever more uncertain, with only this much apparent: that Odysseus and his ships passed through the wide Tunisian Strait into the hitherto scarcely explored Western Sea. Here the chief point of discussion among later scholars in antiquity centered on the dispute whether Homer had any hearsay knowledge of the Atlantic outside the Gibraltar Strait and wove this knowledge into his story. Strabo, echoing Polybius, maintained that when Homer described Charybdis as three times a day sucking the salt water down till the sea bottom showed black with sand, and three times a day again sending up its flood, he was making poetic use of the ebb and flow of the Atlantic tide. If so, we can only assume that he had heard from Ionian sailors, fellow countrymen of his, some report of the striking and even startling phenomenon of the refluent ocean beyond the Pillars of Heracles. For it must be remembered that the Mediterranean is all but tideless, so that the daily repeated rise and fall of the Atlantic must have been as unexpected as it was impressive when first it was encountered. In setting its rhythm at thrice instead of the actual twice in the day (Strabo thought), Homer may have "corrupted his information"—or, as we should say, was indulging his poet's license to exaggerate.

It is the rhythmic alternation of Charybdis' fall and rise that is the characteristic element least likely to have been imagined by anyone who had never learned of the precisely repeated timing of the planetary tide; so that the modern reader of the *Odyssey* may be tempted to agree with Strabo's argument. But the difficulty in crediting the author of the *Odyssey* with any knowledge of the Atlantic is the unavoidable mid-seventh-century date that must then be assigned to his poem, because that date is the earliest that may be attached to the first passing through the Gibraltar Strait by any Greek seamen. My personal feeling is that it is better to face up to the chronological difficulty by accepting the conclusion that the *Odyssey* was composed around the middle of the seventh century B.C.; but the majority of Homeric scholars will probably not agree, any more than the majority of Homeric scholars in classical antiquity saw fit to side with Strabo in holding that Charybdis was a poetical echo of the great Atlantic tides that daily uncover and again conceal the sandbars and shoals along the Andalusian coast. There (to quote the U. S. Hydrographic Office *Sailing Directions* for Spain) the average tidal range is 8.6 feet, the spring tides range around 11.6 feet, with currents up to three knots; and when strong westerly winds are blowing, both tidal rise and current velocity are much increased. So great is the tidal onset that in the Guadalquivir its effects are remarked upriver as much as thirty miles beyond Seville, which itself is more than fifty miles inland from the open sea. All this, of course, proves nothing very tangible about Homer!

Charybdis' companion horror, the deadly dangerous Scylla,

adds nothing toward the settlement of this controversy. There is pretty general agreement that a marine monster with six long arms, each studded with three rows of close-set teeth, that lurks in a sea cave and thrusts out her arms for feeling and fishing around her reef, being destructive not only to sea things but even to human beings, can only be a devilfish of the sort that so greatly excited the imagination of Victor Hugo in his romance, *The Toilers of the Sea*. To be sure, the octopus has only two, not three, rows of suckers on each arm; but it makes up for this lack by having eight arms as against Scylla's six. Being wholly ignorant in such matters, but wondering whether there is any truth to nature in Scylla's menacing attack, I have read with interest what the English marine biologist J. Y. Cunningham once had to say on the subject:

> The celebrated account of the octopus given by Victor Hugo in his *Travailleurs de la mer* is not so fictitious as some critics . . . have maintained. . . . His description is exaggerated, imaginative and· sensational; but it is correct in its most important particulars, and bears evidence that the author was to some extent personally acquainted with the animal and its habits. . . . There is nothing impossible in Hugo's account of the skeleton of a drowned man surrounded by the shells of crabs which the octopus had devoured. Whether an octopus would attack and kill a man is another question, but it certainly might seize him with its arms and suckers while holding to the rocks by other arms, and a man seized in this way when in the water might be in danger of being drowned.[1]

Even so, there seems to be no reason for believing that such a monster was more likely to have been encountered in Atlantic than in Mediterranean waters. Perhaps its only pertinence to our present interest in ancient explorers is the coloring of perilous adventure that it adds to the picture of Ionian seafaring in far-western waters.

From all this it follows that Homer should not be taken as a source of information on early Greek exploration of the western Mediterranean, however likely it is that his *Odyssey* reflects and reproduces in fairy-tale disguise some of the reported wonders of this hitherto unvisited world.

Disregarding the Homeric epics as being too patently ficti-

---

[1] *Encyclopaedia Britannica*, 11th ed., *s.v.* "Octopus."

tious to yield any certain information about Greek knowledge
of the West, we are dependent on Herodotus for our earliest
factual account of Greek exploration of those Mediterranean
lands that could be directly reached by ship without expeditionary marches inland. This ancient Greek author is such a vital
source of information on early classical times that something
should be prefaced here about his claims to being correctly informed about the events of his own lifetime and the century immediately preceding his birth; and some account should be
included of the extraordinary book that he compiled, a work that
still today may be read with intense interest and unqualified en-
joyment. The title of his composition, *Historia,* should not properly be translated as "history," since the Greek word more nearly
signified "inquiry." And an inquiry it was, into everything that
its author could elicit from men of his own and of adjoining
foreign lands when he asked them about themselves, their man-
ners and customs, their religions, their traditions about events
in their past, their knowledge of the geography and natural resources of the lands they inhabited. Behind and beyond all this
questioning was the ambition to write a fully detailed chronicle
of the greatest political event of his own, or of any recent, generation—the conflict between Persia and Greece, in which the
Greek inhabitants of Asia had been forced to submit to the
Persian empire while the Greeks of the European mainland,
with Athens and Sparta leading them, had defeated the Persian
attacks by sea and land and kept Greek independence unde-
stroyed. The outcome of this twofold interest in inquiring into
the character of the motley world around him and at the same
time recounting the conflict between Persia and Greece was a
loosely organized whole, only a part of which was contemporary
history, while the rest (and by no means the least valuable portion) was made up of the This-and-That of his curiosity-impelled
"Inquiry."

His first long chapter (or book, as it is usually referred to)
treats mainly of Asia Minor with its Greek and Lydian and
other nationalities, but deals also in considerable detail with
the Medes and Persians and the growth of Persian power.
Book II is devoted to Egypt and contains, in addition to a
brilliant description of the country of the Nile and its people,
a remarkable attempt to sketch the country's remotest history

without benefit of any knowledge of hieroglyphic writings. Book III continues with the more recent event of Egypt's submission to Persian rule and proceeds to a variety of other matters and in particular the dynastic history of the Persian kings and their spreading empire. Book IV introduces the Black Sea with its tributary rivers and the Scythian steppes of Russia, then turns to the Mediterranean's southern shore to narrate the Greek colonization of Cyrene. Book V is at last more closely concerned with Greece. With Book VI the great war against Persia begins; and to this the rest of the *History* (Books VII, VIII, and IX) devotes itself with magnificently vivid descriptions of the great battles at Marathon, Thermopylae, Salamis, and Plataea.

The tone of this remarkable inquiry into the civilized world of antiquity may be termed strictly factual and extremely accurate if we take into account the unavoidably oral nature of its author's information. What Herodotus records in written words was not taken from other written works, but from the mouths of men—and these, as we all are aware, are often full of vain imaginings and may stray widely from the true course of the events of which they speak. Herodotus was seldom deceived by others' talk, yet felt himself in duty bound to put down everything that might be so, even when he himself misdoubted it. More than once he cautions his readers, "This is what I was told," leaving it to them to accept or reject it as they see fit.

In reading the *History* we should never forget that we are almost never confronted with transcripts of documentary records, chronicles, laws, or other written testimony, but are being told what contemporary men said and thought and chose to believe about themselves and the events in which they had taken part or about which they had heard from others. This makes the accounts more human, more alive with a special sense of intimacy. It would not be correct to say that Herodotus ever deliberately foisted any information that he knew positively to be false or that he had invented outright out of his own imagination.

He lived in the fifth century before Christ, having been born about the year 485 B.C. and having died about 425 B.C. This being his life-span of learning and inquiring, men's memories could have made him pretty thoroughly informed about historical events and human happenings in his own lifetime and

as far back roughly as the middle of the sixth century, a matter
of two to three generations. But whatever had taken place still
earlier could have been only sketchily known to him, with much
forgotten and much none too accurately transmitted. The world
contemporary with Homer was already beyond the horizon of
reliable recall. And since the period in which the Greeks of the
classical age first explored their own Mediterranean world beyond the limits of the Aegean Sea and its adjoining territory
must be assigned to the late eighth century and the course of the
seventh century, it will be seen that the earliest of the great
Greek explorers may not be expected to occupy much space in
the pages of Herodotus nor yet to figure with all the circum-
stantial detail that their exploits deserved. But fortunately there
is sufficient mention of who they were and what they did to
rescue several of these stout adventurers from the oblivion that
would otherwise have overtaken them.

The most comprehensive statement in connection with early
Greek exploration to be found anywhere in the pages of Herodotus is a brief digressive passage in the heart of Book I, to be
translated as follows:

> The Phocaeans were the first of the Greeks to undertake long
> sea voyages. It was they who made Adria known, and Tyrrhenia,
> and Iberia and Tartessos.

This is an extremely condensed bit of exploratory history; but
it contains a great deal of significant information, requiring
much comment to make it comprehensible.

"Adria" must be taken to refer to the northeastern coastal
strip of Italy along the great arm of the Mediterranean to which
Adria has bequeathed its name—the Adriatic Sea. Extending
from about modern Ancona to Venice, this shoreland includes
the delta of the important river Po, whereon there was a trading
station of considerable significance for Greek commercial relations with the interior of Europe. Here, in exchange for the
commodities that Greek ships brought, payment was partly
made in amber. Perhaps for superstitious reasons as much as for
its rarity and ornamental attractiveness, this fossil resin was
greatly prized in classical and even more in Mycenaean times.
Although amber was to be found in Sicily, this potential source
of supply was apparently unknown to early antiquity, when every

bit of amber is thought to have been transported overland from the Baltic Sea, on whose sandy southern shore, between Koenigsberg and Memel, vast quantities of it had been washed up and buried in the strand. We have no means of knowing who first opened up this extraordinary trade route which ran across the entire width of Europe, through Poland and Slovakia to the Danube valley in Hungary, whence in Mycenaean times it may have continued overland through the Balkans. But after the Phocaeans had opened the Adriatic to Greek trade, Baltic amber was diverted through Austria via Trieste to the mouth of the Po and its trading station of Adria. The classic myth, best known from Ovid's poetry, of the weeping sisters of hapless Phaethon who were transformed into poplar trees on the banks of the Po, where their tears continued to fall as drops of amber, indicates that the tellers of the myth knew where amber was to be sought but had no knowledge of how it got there. The amber route can hardly be classed as the track of any overland explorer, since the commercially profitable substance was probably carried in stages and passed from hand to hand, so that no single group of merchant traders covered the entire journey. Nevertheless the unanswered puzzle remains how any knowledge of the existence of an eastern Mediterranean market for amber could have been carried to the far corner of the Baltic Sea. It is not recorded whether Phocaean ships took any active part in the amber trade. Herodotus merely states that they "made known" Adria to the Greeks.

Tyrrhenia, the second on Herodotus' list of Phocaean discoveries, refers to the opposite, or western, coast of Italy and specifically to the two-hundred-mile stretch of land enclosed within the courses of the Arno on the north and the Tiber on the south. This was the adopted homeland of the Etruscans (Greek *Tyrrhenia* being the equivalent of Latin *Etruria*). It is not certain that the Phocaeans were actually the first Greeks to make contact with the Etruscans, since this distinction should more probably be accredited to Euboean settlers of the island of Ischia off the northern head of the Bay of Naples, where Etruscan ships may have passed from their more northern coastal ports. Yet it may be true that the Phocaeans reached some of the Etruscan territory before any others of their race, since they are known to have explored the Riviera coast beyond Etruria sufficiently to have discovered the splendid harbor of Marseilles near the mouth of the Rhone, where they founded a colonial trading post somewhere about the year 600 B.C. Also, it may well have been Phocaeans who constructed the trading port known as Pyrgoi ("The Walls") on the rocky beach near the important Etruscan city of Caere (Cerveteri). If that was their doing, the Phocaeans quite literally "showed" Etruria to the other Greeks.

After mentioning Adria, Tyrrhenia, Iberia, and Tartessos in the previously cited passage, Herodotus continues:

> And they did not make their voyages in round ships but in penteconters.

These words are not open to any possible misunderstanding. "Round ships" were the broad-beamed and rather shallow-bottomed craft, rigged with a single sail and equipped with some six or seven oars on either side, such as are often pictured on sixth-century Greek vases. They were slow in the water, except with a strong wind astern. The "penteconters" were a new type of craft of greatly superior design. The Greek name "pente-conter" was coined from the Greek word for "fifty," in reference to the fifty oars by which they were driven. These ships carried sails, but were in no way dependent upon their use. Being necessarily of considerably greater length in order to accommodate twenty-five oarsmen in a row on either side, and being built much narrower to give them better speed through the water and with deeper keel to diminish sideways drift, they were not intended to carry much cargo. The round ships were therefore the merchantmen for hauling and commerce, while the fifty-oared longships or penteconters were far better suited (as Herodotus implies) for longer voyages and above all for distant exploration.

Despite Herodotus' express statement, the Phocaeans might have reached Etruria without recourse to their penteconters. For it is only a short crossing from the west coast of mainland Greece to the heel of southern Italy; and Greek colonies had been founded on the Gulf of Taranto and on the east coast of Sicily and even as far as the Bay of Naples a generation or two before penteconters were built. On the other hand, Herodotus must have been entirely correct in attributing their use to the Phocaeans in their exploration of "Iberia and Tartessos." For these were truly distant journeys such as could scarcely have been accomplished except with speedy ships that did not rely on the winds.

The introduction of the penteconter was an event almost as revolutionary for the history of navigation in antiquity as the substitution of steam for sails in modern times. Herodotus indicated its importance for Greek maritime exploration when he pointed out that the Phocaeans were the leading explorers in the early classical period and used penteconters instead of round ships for their voyages. He does not state specifically that the substitution of fifty-oared longboats for the older, slower round ships coincided with the first invention of the new type of vessel; but this was almost certainly the case. In view of the crucial role that the penteconter played for more distant exploration, it will not be out of place here to consider this craft somewhat more closely.

In the far remoter past the oar, with its fixed pivotal support giving leverage to the stroke, was evolved out of the much less efficient free-held paddle. And just as more and more men operating together could use an increasing number of paddles simultaneously, so a numerous crew of oarsmen "seated well in order" could "smite the gray sea with their oars." The woven cloth sail, hung on an upright mast raised amidship, was likewise a very early invention, having probably been already in use in neolithic times. Oars and sail could be used together to supplement each other's propulsion; but more generally, the oars were put out only when the wind failed or blew from an unfavorable quarter, and for maneuvering in harbor. Since beating into the wind by tacking yielded little or no progress for ships square-rigged with boomless sails and shallow keels, rowing was often obligatory in Aegean waters, where the summer trade wind sets almost daily from the same northeast direction. (During the winter months squally or heavy weather kept the early ships shorebound.) Under these conditions the great advance in shipbuilding was a wholly new design to overcome earlier dependence on sailing down or across the wind, with only laborious aid from the oars. A narrower hull, with deeper keel and with a much longer body to accommodate a greatly increased crew of oarsmen, made for much greater speed and permitted holding a course without regard for wind or calm or set of current.

On late-eighth-century Attic and Corinthian vases there are

crudely drawn but quite definitely depicted outlines of ships showing twenty rowers in file on one or on both sides of the vessel. These would represent the immediate forerunner of the penteconter, which was in turn developed simply by increasing the number of oarsmen from twenty to twenty-five for each of the two rows of benches. This was apparently judged to be the maximum effective number of oars for a ship of this structural design. In consequence, the fifty-oared longboat became standard throughout the Greek world.

The late-eighth-century-B.C. date of the vases picturing forty-oared ships suggests that the fully manned (i.e., fifty-oared) penteconter was a creation of the early seventh century. And this, or an only slightly later, date is the period to which the Phocaean exploration of the western Mediterranean must be assigned. Its introduction marked such an innovation in Greek navigational history that it left an indelible mark even on Greek legend and poetry. The *Odyssey* is one of the memorials of it; but there was still another epic example, not textually surviving to our own day, but openly referred to by Homer himself in verses put in the mouth of Circe, the banefully beautiful enchantress who bewitches Odysseus' comrades in the *Odyssey:*

For there are overhanging rocks there, against which
Roars dashing the great wave of the black-eyed Sea-goddess;
"Splashers" is the name the blessed gods call them. . . .
There never yet unscathed passed mortals' ship that came there;
But the waves of the salt sea and the blasts of fiery windstorm
Bore away the planks of their ships and the bodies of their crewmen.
Only a single seafaring ship ever passed there safely,
Even *Argo* the swift, to all of us made familiar,
As to King Aietes she journeyed.[2]

As Homer hints at the story, the scene of *Argo*'s adventure past the deadly "splashing rocks" was the far-western Mediterranean; but subsequent legend, in poetry and prose, localized it otherwise. *Argo* the swift, driven by a heroic crew, opened the Black Sea to all Greeks by running the dangerous current of the Bosporus, where previous slower-moving ships had always been caught by the stream and wrecked on the rocky shores. So Pindar set the story in one of his Victory Odes composed shortly before the middle of the fifth century B.C.; and so, in elaborate

[2] Homer, *Odyssey*, XII, 59–70.

detail, a late-third-century Alexandrian poet called Apollonius of Rhodes recounted the tale in a long and by no means unworthy epic. For Apollonius, the building and launching of the *Argo* was in itself a heroic achievement; and the unusual character of the ship was proclaimed by its name, *Argo* ("the swift"). Although Pindar names only ten heroes among its crew, Apollonius names fifty, thereby identifying the ship as a penteconter.

It can hardly be questioned that the plot of the Argonautic expedition in quest of the Golden Fleece, with Jason as leader, was a myth of much older date than the Greek discovery of the Black Sea. In its original telling it may not have had any connection with that event or that body of water. But just as Homer imparted vividness and plausibility to his narrative by introducing actual geographical names and places into his epics, so the unknown author who composed the poem to which Homer seems to refer in the passage previously quoted seized on an actual exploit of which he had heard, and attached this to the myth, thereby profiting from its adventurousness and its wonder of new names of hitherto unknown places to make a marvelous tale seem true. Since the new type of explorer's ship, the fifty-oared penteconter, was first constructed and put to use at the start of the seventh century B.C., and the opening of the Black Sea to Greek trade and settlement seems, on historical and archeological evidence, to have occurred within a decade or two of this same span of time, it is not unreasonable to connect the two events. But the transference of a historically genuine happening to the mythical world of epic romance, coupled with the circumstance that no prose account of the event in its sober actuality has chanced to survive, has left us without knowledge as to what mariners from what Greek city manned the penteconter that first ran the headcurrent of the Bosporus and explored the strange new open sea eastward to the rocky shore of the Caucasus.

Whoever the "Jason" was who captained this ship and set its course for more than six hundred miles along hitherto unvisited coasts, he must rank as one of the Great Explorers. His voyage should have a chapter in any book devoted to Greek exploits on the sea. But the chapter cannot be written in proper documentary form with names and dates and notation of places visited and running time between them, because all these have been lost through their history's having been transmuted and disguised as poetic legend shaped on myth—and out of myth nothing can be made that can claim to be reality.

We can only guess that the historic substitute for the fabled ship of the Argonauts was manned by a crew of Ionian Greeks from some Asia Minor city on the Aegean coast, perhaps the notoriously energetic trading town of Miletus, and that it was very shortly after the year 700 B.C. that her enterprising mariners opened up the swift waterway hitherto untraveled by Greek shipping and made the alien Black Sea an integral part of the Greek world. At first this great body of salt water was known as the "Unfriendly Sea" (perhaps through misinterpretation of some non-Greek name for it), but when it was perceived that it was not inhospitable at all, being easy and not in the least dangerous to navigate, its epithet was reversed in meaning and it became the "Hospitable Sea"—the Euxine. I do not know who was responsible for once more altering its name and calling it the Black Sea; but though its surface is not particularly dark in color, in contrast to the intensely blue Mediterranean the adjective is not wholly misapplied.

However it is interpreted as a historical event, the first running of the swift Bosporus was a high adventure that caught not only the ancient Greek imagination but has inspired a deal of poetry ever since:

> In the ears of the world
>   It is sung, it is told,
> And the light thereof hurled
> And the noise thereof rolled
From the Acroceraunian snow to the ford of the fleece of gold . . .
>   By the Chersonese
Where the thundering Bosphorus answers the thunder of Pontic seas.[3]

Fortunately we are much better informed on the Greek exploration of the Western Sea—thanks chiefly to Herodotus, and not merely by virtue of the brief passage previously cited and partially elucidated. To repeat, that passage read:

> The Phocaeans were the first of the Greeks to undertake long sea voyages. It was they who made Adria known, and Tyrrhenia, and Iberia and Tartessos.

[3] Algernon Swinburne, "Atalanta in Calydon."

Of these four exploratory goals, Adria and Tyrrhenia have already been discussed. There remain for more detailed investigation Iberia, which in Herodotus' day signified the Mediterranean *shoreland* of the Spanish peninsula, and Tartessos, which was also in Spain but was situated on the Atlantic beyond the Gibraltar Strait.

In order to reach either of these more distant regions the Phocaeans in their penteconter would have traversed the already familiar sea route to the Tyrrhenian-Etruscan coast as far as the island of Elba (already dark with slag of iron ore from Etruscan furnaces, two and a half millennia before Napoleon spent his brief first exile there). Thence they would have crossed to the mountainous northern spur of Corsica, whose steep, wild, and densely forested ridges would have been in sight from the start. Turning south again along the Corsican coast, after some fifty miles they would have reached one of the few stretches of level shoreland that rugged Corsica can show, a fairly broad alluvial plain built out into the sea by the river Tavignano. Here, almost a century after their first voyage to Spain, the Phocaeans were to take refuge when the encroaching Persian domination of Asia Minor besieged their home city at the mouth of the Gulf of Smyrna. Rather than submit to the Persians, they had embarked themselves with their wives and children and all their movable possessions aboard their penteconters, to start life anew on the wild western island where they had already established a small settlement. They were not destined to stay long in Corsica because—as Herodotus tells the story—they raided nearby Italy and made themselves intolerable to the Etruscans, who called on Carthage for aid. A great sea battle was fought in which all three contestants suffered such injury and losses to their ships that, though the Phocaeans counted themselves the victors, they saw that they could no longer maintain their hold on Corsica. Accordingly they emigrated once more, to find still another dwelling place, this time close to their fellow Greek countrymen and safely south of the Bay of Naples. All this adds to our picture of these ancient "Vikings" of the southern sea; but otherwise it has been a digression from their first great voyage westward to Spain and the Atlantic.

Continuing to keep Corsica to starboard as they journeyed southward, the Phocaeans discovered the passage between Cor-

sica and Sardinia with its marvelous cliff-girt harbor on the
Corsican side of the strait, which took its modern name of Boni-
facio a thousand years ago from a hardy Tuscan sea dog who
fought the Saracens hereabouts.

It is conceivable that the report that the Phocaeans brought
home about this deceptively safe haven in a savagely hostile
land may have been poetically transformed by the poet of the
Odyssey into the dreadful adventure in which only the wily
Odysseus took the precaution of mooring his ship to the rocks
outside "the famous harbor, the wide-gated sheer citadel of
Rockpidgeonland," while all the rest of his fleet of ships took
trusting refuge within the harbor, only to be destroyed by the
wild giants that kept the land.

The uncivilized Corsican natives may indeed have been un-
helpful; but presumably the Phocaeans proceeded to explore
the yet larger neighboring island of Sardinia. And there—
somehow, although one wonders at their means of communication with people of such totally different speech—Sardinian
fishers who knew where Spain was (because they seem to have
been themselves of Iberian descent) conveyed the information
that there was other land far to the west. For otherwise why
would the Phocaeans have attempted the couple of hundred
miles of completely landless sea that separates Sardinia from
the easternmost of the Spanish Balearic Islands, and how would
they have known that they must set a course precisely west southwest if they expected to find these islands far out at sea, to show
them the way to the great continent of the West? On all these
matters Herodotus is silent. But we must trust his word that
the Phocaeans reached the southeastern coast of Spain; and
there is evidence of rather an involved sort to indicate that they
came by way of Sardinia and the Balearic Islands. It must be
taken into account that wind and wave—which is to say, the
summer trade wind and the westward set of the Mediterranean
current—facilitated a crossing from Sardinia to the Balearics
under sail without continuous use of oar, whereas the trades do
not blow so far north as the gulfs of Genoa and the Lion (or
Lyons), where the prevailing westerlies would have set a head
wind counter to their course if the Phocaeans had attempted to
reach Spain by following the continental coast of Europe the
long way round, past northern Italy and southern France.

Almost from the time of its first discovery by the ᵀ
which occurred perhaps as early as the middle decaᵤₑ
seventh century B.C., Mallorca (or Majorca), the largest islaᵢ,
the Balearic group, came under Greek influence, whereas thᵤ
smaller island of Iviza, nearer the Spanish mainland, fell somewhat later under Carthaginian control, to become for Punic
Carthage a permanent point of vantage for her Spanish trade.
Excavation on Iviza has unearthed a long line of Punic graves
containing offerings that date from the first half of the sixth
century B.C. onward. In contrast, Mallorca has yielded a considerable quantity of Greek bronze figurines, some of fine quality,
the earliest of which are roughly contemporary with the earliest
graves on Iviza. The rivalry between Greek and Carthaginian
merchants for the rich Spanish trade in metals and other native
products, which was to exert such a decisive influence on the
political and economic history of the Western Sea, stands out in
sharp relief in the cultural opposition between these two islands
in the same mid-sea group. But all this tension of rivalry had not
yet developed when the Phocaeans first came this way—even
though it is not entirely certain that the Phocaeans were the
predecessors of the Punic traders in these waters. For, when the
Greeks discovered Spain, Carthage had already been founded
almost a century previously by Phoenicians from Tyre on the
Syrian coast; and Carthage had in turn founded settlements on
the western shore of Sicily lying opposite across the Tunisian
Strait and had occupied parts of southern Sardinia. But, as we
shall see, the widely prevalent idea that Phoenicians, whether
from their eastern homeland or from their outposts in the
Western Sea, had been trafficking in Spain long before any
Greek ship reached its shores is a mistaken notion. It is much
more likely that it was a Phocaean penteconter and not a Punic
round-ship merchantman (such as the Greeks contemptuously
referred to as "buckets" or "tubs") that opened up the island
bridge from Sardinia to the Iberian shore of Spain.

Nowadays it is perhaps only the yachtsman vagabonding in a
small sailing craft in these waters who can appreciate the sensa-
tions of the Phocaeans in their penteconter as they sighted these
faraway islands with their abrupt limestone cliffs rising out of
deep-blue water and ringed by ceaselessly shifting lines of sunlit
foam. But even such a make-believe Odysseus, because he has

s charts and knows what lands to expect to encounter and where to find them, cannot quite recapture the sense of excited wonder that must once have attended on voyaging in pursuit of the setting sun over windy seas where no one knew what land might next come up above the horizon.

From the westernmost of the Balearic group, Iviza, which the Carthaginians were soon to make their own, there is only a fifty-mile stretch of sea to the Spanish mainland, whose higher coastal ridges are sighted long before the actual shore is visible. I venture to quote from an early book of mine (now long out of print) an eyewitness description of the landfall as it must have appeared to the Phocaeans in their penteconter:

As they neared, they beheld a coastline of hundred-foot cliffs behind which a stretch of green undulating land ran back to higher ridges. The headland is called today the Cape of the Ship, *Cabo de la Nao,* and offers no landing place or harbor. But south along the coast after eight or nine miles there is a sort of fishers' haven (now called Moraira) and then, a few miles farther, comes a deep bay with a shingle beach and a tiny stream of fresh water. At the end of the beach against the open sea, as though expressly reared for shelter, there stands a gigantic isolated towerlike mountain of rock, a lookout post guarding the "island bridge" that leads over the Balearic Islands to Sardinia. It is a wonderful watching place over the sea. From the top of it I have seen northeastward against the sunrise the peak of Balearic Iviza, distant more than sixty miles, and looking southwestward the bays and coastline heads and islets of the Spanish coast for almost as many miles in the other direction. Only the coast northward is hidden from view by the hills and mountainous ridges of the Cabo de la Nao.

What wonder that this marvelous observation-point, rising abruptly like a second Gibraltar out of the sea, impressed the Phocaeans who drew up their ship behind its shelter; and what wonder that they gave it a picturesquely descriptive name and called it *Hemeroskopeion,* "The Lookout"?

Plate ZZ shows the great isolated thousand-foot rock (known today as the Peñon de Ifach) almost surrounded by sea. In the middle distance a wide bay sweeps in behind the shelter of the Lookout, where the land to the left is fringed by a low reef of rock backed by river sand. Here a silted-up cutting through the reef leads to a small landlocked harbor, long since sanded up save for a pool of stagnant saline water from which salt, until rather recently, used to be evaporated. Beyond the picture's left-hand margin there are scant traces showing where once a small temple stood. On the slope leading up to the great rocky head there are indications of once-massive walls; and there are quantities of fragmentary potsherds in the soil, from Hellenistic Greek, native Iberian, and earlier fourth-century Campanian Greek ware.

Until the Spanish authorities show interest in excavating this remarkable site, that is all that can be said about ancient Hemeroskopeion. No doubt, it was at first a mere shelter station for the Phocaean ships before or after the four-hundred-mile run across the Balearic "bridge" from Sardinia.

That it ever had much importance as a trading point and market is unlikely, as it lay in the territory of backward tribes, whence neither road nor river led to the mining districts. But as a stopping place for food and water and for waiting on wind and weather, commanding the route to Italy, it must have gained in importance as long as Phocaean or other Greek merchants traded with Tartessos.[4]

It has been very plausibly suggested that this Greek settlement was destroyed by Carthage in the days when Hannibal was gathering his forces in Spain for his famous invasion of Italy at the start of the Second Punic War, 2,200 years ago. However that may be, subsequent history has been silent about the great headland of Ifach except for a single mention. Although this has no immediate connection with the Phocaean explorations with which this chapter deals, its occasion is of such historic interest and makes so dramatic appeal that this must be the excuse for its inclusion here.

It happened in Roman times, in the period of the Late Republic when a particularly vicious civil war had split the Romans into partisans of Sulla and partisans of Marius. A brilliant military commander named Sertorius, who had served under Marius, finding himself on the losing side, withdrew to Spain in the hope of maintaining his opposition to his ever more successful adversaries in the party of Sulla. Sertorius was familiar with the land and its heterogeneous native tribes through having held a previous command in Spain. In spite of strict notions of

[4] Reprinted, with slight verbal changes, from Rhys Carpenter, *The Greeks in Spain* (Bryn Mawr: Longmans, Green & Co., 1925), pp. 19-23.

military discipline and his unyielding Roman ways, he succeeded in building up a native following of almost fanatical devotion. While suffering all manner of reverses and mishaps, he managed to hold out for years against every effort of the ruling faction in Rome to destroy him. As Plutarch tells it in his *Life of Sertorius*, the story is long and intricate, though lightened by picturesque anecdotes such as that of the tame white fawn that followed Sertorius everywhere and was regarded by the natives as his familiar spirit through which he communicated with the great goddess Diana. After having raised all Spain south of the Ebro in open revolt against Rome's authority and defeating every expeditionary force sent against him, even under such notorious generals as the great Pompey, Sertorius saw his astonishingly high fortunes threaten to forsake him just at the moment when he was reaching out for control of the seas to assure him victory over Rome. By negotiating a treaty with King Mithridates, Rome's inveterate foe in the east, he was promised a fleet of forty ships of war. And here the great rock of Ifach enters the story. According to the annoyingly brief account in Strabo, Sertorius made Hemeroskopeion his maritime base for his own and his expected ships "because it was a stronghold suitable for buccaneering and because it is visible from a great distance to vessels approaching." Except that Strabo might better have said, "because approaching vessels are visible at a great distance from it," it is a fine and very accurate description of the Lookout.

But here the high adventure comes to a sudden end when Sertorius' second-in-command, a Roman noble named Perpenna, played the part of Brutus to this forerunner of Caesar and conspired at his assassination. With Sertorius out of the way, Pompey had no further difficulty in putting a speedy end to the Spanish revolt.

To return to earlier times when first the Phocaean longboat put in at the Lookout and its crew got their first glimpse of Iberia from its tall summit, the course that they had been steering, the prevailing direction of the wind and the sea current, and their own curiosity for exploring the more distant unknown all conspired to make them choose to follow the coast south-westward rather than double back toward the north. We cannot doubt that this was their decision, because Herodotus says that they discovered Tartessos, and there is no possible doubt as to

THE GREEKS EXPLORE THE WEST 51

where Tartessos lay. If they were indeed the first Greeks to find it, then they were the first of their race to have seen and passed through the Gibraltar Strait and to encounter the Atlantic tides.

A land of fabulously abundant silver, set at the very end of the navigable sea on a shore of the great ocean-river that encircled the entire habitable world, made great appeal to the Greek imagination—particularly as this land was discovered only to be lost again after little more than a century when Carthaginian commercial rivalry shut the Atlantic strait to all Greek shipping. It has struck the modern imagination even more forcibly, transforming itself into a mythical realm almost as fabulous as the lost Atlantis, which Plato's fertile mind located in the same remote corner of the known world. To the Greeks of the classical age Tartessos could take on the glitter of fairy tale because, like fairyland, having once been seen it could never be revisited. Fortunately, before all memory of it had become transformed, Greek literature took note of its actuality; and more fortunately still, Herodotus had occasion to insert a fairly substantial account of it in his *History*.

He makes mention of Tartessos in two completely unconnected narratives, only the first of which concerns the Phocaeans. This connects directly with the passage already twice cited, of which it is the immediate continuation. After asserting that it was the Phocaeans in their fifty-oared ships who made Tartessos known, Herodotus gives this account of their relations with the local monarch:

> On their arrival at Tartessos they became friended with the king of the Tartessians, whose name was Arganthonios. He held sole rule over Tartessos for eighty years, and himself attained the age of one hundred and twenty. Now, the Phocaeans became so endeared to this man that when they were abandoning Ionia he first bade them settle wherever they wished in his own land and then, when he did not succeed in persuading them to this and he learned how the power of the Mede was waxing great amongst them, he gave them funds for constructing a wall around their city. And he gave unstintedly. For the circuit of the wall was several miles in length and it was all built of large well-fitted blocks of stone.

The dates here are somewhat misleading. The Phocaeans first

reached Tartessos shortly after the middle of the seventh century B.C. The trouble with "the Mede" occurred almost a hundred years later. During that interval there must have been repeated Phocaean visits to Tartessos to make the story consistent and to cement the fast friendship between Arganthonios and his Ionian Greek visitors. The eighty years during which Arganthonios ruled his land may synchronize with the span of time during which the Phocaeans frequented him up to his death, which Herodotus records as having occurred before the Phocaeans abandoned their city to the Persians and emigrated to Corsica. (In order to keep the chronology firm, let us say that the Phocaeans built their fine wall around their city shortly after the year 560 B.C.—"the Mede" was succeeded by the Persian Cyrus in 550. Then the first Phocaean arrival in Tartessos would have taken place *ca.* 640–35 B.C.).

All this may appear to be simple and self-consistent. But Herodotus makes the matter thoroughly confusing by telling elsewhere in his *History* (in Chapter 152 of Book IV) a totally different story of the opening up of Tartessos to Greek commerce. Like most of the anecdotal narratives in Herodotus, this is well and vividly told. Nor does it lose much in translation, for which reason it is here reproduced in full:

> A Samian ship whose captain and owner was a man named Kolaios put in at the island of Platea on his way to Egypt. . . . But as he was putting to sea again with intent of sailing thither, he was carried off course by an east wind. And because the tempest did not abate, the mariners, thanks to divine guidance, passed out between the Pillars of Heracles and came to Tartessos. Now, at that time this was an untouched virgin market, with the result that when they reached home again they made the greatest profit from their cargo of any Greeks about whom we have any reliable information—except, of course, the Aeginetan Sostratos, son of Laodamas: no one could rival *him!* So the Samians took out a tenth part of the profits, namely six talents, and had a bronze cauldron of Argolic type made, with heads of griffins jutting out around it; and this they dedicated in the temple of the goddess Hera; and under it they set three huge ten-foot figures of men kneeling.

Here is indeed a nest of difficulties!

Platea ("Flat" Isle), at which Kolaios touched while bound for Egypt, causes no trouble. It can be identified on the modern

map as lying close offshore in a bight of the east coast of Cyrenaica, where the direct crossing from Crete strikes the African
shore. A current of moderate strength runs east along this coast,
and on this, with the aid of gentle westerly winds, the early
Greek ships relied for reaching the mouth of the Nile.

As the ship set out from Platea along this route it could
perfectly well have been caught by the head wind of an easterly
or southeasterly gale and been blown wide of its course out into
the open water of the African Sea. But it would be a violent
strain on our credulity to believe that such a storm could have
carried a sailing vessel 750 miles so exactly west northwest as
to drive it through the Tunisian strait without wrecking it
either on the Tunisian or the Sicilian coast or against any of
the interspersed islands, and thereafter have veered into the
east to continue driving the ship for another 750 or 800 miles
past the northern African coast of Algeria and Morocco, and
so out past Gibraltar into the Atlantic!

Not that Mediterranean storms cannot be violent, or that an
oldtime merchantman with only a single sail and a scant
complement of oars would not have to run helpless before the
gale. Today's visitors to the Mediterranean, cruising aboard a
large ocean liner, do not appreciate the dangerous power of wind
and wave for a sailing vessel caught in one of the sudden storms
that at times sweep across that reputedly mild and sunny sea.
There are many references in ancient writers to ships beset by
unmanageable winds; but far the best description of a vessel
swept away by a tempest is to be found in the New Testament in
the Acts of the Apostles, in which Paul is sent under arrest to
Rome to be tried before "Caesar" and the ship on which he is
being conveyed is caught by a storm and wrecked on the island
of Malta. As many parts of the Testament are not so familiar
to our generation as they were to that of our forebears, and as
this description of a Mediterranean storm is pertinent to any
imaginative portrayal of the risks and perils to which the ancient
explorers were exposed, it is included here among our sources
on seafaring in antiquity:

> And when it was determined that we should sail unto Italy
> . . . And entering into a ship of Adramyttium we put to sea,
> meaning to sail by the coasts of Asia. . . . We sailed below
> Cyprus, because the winds were adverse. . . . And when we

had sailed slowly for many days, and scarce were come opposite Cnidus, the wind not suffering us, we sailed under Crete . . . and hardly passing it, came to a place called Fair Havens. . . . Now when much time elapsed and sailing was become dangerous . . . Paul admonished them, and said, "Sirs, I perceive that this voyage will be with hurt and much damage, not only of the cargo and ship, but also of our lives." . . .

But when the south wind blew gently, supposing their purpose attained, they unmoored thence and sailed close under Crete. But shortly thereafter there arose a tempestuous wind from the southeast, the wind that is called Euroclydon. And the ship was caught thereby and could not bear up, so we let her drive before it. Running under a tiny island called Clauda, we were barely able to control the skiff, so hauled it aboard; and for greater security we passed cables underneath the hull. Then, fearing lest we should run aground on shoals, we loosed the tackle and let the vessel drift.

Next day, being mightily stormtossed, they threw out cargo and on the day following cast likewise the tackle overboard by hand. But when after many days neither sun nor star were to be seen, and a mighty tempest beset us, all hope that we should be saved was taken from us. . . .

But when the fourteenth night was come and we were being carried about in the Adriatic, about midnight the crew suspected that land was nigh, and sounding they found twenty fathoms and a little later casting again they found fifteen fathoms. So, fearing lest we should fall among reefs, they cast four anchors astern and prayed for daylight. . . .

But when day came they did not recognize the land; but they discerned a sort of cove with a beach, and there they planned to save the ship if so they could.[5]

Hoisting sail, they ran the ship aground, to its complete destruction; but the crew and passengers managed to reach the land, those who could by swimming, the rest with help of planks and timbers from the wreck.

The foregoing may serve to impart some notion of the troubles that overtook Kolaios and his ship when caught in just such a storm of wind from the southeast, to be carried before it, like Paul six centuries later, but, unlike Paul, not to be cast ashore and wrecked. Malta lies some five hundred miles due west of the western tip of Crete; and it must be granted

[5] Acts XXVII.1–39.

that this was a great distance for Paul's ship to have been carried through the Mediterranean, even by a severe early-autumn storm. Nevertheless, what Kolaios claimed to have happened to him remains utterly incredible—not only because no gale could have persisted so long and no ship been driven so far, but because the chances of being thus transported without further incident or calamity precisely to Gibraltar and through the Straits are incalculably minute.

We must conclude that Captain Kolaios, on finding himself headed toward the west against his will, decided to make the best of his mischance and seek another market than Egypt for his cargo of Samian goods. Even so, he would not have thought of Andalusian Spain nor known how to steer a course to reach it, unless he already knew where and what Tartessos was or somewhere on his way westward had gained word of its whereabouts and its fabulous wealth of silver.

It might be suggested that he derived this information from Phoenician traders at Utica or Carthage on the western shore of the Tunisian Strait. But there are three considerations that make such a notion extremely implausible:

1. In view of the keen commercial rivalry that developed between Greek and Phoenician traders in the Mediterranean, the last thing that the Carthaginians or any of their countrymen would be inclined to do would be to reveal to their competitors an untapped source of wealth from which they could make "the greatest profit" of any traders of their time.

2. If Tartessos was, as Herodotus asserted, "an untouched virgin market," it would seem that the Phoenicians had not yet visited it and so could not have given Kolaios any word of its whereabouts.

3. The archeological evidence does not encourage the supposition that the Phoenicians, whether based on their Syrian homeland ports of Tyre and Sidon or on their western colonies of Utica and Carthage, had anticipated the Phocaeans in exploring the farthermost regions of the western Mediterranean. This is a question that has given rise to much difference of scholarly opinion in recent years. The ancient historians were entirely convinced of Phoenician priority; but their position was the result of their firm belief in the historical actuality of everything narrated by Homer. And in the Homeric epics,

particularly in the *Odyssey,* Phoenician ships and Phoenician traders sail the Aegean and the Sicilian seas. But modern archeological investigations, by introducing a great amount of hitherto unfamiliar evidence, has set the problem in a different light and encouraged the very opposite conclusion—that it was the Ionian Greeks who first explored the far-western Mediterranean, although granting freely that their commercial rivals, the Phoenicians, may have followed close on their vessels' heels.

It would seem, therefore, that Kolaios must have heard rumor, in his native port of Samos, of the Phocaean exploration of "Iberia and Tartessos" and in this manner had learned where these lay and how they could be reached by ship, and, having been carried by storm far to the west of his projected course to Egypt, had decided to take the best way out of his predicament by continuing westward to try his luck beyond the Pillars of Heracles in the land which the Phocaeans had discovered. How, then, it may be asked, if the Phocaeans had already visited Tartessos, could Herodotus have referred to it as an "untouched virgin market"? To this the simplest reply is that the Phocaeans, in their swift penteconter, were bent on exploring and were not equipped with cargo for trading. But while they had nothing aboard their ship for barter or sale, they might very well have reported home that anyone who brought a marketable cargo to Tartessos to exchange for silver from the mines could make a "killing"—precisely as Kolaios is said to have done!

But was there ever such a person as Kolaios the Samian? And if he existed, did he ever make the four-thousand-mile sea voyage to Andalusian Spain and back? Since he carried—and, by exchange for silver, brought home—a considerable cargo, he could not have commanded one of the long, narrow, and speedy ships with a crew of fifty oarsmen such as the Phocaeans are reported by Herodotus to have used for exploring. Instead, he must have made his epochal trip to outer Spain in one of the clumsier and much slower round ships, which depended mainly on their sails and took to oars mainly for working in and out of harbor and for dealing with windless days. These tubby merchantmen were square-rigged with a single sail (without any lower boom) rigged slightly forward of midship. In consequence they relied largely on a following wind or one on a stern quarter. Although it has been denied by some writers on the subject of ancient navigation, a ship thus built and rigged could hardly have maneuvered successfully against a head wind or pointed well up across it. Much later, in Roman times, when improvements in ship construction might be presumed, it still was a difficult matter to contend against contrary wind. According to Strabo:

> Posidonius tells us that in his journey back from Spain [6] he observed the singular phenomenon that in this sea, as far as the Gulf of Sardinia, the east winds blow continuously.[7] On this account he strove in vain for the better part of three whole months to reach Italy, being driven by the wind to the Balearic Islands and Sardinia and the opposite shore of Africa.

If Kolaios had any comparable experience, it must be admitted that his exploit was little short of heroic, carried away as he was by storm on his outward voyage and having to struggle against persistent contrary winds for much of his return journey. Must we believe that he actually accomplished this feat? (The Greeks, from wily Odysseus on into fully historic times, saw little shame in concocting effectively plausible lies.)

To so skeptical a query it should be replied that Kolaios could hardly have invented any convincing report about a land that he had never seen, and that it is impossible to suggest where else than in Tartessos he could have taken on the prodigious cargo of raw silver with which he returned. Of the existence of that cargo and of its great value there cannot be any rational doubt. Herodotus had resided for some considerable time on the island of Samos and must therefore have been describing from firsthand inspection the "bronze cauldron of Argive style" with its griffin heads projecting around its rim and its trio of more than lifesize kneeling figures in bronze supporting it. Nor could he have been mistaken about the approximate date of such a dedication, because bronze griffin-head attachments for cauldron rims were fashionable throughout the seventh century B.C., but ceased to be made very long thereafter. Specimens have been found on the sites of the greater sanctuaries of ancient Greece, in the tomb of the Phrygian king Midas (who died in the opening decade of the seventh century), and even,

---

[6] He had been spending a month in Cádiz.
[7] Posidonius should more properly have said that the wind set in from the northeast. Patently, the summer trade wind was keeping to its daily habits.

most pertinently of all possible places, in Andalusian Spain in an example that may well have originated in the famous bronze foundries of Samos itself. Furthermore, such an ambitious dedication would certainly have carried an incised inscription proclaiming the name of the dedicator and very probably the occasion of its dedication, the reading of which would have confirmed to Herodotus any account·that the temple attendants might have given him. Even the value of the cauldron might have been stated. Religious superstition dictated that a tenth of the proceeds of any greatly profitable gain or any sudden windfall, as of hidden treasure, must be dedicated to some deity, so that Herodotus' statement that "the Samians took out a tenth of the profit, six talents," and with that sum paid for the great cauldron and its supporting statues, corresponds precisely to the ancient norm. It follows necessarily that the proceeds from Kolaios' Spanish voyage must have been accounted at sixty talents. Now, the talent was a measure of weight rather than of monetary value, so that it would seem that Kolaios' cargo of silver weighed in at more than 3,400 pounds net. It would be idle to calculate the present dollar value of such a load, since the only true value of precious metal is its purchasing power in the current market. In Tartessos it would seem that Arganthonios and his subjects had a very different conception of the value of silver from that entertained by his Greek customers. Yet the rarity and desirability of the wares that Kolaios had to offer—whether it was wine in earthen jars or olive oil, brute or refined and perfumed, or (as seems to me more likely) sets of Greek bronze armor and weapons from the Samian foundries —would have offset any thought that the Tartessians had been cheated by the strange-tongued foreigners in their even strangerlooking ship.

We hear no more of Samian trading with Tartessos. But the Spanish market was now open and known to all Greek comers; and the previously cited account from Herodotus' first volume (or book) bears witness that the Phocaeans became frequent visitors to the "silver-rooted river" (as the early sixth-century Greek poet Stesichoros referred to Tartessos) where Arganthonios took such a liking to them that he gave them silver in generous measure that they might build a wall around their home city in order to keep out "the Mede."

What, then, and more precisely where, was this wonderful western realm of Tartessos that the Phocaeans discovered and the Samians first exploited, this land of prodigiously abundant silver where Arganthonios was king for eighty years and lived to be a hundred and twenty? Some of the later ancient writers thought that Tartessos was a great city that had been destroyed or had for other reasons disappeared, with Gades taking its place. But none of the earlier authors ever speak of it as a city, whether great or small. Herodotus does not say what he thought it was, except that, since he spoke of Arganthonios as king, he implied that Tartessos was a kingdom. But in the Greek usage of the word (*basileus*), such a king might rule any sort of territory or any sort of tribal community. The Greek poet Stesichoros, who lived more than a century before Herodotus and was a contemporary of the Ionian Greek mariners who traveled the Spanish trade route, understood Tartessos to be the name of a river. We have only a scant fragment of one of his poems, preserved for us only because Strabo saw fit to quote it, having to do with the fabulous three-headed Geryon and his marvelous herd of oxen guarded by the two-headed dog Orthros. According to the Stesichoros excerpt Geryon had been born

> Nearly opposite to famed Erytheia,
> In a hollow of the rock,
> Beside the boundless silver-rooted springs
> Of the river Tartessos.

There is abundant evidence to tell what was meant by "famed Erytheia." It was the island in the Bay of Cádiz that, by later silting, has become united with the longer but narrower island on which Phoenician Gadir and Roman Gades were built. Enlarged by deposition of sand washed in from the nearby Guadalete River, it is today called the Isla de León. All this being so, the river Tartessos of Stesichoros' verses should be the Guadalete, since this is "nearly opposite" Erytheia, or—because the "springs of the silver-rooted river" make clear that something else is meant—the much larger Guadalquivir that draws its headwaters from the silver-bearing slopes of the Sierra Morena and flows past Cordova and Seville to reach the Atlantic only a few miles north of the entrance to Cádiz Bay.

In Roman times the Guadalquivir was known as the "River

Baetis"; but it was remembered that it had a different name in earlier days, and Livy gives the important clue that its native name was "Tertis." This was the non-Greek and non-Phoenician word that the Greeks Hellenized into "Tartessos" and the Carthaginians identified with a Semitic word already familiar to them, "Tarshish." There are several passages in the Old Testament that make reference to "Tarshish ships." So, in I Kings XXII.48, "Jehoshaphat made ships of Tarshish to go to Ophir for gold; but they went not, for the ships were broken at Eziongeber" (with which II Chronicles XX.35–37 should be compared). Again, in a more frequently cited passage in the same Book of Kings (X.22), "For King Solomon had at sea a navy of Tarshish [*sc.* "Tarshish ships"] with the navy of Hiram; once in three years came the navy of Tarshish, bringing gold and silver, ivory and apes and peacocks." But in both of these passages (in the former because of the mention of Ezion-geber, which was the port at the head of the Gulf of Aqaba whence voyages in the Red Sea were undertaken, and in the latter because peacocks were available only in the Far East and not in the western Mediterranean), the Tarshish ships can have nothing to do with Spain. There are other references in the Old Testament, mostly to "Tarshish ships" (*anyoth t'ršiš*), but also to Tarshish as a place or country. In none of them is there any plausible reason for maintaining that Andalusian Spain is intended. My personal opinion favors identifying Tarshish with the Greek trading town of Tarsus in Cilicia, only a few miles along the southern coast of Turkey from the Phoenician shoreland, and suggesting that a particular type of ship introduced by Greek shipbuilders and becoming known to the Phoenicians from its use by merchants from Tarsus was called a "Tarsus ship" when it was adopted by Phoenician shipwrights. A better authority than I in Semitic questions, Professor Albright of Johns Hopkins, has given it as his opinion that "Tarshish" is to be connected with a Semitic word referring to mines and metallic ore, so that the "Tarshish ships" would have been cargo vessels for transport of ore or bulk metal. On either view, there is no necessary or even probable connection with Spain.

This is not a recondite philological dispute without significance for the understanding of history; for there is a widespread notion that the Old Testament affords irrefutable testimony that Phoenician ships passed through the Gibraltar Strait to Tartessos on the Atlantic as early as the reign of Solomon and that this belief is supported by the undeniable fact that Tartessos and Tarshish are one and the same word. It is consequently a matter of some moment that this fallacy should not find continued acceptance, because it gives a completely erroneous idea of the scope of Phoenician navigation at the close of the second millennium before Christ and deprives the Ionian Greeks of their rightful title as the original explorers of the far-western Mediterranean.

To return to Tartessos, if "Tertis" (or "Turdis," or some such sounding word) was the name of a river (namely the great Guadalquivir) and not of a city or a land, where shall we localize "King" Arganthonios? His very name gives us the answer to this query.

Again, as for the Tarshish ships, we must dip briefly into philological discussion. It has long been recognized that the name "Arganthonios" was compounded of the normal Celtic word for silver—*argant*—which is presumably the source of the Latin word for the same metal—*argentum*. But since there is no possible connection between Latin-speaking Italy and southern Spain in the time of Herodotus or the still earlier period of Phocaean exploration, we must accept the Celtic connection for Tartessos. It has thence been inferred that the name "Arganthonios" may be translated into English as "Silverman"; but this is not quite correct. Out of Celtic *argant* (silver) the Greeks coined *Arganthōn* as a name for the mountain range where the silver was mined (compare such Greek names for mountains as *Parnōn, Koryphōn, Tretōn,* and *Helikōn*). That the Iberian mountain was actually known as "Mt. Silver" is attested by Strabo and proved by the later Roman name for it, *Mons argentarius,* cited by Pliny. Greek *arganthonios* thus turns out to be an adjective rather than a proper noun, meaning (as it must) "of the Silver Mountain," just as *Helikonios* (an epithet of the Greek god Poseidon) signifies "of Mt. Helikon." So "Arganthonios" was a Greek epithet constructed out of the Celtic word for silver, meaning to the Greek mind "He of the Silver Mountain." Whoever was chief of the mining folk who worked the silver mines in the Sierra Morena near the Guadalquivir would have carried the Greek nickname; and this would explain how for eighty years there would have been an "Arganthonios" for the Greeks to deal with.

The foregoing discussion does not depend on any novel interpretation of the ancient texts. Strabo held that Tartessos was a river name when he wrote:

> Not far from Castalo is the mountain in which they report that the river Baetis has its rise. They call this the Silver Mountain because of the silver mines which it contains. It seems that the ancients knew the Baetis under the name Tartessos, and Gades with the neighboring islands under the name of Erytheia.[8]

Similarly, in Aristotle Tartessos is the name of a river.

But if Tartessos was the Guadalquivir River and Arganthonios was a Celtic chieftain controlling the barter of silver from upriver mines in the Silver Mountain, what becomes of the populous city and the fabulous realm of the Kingdom of Tartessos? Like most fables, they dissolve into mist and airy nothingness.

But Pausanias in his *Guide to Greece* has troubled the Tartessian waters by adding a passing comment to his description of the antiquities visible at Olympia in his day, in order to explain what he meant by Tartessian bronze:

> "Tartessian" refers to a river in the land of the Iberians. This is said to descend to the sea by two mouths. The same name as that of the river is also that of a city situated between the river's outlets.[9]

Pausanias seems here to be echoing Strabo, who in the third book of his *Geography* perpetuated the same mistaken tradition, to the needless confusion of modern minds. In particular, a distinguished, archeologically inclined German historian of ancient Spain, Adolf Schulten by name, trusting to this false helpmeet for guidance, spent several seasons digging the barren sands to the north of the Guadalquivir estuary in the conviction that an old variant course of the river, geologically attested for much remoter times, must mark the second mouth recorded by Pausanias and Strabo and that consequently the lost great city of Tartessos must lie buried under the desolate dunes "between the two outlets." He found nothing whatever to reward his long

[8] Strabo, *Geography*, III.2.11.
[9] Pausanias, *Guide to Greece*, VI.19.3.

searching except a single small iron finger ring with some unintelligible letters engraved inside it!

The truth of the matter is that there was no city of Tartessos; for the Celts were not city builders. At most, there would have been a string of villages or groups of small settlements throughout the fertile basin of the Guadalquivir, the great Andalusian river that was the Baetis of the Romans, the Tertis of the natives, and the Tartessos of the Greeks.

It was up this broad tidal stream that the Phocaeans took their fast fifty-oared ship in their exploration of this far-western Atlantic world. Before entering it—as seems to be implied by Greek legendary references to Erytheia as the place where Geryon kept his herd of cattle when Heracles sailed west in search of them—Greek mariners made use of the landlocked, seagirt, and storm-sheltered little island in Cádiz Bay that has since grown into the Isla de León, as a resting and watering place conveniently located within a few hours' sail of the wide mouth of the Tartessos. Here they would have put in both before and after the upriver journey to the mines of "King" Arganthonios.

There is no evidence, archeological or literary, whether the larger island, long and narrow and immediately adjoining on the seaward side of Erytheia, which the Greeks named Wild-olive Island (*Kotinoussa*) and we today know as Cádiz, was likewise in use as a stopping point for Greek ships bound for Tartessos. But it was this, the larger of the two islands in Cádiz Bay, that Carthage elected to fortify into a stronghold (*Gadir* in Punic speech) from which to block seaborne access to the silver mines to all but Phoenician traders.

The date of this well-considered and stringently enforced Carthaginian blockade against Greek trading with Tartessos has been much debated, with astonishingly wide differences of expressed opinion.

A late Roman tradition of dubious validity set the foundation of Cádiz by the Phoenicians at a date that corresponds to the year 1100 B.C. of our reckoning. The unfortunate belief that the "Tarshish ships" of the Bible, reputedly active on the seas as early as the reign of Solomon, took their title from Spanish Tartessos, gave countenance to this completely unacceptable dating. Modern archeology has advanced a totally different verdict. While granting that a rise in the planetary ocean level since classical times has made portions of low-lying Cádiz inaccessible to excavation and that the city's protecting seawalls, thirty to fifty feet high and nearly twenty feet thick, have further hampered archeological probing, nonetheless it remains extremely significant that no Phoenician or Punic object of earlier date than the fifth century B.C. is anywhere on record as having emerged from the sandy soil and seagirt rock of Cádiz. On the other hand, the presence of Greeks on the Atlantic coast of southern Spain during the period defined by Herodotus in his brief accounts has been attested in a most dramatic manner by two wholly casual finds rather recently made in shallow ocean waters.

In 1938, while the estuary of the Guadalete River in Cádiz Bay was being dredged to clear the ship channels, there was brought up from bottom mud and sand a crudely shaped and rudely fashioned bronze helmet. The nose guard has been broken off and the interior leather lining is indicated only by the punched holes for lacing it fast. Battered and corroded, it would scarcely be an object for museum display were it not that, beyond all possible challenge, it is a piece of late-seventh-century-B.C. Greek armor—dating, that is to say, from the very period when Kolaios or some immediate successor put in at Erytheia island within half a dozen miles of where it was dredged up. Whether it had been lost from a Greek head or had passed into native hands in exchange for Tartessian silver is a matter of indifference, since only a Greek ship could have brought it to Cádiz Bay. Because this uncouth type of helmet was very soon outmoded and replaced by a more attractive and efficient model by Greek armorers, it would not have been in use or been offered on the market any later than the last quarter of the seventh century B.C.

The more efficiently shaped and more finely wrought type of Greek helmet that succeeded this archaic "pot helm" from the Guadalete is exemplified by a second bronze headpiece also dredged up from the sea bottom but recovered some fifty miles farther west along the Andalusian coast in the estuary next beyond that of the Guadalquivir. Here two rivers, the Odiel and the Tinto, run together a little below the important modern seaport of Huelva, from which (as in Roman and probably in earlier classical times) are shipped great quantities of copper and sulfur ores from the mines of Ríotinto and the nostalgically named mines of modern Tharsis. Access from the sea must therefore be kept open for the heavy seagoing vessels, and dredging of the shifting sand bars and heavy sediment is a constantly recurring necessity. The dredges bring up astonishing finds. Among these have been numerous Celtic swords and daggers finely wrought in bronze. But none may yield in historic interest to the late-sixth-century-B.C. Greek helmet. When this was cleaned there became visible beyond the outer margin of each eye slit a delicately engraved palmette of a pattern that, even more definitely than the general fashion of the headpiece itself, proves the date of manufacture to have been the final quarter of the sixth century—which is to say, the period just before Carthage put an end to all Greek traffic in these waters by fortifying Gadir in Cádiz Bay to block Greek access to the Tartessos river and its adjacent mining territories.

No Greek finds of later date than this have ever been made in southwestern Spain. But from approximately this period onward, the Punic finds begin. From such concurrent evidence the conclusion is to be drawn that Carthage, after having followed Samian and Phocaean example and found great profit in Tartessian silver and the other products of the Andalusian mines, decided to eliminate Greek competition so as to divert this great source of wealth exclusively to her own coffers.

Carthage had warships and an effective naval personnel. By stationing these in Cádiz Bay under the walls of a well-fortified stronghold on the narrow island athwart the bay, Carthage put herself in position to intercept and, if resisted, to sink any merchant vessel of other nationality attempting to enter the estuary of the Guadalquivir.

There is a chance notice in Strabo that merits quotation here:

> As one sails from our own into the outer sea, Kalpē [10] lies to the right and by it, at a distance of some five miles, there is the ancient and noteworthy town of Karteia, which once served as marine base of the Iberians. Some claim that it was founded by Heracles; and among these is Timosthenes, who says that in olden days the town was called Heracleia and that wharfing-

[10] The Rock of Gibraltar.

slips for vessels and ship-sheds of very considerable extent are still to be seen there.[11]

As it is not clear what use the Iberian natives would have had for such an installation, it is a legitimate supposition that the site of present-day Algeciras, five miles west across the bay from Gibraltar rock, was fitted out by Carthage as a naval base from which to control the passage of the Gibraltar Strait. For it was not the Bay of Cádiz but the Pillars of Heracles that figured as the limit of permissible navigation in the minds of the Greek poets of the fifth century, after Carthage had imposed her embargo. Notably in Pindar, the greatest of the early-fifth-century lyric poets, there recurs again and again this theme:

Not easy it is to travel the inaccessible sea
Beyond the columns of Heracles that the god-hero set
To be witnesses of his utmost voyage.
Huge sea-beasts he conquered on the main
And through shallows explored the river-streams
Till he came to the end that turned him homeward.[12]

Now has Theron touched the very limits of bravery,
As it were coming home from the Pillars of Heracles,
Beyond which may travel neither wise men nor foolish.[13]

By their family's valourous deeds they have
   touched on Heracleian Pillars:
Unattainable farther beyond is any glory.

Yet Pindar once specifically names Gadir rather than Gibraltar as the limit of shipborne voyages:

Westward of Gadeira none may pass:
Turn back ship's tackle to Europe's land! [14]

If we are to take literally the Greek conviction that the Gibraltar Strait was not to be traversed by any Greek mariner, it would seem that the Strait must have been patrolled and blocked by the Carthaginian navy, in which case Karteia-Algeciras in Gibraltar Bay must have been used as its base of naval opera-

---

[11] Strabo, *Geography*, III.1.7.
[12] Pindar, *Nemea*, 3.20–26.
[13] Pindar, *Olympia*, 3.44–45.
[14] Pindar, *Nemea*, 4.69–70.

THE GREEKS EXPLORE THE WEST

tions, and we have the extraordinary illustration of history's tendency to repetition in twice bringing a foreign power to hold the Mediterranean Strait at this point by virtue of superior naval strength!

Although Phocaean warships had once (in 535 B.C.) worsted a combined Carthaginian and Etruscan task force in Corsican waters, neither the Phocaeans nor any other combination of Greek cities seem to have attempted to break the Carthaginian blockade of Tartessos and reestablish relations with Arganthonios, to partake of his openhanded generosity with his silver. By all odds, Carthaginian exclusion of the Greeks from the Andalusian mines and the Atlantic trade (which dealt in tin, gold and amber, as well) was the shrewdest blow that was ever struck against Greek commerce anywhere in the Mediterranean.

The ancient Greek explorers had manfully done their part by discovering the great western gateway to the Atlantic. But their successors, the merchant traders, had been unable to keep the gateway open for more than a century of use. Carthage had slammed the door shut in their faces. As far as we know, it was not until nearly three hundred years later that any Greek mariner was allowed to steer his ship unmolested into Cádiz Bay. The first to perform this hitherto forbidden journey hailed from the Phocaean colony in southern France that was to transmit its ancient name of "Massalia" to the great modern seaport city of Marseilles, situated on the same magnificent harbor. The man from Massalia was himself a Great Explorer: his name was Pytheas.

❦ III ❦

THE AFRICAN COAST

THERE are no records—not even archeological ones from wordless objects—to tell by what routes or in what remote periods men first found their way through the huge southern continent that the Greeks called "Libya" and that we call "Africa." It is idle to ask what human beings first penetrated its equatorial forests or what races first drove cattle over the green uplands that, during the Ice Age, preceded the inhospitable Sahara of modern times. Because we are so greatly dependent upon the written word for our knowledge of the past, it is only the literate people of the eastern Mediterranean region who might tell us anything about ancient Africa; and none of these knew that vast continent's remoter history or ever explored its distant interior. For this reason, because it is only as written notices exist that the story of ancient exploration can be compiled, our picture of African discovery is only a partial glimpse through Egyptian or Phoenician or Greek or Roman eyes. And because the habitants of the Mediterranean world moved abroad by sea so much more freely than by land, their exploration of the African continent was largely confined to its seaward fringe, the tremendous ocean-washed coast along which ships might sail for weeks yet have no sight and gain no knowledge of the land within. Only the occasional great river mouths —the Nile in the north, the Senegal and the Gambia on the west, perhaps the Niger and the Congo farther south—offered any opening for the shipborne voyager to penetrate interior territory. The only easy, ever-open road for trading, colonizing, and exploring was the sea; and that highway only skirted the land.

This notion that the traveler's proper path led over water and that he must take to ship if he would journey far suggested itself almost inevitably to the Mediterranean mind. Egypt south of the delta was a habitable land only as the Nile cut its narrow swath of fertility through the waterless desert; and there in antiquity the river was the highway of communication, while roads ashore were only lanes and byways between adjoining villages. Even in the Delta, where geography had a two-dimensional spread over wider land, the diverging arms of the Nile with their network of interconnecting canals made travel by boat or barge more convenient than trudging afoot or riding donkeyback.

In Mesopotamia the situation was virtually the same as in Egypt except that there were two rivers, the Euphrates and the Tigris, instead of only one as in Egypt. There, too, there was wide desert and mountain on either hand of the riverland; and within, as in the Nile delta, there was a network of interconnecting canals. Whether upstream or downstream, one traveled and moved merchandise better by water than by land.

In the Aegean homeland of the Greeks there were communities on more than fifty separate islands, with no communication possible among them except by sea. Even on the Greek mainland, because the hills were high and the roads were bad and none of the larger towns lay far inland, the all-penetrating sea made travel by ship the easier way of reaching another city's territory. For longer journeys to more distant lands the Mediterranean was usually the only practicable road. One could cross from continental Greece to the Asia Minor coast in a single day and night if one went by sea; whereas it was more than two weeks' heavy travel on foot or by animal if one followed the long way around by the shore. To reach southern Italy from Greece or Asia Minor, no one even considered going overland. There was the additional advantage in ship travel that, despite the possible mischances of storm and reefs and difficult headlands, the seas were comparatively safe, whereas overland passage set much greater perils from foreign hostility and lack of food by day and want of shelter by night. On shipboard one was one's own hospitable host, with food provided and a sure bed for sleep.

The Nile, as was just pointed out, constituted a natural and

inevitable road for Egyptian travel; but the Red Sea, too, offered
an unfailing highway to the south, vastly easier to negotiate
than its hot and wild and waterless shoreland. Between the two
avenues of travel, the Nile and the Red Sea, there was the important difference that, whereas the Nile led to impassable
reaches of gigantic gorges in Abyssinia and marshland in the
Sudan, the Red Sea offered a course free of peril or obstruction,
to lead the mariner to ever wider waters and more abundant
tropical climes. The narrowness of the Red Sea, combined with
the existence of only a single exit from its farther end, made
Egyptian penetration of the Indian Ocean inevitable. As previously mentioned, Egyptian ship voyages to "God's Country" in
the land of "Punt" prove that from surprisingly early times the
Egyptians of the Nile had been sailing at least as far as Eritrea
and perhaps as far as the Gulf of Aden and the outer Somali
coast of Africa. "Earth's ocean-stream," Africa's encircling Atlantic and Indian Oceans, was therefore known to them long
before any other Mediterranean people—unless perchance the
Phoenician ships that sailed from Ezion-geber to Ophir in King
Solomon's time had precursors manned by earlier Phoenicians
dwelling by the Gulf of Aqaba.

So likewise, but much later, when Phocaean Greek explorers
discovered the Gibraltar gateway to the Atlantic, the Greeks too
became aware that endless ocean held in the habitable land. If
one put together in common knowledge what the Egyptians
and the Phoenicians and the Greeks had learned, it would seem
certain that the world was encircled by water. And since this salt
water's flood ran in unceasing current past Gibraltar into the
Inner Sea, and similarly streamed through the strait at Aden
into the Red Sea, it was clear that the encircling ocean must act
like a gigantic river, running endlessly around the world.

About the year 600 B.C., after the outer ocean beyond Europe
and Africa on the west had become familiar to Greek and Phoenician mariners, even as the outer ocean beyond the Red Sea
had long been familiar to the Egyptians, the reigning pharaoh
Necho (whom we have met before in connection with the Nile-
Suez canal) seems to have been struck with the idea that Phoenician seadogs who had been able to work their way from Tyre
to Tangier and from Suez to Somali might succeed in making
the trip from the Red Sea to the Mediterranean by following

the outside track of the ocean's stream from Aden to Gibraltar and thus return to Egypt from the west, after having set out from it toward the south. Accordingly Necho issued a royal decree that a fleet should be equipped for such a voyage and that it should be put under a Phoenician captain's command and manned by a Phoenician crew.

No one in the Egyptian court or the Phoenician merchant marine could have had the least conception of the magnitude of this undertaking. Captain and king alike must have imagined that the external ocean-river circled directly from one sea to the other, so that the voyage to Spain by way of Africa's southern shore would not greatly exceed that along its northern coast through the Mediterranean. Presumably it was known that, once a ship had passed the Gulf of Aden and rounded Africa's eastern tip, the coast turned abruptly south and thereafter swung southwest. By continuing to veer westward, it would have led directly around through the Gulf of Guinea and along the Atlantic shore to Morocco. A glance at the map will show how mightily such an expectation was deceived!

The human mind tends to think in terms of simple geometrical shapes and symmetrical arrangements. In early classical times, before exploration brought better knowledge, men imaged the inhabited world as a huge disk of land with the Mediterranean Sea at its center and a symmetrically balanced grouping of continents about it on the north and east and south. Round the rim of the disk, like the felly holding in a wheel, there ran the endless stream of ocean, passing north of Europe, east and south of Asia at approximately equal remove. On such a view the extravagant asymmetry of Africa, with its protrusion southward through forty-five degrees of latitude from Cape Guardafui (opposite Aden) to the Cape of Good Hope and back again on the west to the Gulf of Guinea, could never have been anticipated. Captain and crew of the Phoenician fleet, setting out on the voyage around Africa pursuant to Necho's order, must have suffered a shock of surprise, bewilderment, and deep discouragement on finding that the African coast ran on and on without making the wide-sweeping turn to the west which they had so confidently expected.

One cannot too much wonder at the courageous persistence of these first circumnavigators of the immense equatorial and subtropical continent, who did not turn back in dejection and despair, to report to Necho that his project was impossible of execution, but instead held to their onward course, month after month through the varying seasons and changing climes, till their own sea came at last into view through the Gibraltar Strait.

Such, at any rate, was the surprising report about their voyage that Herodotus heard from his countrymen on the Nile when he visited Naukratis, the trading center that Necho's father had set aside for Greek merchants frequenting his land. Since all our knowledge of the event depends exclusively on the account in Herodotus, no better method of narrating it exists than by reproducing his text here in translation. This is the story as Herodotus tells it:

> Africa proves to be completely surrounded by water except for as much of it as borders on Asia.[1] Of all men of whom we have any knowledge, the Egyptian king Necho was the first to establish this fact. After he had ceased from trying to dig the canal that extends from the Nile to the Arabian Gulf, he dispatched some Phoenicians in ships with orders to sail back into our northern sea by passing through the Pillars of Heracles and so to return to Egypt.
>
> Accordingly these Phoenicians set out and from the Red Sea sailed into the southern ocean. Whenever autumn came, they went ashore wherever in Africa they chanced to be on their voyage, to sow grain in the earth and await the harvest. On reaping the new grain they put again to sea. In this wise, after two years had elapsed, they rounded the Pillars of Heracles and in the third year reached Egypt.
>
> Now, they told a tale that I personally do not believe (though others may, if they choose), how they had the sun *on their right hand* as they sailed along the African coast.[2]

In order to round the Cape of Good Hope, a ship must travel as far south of the equator as the Mediterranean lies north of it. In consequence of their deep penetration of the southern hemisphere the Phoenicians must have witnessed the reversal of a celestial phenomenon that every Mediterranean sailor regarded as fixed and immutable. Being without compass, the ancient mariners steered their course when out of sight of land

[1] I.e., at the Sinai Peninsula.
[2] Herodotus, *History*, IV.42.

by watching the position of the sun (just as at night they looked to the constellations of the northern Bears, or Great and Little Dipper, for guidance). Were a ship heading west, the sun in midsummer might rise somewhat left of the stern and set somewhat right of the bow; but otherwise throughout the day—as throughout the year—the sun in heaven would keep unvaryingly to port, holding the sky on the steersman's left. But in the southern hemisphere the situation is precisely reversed: the daily sun passes on the right of a ship headed west. At Africa's southern tip between Port Elizabeth and Cape Town, the coast tends almost due east and west for some five hundred miles; so that a ship following that stretch westward in order to round the Cape would necessarily have the sun north of it in the sky, that is, on its starboard or right-hand side. It was this novel experience that struck the Phoenician seamen as so extraordinary and, because its physical explanation escaped him, seemed completely incredible to Herodotus.

It is important not to misunderstand the intention of the Phoenician report about the behavior of the sun over southern waters—as the poet Coleridge seems to have done when he introduced it into his *Rime of the Ancient Mariner*. Like every well-educated Englishman of his day, Coleridge was thoroughly familiar with Greek classical literature; so that there is nothing surprising that more or less unconscious memories of Herodotus (as of Homer's *Odyssey*) color his famous poem. As the Mariner's ship sailed south on its outward voyage,

> The Sun came up upon the left,
> Out of the sea came he!
> And he shone bright, and on the right
> Went down into the sea.

But when, after having been "drawn by a storm toward the South Pole," the ship was returning northward again before "a good south wind,"

> The Sun now rose upon the right;
> Out of the sea came he,
> Still hid in mist, and on the left
> Went down into the sea.

If the Phoenicians of Herodotus' account had meant no more than this, that as they voyaged south through the Red Sea and the Indian Ocean the sun rose on their left, whereas after they had doubled the Cape and turned north it rose on their right, it would have been impossible for Herodotus to have found anything incredible in such an entirely obvious occurrence. What Herodotus refused to credit, and the Phoenicians asserted that they had seen, was a celestial phenomenon of a totally different order. Many modern critics have denied that an ancient Phoenician flotilla (Herodotus speaks of "ships," in the plural) could have performed the feat of circumnavigating Africa. But none of these skeptics has ever managed to explain how the Phoenician explorers could have thought of saying that they had seen the sun travel across the sky on the wrong side of their ships if they had not actually beheld it doing so.

It was a fortunate circumstance that the skeptical old historian, in keeping with his custom of repeating what he heard, even when he did not believe it to be true, gave the Phoenician story about the aberration of the sun during their journey and, at the same time, recorded his own conviction of its absurdity. For we may reasonably infer that, if Herodotus considered it an idle invention, others in King Necho's day would have greeted it with similar disbelief; so that it would have been a thoroughly unlikely invention to have been thought up by the Phoenicians to support a fictitious claim that they had circumnavigated Africa if they had not truly done so. And further, the very idea of attributing peculiar behavior to the sun in contradiction to its well-known and invariable habits would never have entered their minds, had it not been forced on their attention by an actual experience. The curious detail that Herodotus refused to believe thus turns out to be our surest warrant for believing the Phoenician claim that they circumnavigated Africa. For only at the southern end of the continent, on the five-hundred-mile stretch between Port Elizabeth and Cape Town, would their ship have been heading west in the southern hemisphere and only while it was so headed would they have had the sun consistently on their right hand. But if they succeeded in reaching the Cape, there is no good reason for refusing to believe that they kept on around it, to follow the retreating coast northward toward their now certain goal—especially as wind and ocean current alike would not merely have encouraged, but would practically have forced them on this course.

The direction in which the winds blew and the ocean currents flowed were factors of the greatest moment to ships under
sail that had extreme difficulty in working into the wind and
could not do so at all if the current flowed strongly against
them. By what can only be termed a happy stroke of fortune
the Phoenician voyage around Africa was attempted from east
to west around the Cape instead of in the opposite direction.
Winds and currents conspire greatly to favor the vessel that cir-
cumnavigates Africa in this clockwise manner. Along the East
African coast from Cape Guardafui, the southern "horn" of the
Gulf of Aden, all the way to Mozambique, through thirty degrees of latitude, the northeast monsoon blows pretty steadily
during our northern late-autumn and early-winter months, and
a strong ocean current travels with it. Thus, for three thousand
miles there is much to help and little to hinder progress. After
the Cape of Good Hope has been turned, the navigational conditions are exactly reversed. The so-called Agulhas current leads
into the equatorial current along the African west coast in unbroken run from the Cape to the equator, accompanied and
encouraged through most of its course by the southern hemisphere's trade wind blowing from the southeast. Beyond the
equator westward through the thousand miles of the Gulf of
Guinea the winds are fitful and the currents variable; but there
is no real obstacle to a ship's progress past Nigeria and Ghana,
the Ivory Coast and Liberia, until the long last stretch is reached
around the huge bulge of northwestern Africa.

Throughout this long journey from the Gulf of Aden to the
Guinea coast natural conditions of the shorelands would in
general have been propitious for landing to secure water and
food and for camping out. But there is a long, rough stretch of
extreme aridity on the southwest coast north of the Cape—the
redoubtable Kalahari Desert. Yet this would not overmuch have
appalled Phoenicians accustomed to voyaging the equally arid
Egyptian coast of the Red Sea. Only the next-to-final stage of
the voyage to the Gibraltar Strait—the thousand miles of almost
waterless, dune-surfaced Saharan coastland lying athwart the
tropics—need have proved really formidable, with the northern
trade wind blowing persistently in their faces, the currents in
general running against them, and the long Atlantic swell
pounding hard on the beaches or against the low rocky shores.

But by this time the sailors must have seen from the set of the constellations that they were back under familiar skies and could not be too far from their Mediterranean goal.

Among the critics who accept the voyage around Africa as historic fact rather than dismissing it as Herodotean fiction or Phoenician pretense, several have attacked the problem realistically by constructing a detailed timetable for the journey with its various stopovers. Given the total length of the African coast as roughly 16,000 miles and the duration of the voyage as somewhat more than two years, or rather less than a thousand days, there is nothing discordant between these two sets of figures. An average run of only forty miles per day during periods of active sailing would still leave time for idling through unfavorable weather and for biding ashore during more than half of the voyage. Basing their suggestions on Carl Mueller's reconstruction, Cary and Warmington in their authoritative treatise *The Ancient Explorers* have given the following itinerary for the Phoenician expedition:

> They left Egypt, we may suppose, late in November and rowed against a then unfavorable current of the Red Sea and the N.E. monsoon as far as the headland of Guardafui. Turning south here with the coast they had the N.E. monsoon and drift-current behind to the equator, after which, in early northern spring, the S.E. trade wind blew at the side. Soon after crossing the equator . . . the swift Mozamique current swept them on, the Agulhas current taking them round the Cape, on the western side of which (perhaps in Great Bushman Land at St. Helena Bay, south of the Kalahari desert) they landed during May of the first year in a subtropical climate where wheat could grow, sowed the grain in June, reaped in November, and set sail in December, being now in the second year of travel. . . . The Bight of Biafra at the equator, where the coast turns abruptly west beside the great Gulf of Guinea, was reached late in March. . . . After this . . . a S.W. wind and calms, in spite of the Guinea current, caused hard rowing along the coast to and round Cape Palmas which marks the frontier between Ivory Coast and Liberia at the extreme western end of the Gulf of Guinea—late in June, whereupon the N.E. trade wind and the ever-lessening Canaries current fought unsuccessfully against them all the way towards the Straits of Gibraltar. Passing the tropic at the end of September, they landed again some-

where in Morocco (suitable for wheat) in November, sowed in December, reaped in June, and went on, quickening up in home waters. Once inside the Straits, the joy of home-rushing coupled with neutral winds and a favorable current made the last lap to the Nile easy. Such may have been the voyage taken by these Phoenicians.[3]

In connection with this proposed timetable for the voyage an alternative suggestion may be made:

Herodotus' report that "whenever autumn came" the crews disembarked "wherever in Africa they chanced to be, to sow grain and wait for the harvest to ripen," hardly sounds probable, since the African shoreland was everywhere inhabited and the natives would presumably have been willing to supply food in exchange for such trinkets and articles of trade as Phoenician ships habitually carried. (Compare Homer's *Odyssey* XV.415–16 and 459–60: "Then there arrived Phoenicians, skilled mariners, in a dark ship with many a trinket. . . . And a crafty man came to my father's house with a golden necklace strung with amber, which my mother and her housemaids took in hand and examined, offering a price for it.")

It would be a much more plausible assumption that the prolonged interruptions in the voyage around Africa were occasioned not by any lack of grain for bread, but through the onset of contrary winds, by which the flotilla was obliged to wait for the alternate changes of air currents prevalent in those southern latitudes.

Despite the various doubts and queries and rational objections that may be raised about an exploit demanding so much courage and persistence, such skill of seamanship, such resourcefulness in the face of adversity, let us content ourselves with asserting that there is good reason to accept Herodotus' report as accurate in its essentials, that we may take it for historic fact that the pharaoh Necho (who ruled Egypt from 609 to 593 B.C.) commanded such an expedition of exploration about 600 B.C., and that, obeying his orders, a group of Phoenician mariners actually accomplished the task of sailing clockwise around the entire continent of Africa from Egypt back to Egypt.

A hundred years passed before anyone again attempted the

[3] M. Cary and E. H. Warmington, *The Ancient Explorers* (Baltimore, Md.: Penguin Books, Inc., 1963), p. 94.

circumnavigation of Africa. And when the attempt was made, it resulted in failure. Again it is Herodotus who gives us the story; but this time his account is so interwoven with personal anecdote and salacious incident that it is difficult to unravel the historic thread from the picturesque loomwork of popular romance. Before repeating the tale as Herodotus tells it, it would be well to look at the tyrannical and heartless Persian despots through more sympathetic eyes than those of their Greek contemporaries. For where the Greek saw only an Oriental monarch in barbarian cruelty indulging his arbitrary will, today's impartial historian discerns a statesmanlike and truly great ruler intent on enlarging a mighty empire. If Xerxes was interested in learning the size and shape of the African continent and dispatched his own cousin on a voyage of exploration to bring him word of the nature and extent of this possible increment to the already enormous Persian empire, we may look beyond the court scandal and gossip that reached Ionian Greek ears, to catch a glimpse of world politics and the higher strategy of empire. Even so, we must start from the story as Herodotus tells it:

> So this was the first exploration of Africa.
> The next is claimed by the Carthaginians. For Sataspes, son of Teaspes, a Persian Achaemenid, did not succeed in circumnavigating Africa, although he had been dispatched for this very purpose, but became frightened at the length of the voyage and the emptiness of it and therefore returned without accomplishing the task that his mother had set him.
> Now, Sataspes had done violence to the virgin daughter of Zopyros, Megabyzes' son; whereupon Xerxes the king was about to have him impaled for this offense. But Sataspes' mother, who was sister to Darius, begged him off, saying that she would impose an even heavier penalty than the king himself: he would have to circumnavigate Africa till, by so doing, he reached the Arabian Gulf!
> Xerxes agreed to these terms. So Sataspes went to Egypt and there engaged a ship and crew. With these he proceeded to the Pillars of Heracles and sailed through them and doubled the African cape of Soloeis. He continued to journey south, traversing a vast expanse of sea in the course of many months, yet always there was more ahead of him. So he turned back and returned to Egypt.
> Appearing before King Xerxes, he related to him how at the

farthest point of his voyage he encountered a race of little men
who wore palmleaf clothing and fled into the hills whenever
he landed near them, abandoning their villages. Yet neither
he nor his crew did them any injury, except only that they
seized some of their cattle. And he declared that the reason why
he had not sailed all the way around Africa was that the ship
was unable to move any further forward but remained fast in the
water. But Xerxes refused to admit that he was telling the
truth and, because he had not accomplished the task that had
been set him, imposed the original sentence and had him
impaled.

Now, a eunuch who belonged to this same Sataspes, the
moment he learned that his master was dead, fled to Samos
with a large sum of money; and this a Samian took away from
him. (I know this Samian man's name, but do not intend to
divulge it.) [4]

We have already noted that Herodotus was well-acquainted
with Samos; so that there is every reason for thinking that his
account of Sataspes, the Persian nobleman, reached him from
the lips of the fugitive eunuch slave. We may be well enough
convinced that the unfortunate eunuch was robbed of his stolen
wealth by some Samian Greek; but we cannot be equally sure
in regard to the long rigamarole about the ravished maiden and
the curious penalty for the act—as though a reasonable way to
expiate rape was to sail around Africa! It may be that the eunuch
actually accompanied his master on his unsuccessful expedition
and had himself seen the little men in palmleaf clothing flee in
terror of the strange ship and its stranger occupants. If not, then
he learned about them directly from Sataspes, who no doubt re-
galed his household with tales of his adventures before seeking
audience with his unforgiving sovereign. It is possible that mere
failure to carry out the royal command was the actual cause of
his execution; and all the rest may have been mere court scandal
and gossip. In any event, Sataspes was a real person and his expedition was a historical event. Since he collected his ship and
his crew in Egypt, these would have been Phoenician, not native
Egyptian because the Egyptians did not sail widely over Mediterranean waters, and not Greek because during Xerxes' reign,
which lasted from 485 to 465 B.C., the Gibraltar passage was
already closed to Greek vessels.

[4] Herodotus, *History*, IV.43.

At that period the Carthaginians not only held Gadir in the Bay of Cádiz, but had already explored the Atlantic coast of Africa and founded trading settlements on the Moroccan shore. It was therefore very natural for Sataspes' Phoenicians to set the course of the voyage by way of the Gibraltar Strait and Morocco, where the "cape of Soloeis" is to be sought—probably in the precipitous headland known today as Cape Cantin, some three hundred miles beyond the Straits. The "emptiness" and desolation that appalled Sataspes thereafter may readily be identified with the long reaches of the Río de Oro coastland, low, arid, and skirted with sand dunes for hundreds of miles—conditions that continue with unabated dreariness until Mauretania is passed. For it is here that the thousand-mile-wide zone of the water-poor Sahara touches on the ocean. The undersized race that dressed itself in palmleaves could not have been encountered here; so it is certain that it was not the emptiness of the Sahara that turned Sataspes back, however much it may have affrighted him. Beyond Dakar there is woodland again and still farther south, past Guinea and Sierra Leone, equatorial fertility reigns.

Somewhere here, or perhaps still farther along in the Gulf of Guinea, must have occurred Sataspes' experience with the little men who fled at his approach. And a little farther along, in the deep pocket of the Gulf, his ship stuck fast in the sea and could not be made to move forward. The explanation is simple: Sataspes had encountered the current of water that the southern trade wind drives before it along the west coast of Africa toward the equator and into the Gulf of Guinea. It was not the equatorial calms, the so-called doldrums, that turned him back, since the crew could have coped with desultory or failing winds by use of oar. But when the prevailing direction of the wind and the steady drift of the surface water combined counter to his course, no toiling at the oars could accomplish any visible progress. Even when occasionally the ship moved forward during daylight hours, during the night it would always have drifted back to where it was before. In this sense it "stuck fast" in the sea, so that nothing was to be done except to give in to this baffling perversity of the southern ocean and turn the ship's prow back on the course that it had come (whereupon, of course, the vessel would have moved agreeably on, as though every whit as anxious as its commander to begin the journey home).

The only obscurity in this entertaining narrative is lodged in the opening statement about the Carthaginians' title to having been the next true explorers of Africa subsequent to Necho's expedition, inasmuch as Sataspes' attempt (in Herodotus' estimation) did not qualify because he had not "sailed around Africa." But who were these Carthaginian explorers who were more successful than Sataspes and who, by implication, made a later voyage? To this question Herodotus supplies no answer, either in the passage cited or elsewhere in his *History*. It is tempting to think that his remark about the Carthaginians conceals a reference to the exploit of Hanno of Carthage; but if so, it is very strange that he nowhere found occasion to introduce that spectacular achievement into his liberally discursive narrative about people, places, and events.

Clearly, if anyone outdid Sataspes in the exploration of Africa by sea, he must have been a Carthaginian, whether a citizen of Carthage itself or a colonial from one of that city's more western settlements, since only Punic ships were allowed through the Gibraltar Strait during the two and a half centuries succeeding Sataspes' ill-starred venture. And at the other starting point for sailing around Africa, there was no one in Egypt interested in sending out an exploratory expedition of this magnitude until the days of the second Ptolemy, the Macedonian Greek ruler who received the title of Philadelphus and expressed an enlightened concern for natural history and geographical knowledge. But all this was, of course, long after Herodotus' lifetime —which leaves us with the difficulty of finding any Carthaginian navigator who might have bettered Sataspes' record some time in the fifty years intervening between the violent death of Sataspes and the peaceful demise of Herodotus. The only candidate anywhere mentioned by ancient writers is Hanno.

No more curious document has survived from classical antiquity than the Greek manuscript entitled *Periplous of Hanno,* which was copied out in the tenth century of our era and preserved in the library of the University of Heidelberg. Few texts of such limited length have elicited so much discussion and critical comment or led to more contradictory opinions. The pretense that this extraordinary narrative makes to historical veracity may seem so improbable at first sight as to raise doubts on its authenticity. Yet, certainly, it is not an ancient forgery or fraud, but must be accepted at face value.

The manuscript is headed:

> Voyage of Hanno, king of the Carthaginians, to the Afric lands beyond the Pillars of Heracles, an account of which he dedicated in the sanctuary of Baal, as follows:

This preamble should be taken as an explanatory title affixed by the Greek translator of the original document, which must of course have been composed in Hanno's own native language, i.e., the North Semitic Phoenician dialect known as Punic, current in Carthage in his time. As one reads on, a score of questions at once arise: Is the Greek translation complete and entire? Is it linguistically accurate, correctly reproducing the sense of the original Punic? Is it a word-for-word rendering, or has it undergone recasting into conventional Greek literary form?

More drastic doubts extend to the original Punic document that the Greek translator purported to have consulted: Was there ever such a document? Would a high Carthaginian official with the title of "king" have absented himself on such a lengthy and perhaps precarious expedition? If he had done so, would he have published a detailed account of it, for any chance visitor to Baal's temple to consult and write down? (The Carthaginians had a reputation for scrupulously concealing from other nationalities everything connected with their commercial enterprises "beyond the Pillars.") Were records of contemporary events and undertakings thus posted in the sanctuaries of Carthage? And if they were, would a Greek visitor have been allowed access to them?

That there were Greeks capable of deciphering the Punic alphabetic script and understanding what was written in it is certainly possible, even though the classical Greeks were notoriously uninterested in other languages than their own. The dies for some extremely beautiful silver coins issued by Carthage in the course of the fifth and fourth centuries B.C. are unmistakably the work of Greek artists, who presumably would have superintended their manufacture in the metal workshops of Carthage itself. In the course of the frequent and vehement battles between Carthage and the Sicilian Greeks, great numbers of prisoners were taken by both sides; so that a certain degree of bilingual communication must have developed between the speakers of the two basically unrelated tongues. Accordingly, a document composed in Punic would not necessarily have been unintelligible to a Greek who chanced to be in Carthage.

To all these variously inspired doubts and hesitations there are no completely reassuring replies. Yet the all but universal verdict of modern scholarship has been that an original Punic document actually existed, that it was publicly displayed in the chief temple of Carthage, and that this same document—perhaps in condensed or otherwise abbreviated form and with a discreet amount of literary embellishment by the Greek translator—has been in most respects faithfully reproduced in the Greek version. But the translator's name, provenance, and precise or even approximate date of activity remain undiscoverable. All that is certain about him is that he must have published his brief work sometime during the third century B.C. (because the compiler of the pseudo-Aristotelian collection *Remarkable Reports* made use of it, whereas Aristotle himself seems not to have known it) and that it was widely circulated among educated Greeks and Romans, for Hanno's name and references to his report occur frequently in the Greek and Latin authors. As to the date of the expedition itself, practically nothing more certain is known than can be inferred from Pliny's notice that Hanno was commissioned to "explore the circuit of Africa while the power of Carthage was at its height"—a remark that is usually interpreted as referring to the early fifth-century B.C., but would equally well (or even better) fit the early third century before the opening of the Punic Wars with Rome.

If these preliminary notices have stimulated the reader's curiosity sufficiently to make him wish for a closer look at Hanno's account of his African expedition of exploration, here will be a proper place to satisfy it. Here, then—in a retranslation of a translation—is the text of the famous document:

1. The Carthaginians decreed that Hanno should make a voyage outside the Pillars of Heracles and found cities for the Phoenicians of Africa. Accordingly he set sail in command of

sixty penteconters, with a multitude of men and women to the number of 30,000 and with provisions and other equipment.

2. After having put to sea, when we had passed the Pillars and voyaged two days outside them, we founded our first city, which we named Thymiaterion. Below it was a broad plain.

3. Thereafter we set out to sea toward the west and assembled at Soloeis, an African headland overgrown with trees.

4. After dedicating thereon a sanctuary of Poseidon, we reembarked and proceeded half a day toward the sunrise until we came upon a lagoon situated close to the sea and full of tall reedbeds. In these there were elephants feeding and many other sorts of wild animals.

5. After voyaging past this lagoon about a day's run we stationed colonies along the coast, naming them Carian Fort, Gyttē, The Heights, Melitta, and Arambys.

6. Thence we again set sail and came to the Lixos, a large river flowing from [the interior of] Africa. Along it the Lixite nomads were pasturing their herds; and among them we remained for some considerable time, making friends of them.

7. Beyond them higher up there dwelt inhospitable Ethiopians, tending a country infested by wild beasts and hemmed in by great mountains, out of which the Lixos is said to flow. Peculiar races inhabit the mountains, cave dwellers, whom the Lixites declared to be fleeter of foot than horses.

8. From these Lixites we took aboard interpreters and continued our voyage southward past the desert for *nine* [5] days, whereupon we turned again toward the sunrise for a day's run. And there in the recesses of a gulf we discovered a small island with a circuit of about *fifteen* stades. This we occupied, giving it the name Kernē. We conjectured that in terms of our voyage it lay on a direct line with Carthage, inasmuch as the journey from Carthage to the Straits was about the same length as that from the Straits to Kernē.

9. Thence sailing along a great river called Chretes we reached a lake that contained three islands larger than Kernē. From these, by completing a daylong voyage, we came to the head of the lake, beyond which there extended some very high hills full of savages clad in wildbeast hides. These drove us off by hurling stones at us and would not let us land.

10. Proceeding thence we came to a second river, great and wide, and swarming with crocodiles and hippopotamuses. So we turned back again and retraced our course to Kernē.

[5] Asterisks indicate amended text. See pp. 92–3.

11. From there we sailed south for twelve days, holding to the land, all of which was inhabited by Negroes who fled and would not abide us. They uttered words unintelligible to the Lixites in our company.

12. And so, on the final day, we moored by great forest-clad hills. And the wood of their trees was odorous sweet and of great variety.

13. Past these we journeyed for two days and found ourselves in an enormous inlet of the sea. On the landward side was a level plain, from which at night we beheld fires leaping up everywhere at varying distances, now greater and now less.

14. We took on water and proceeded thence along the coast for five days until we came to a large gulf that our interpreters said was called "Horn of the West." Therein there was a large island; within the island there was a sea-like body of water containing a second island. Here we landed. And from it by daytime we saw nothing except forest; but at night we beheld many blazing fires and heard a sound of pipes and the rattle of cymbals and drums and an endless shouting. Thereupon fear seized on us and our soothsayers advised us to quit the island.

15. At once putting out to sea we coasted past a blazing land filled with the odor of aromatic shrubs. And from it fiery torrents cascaded into the sea. The earth was so hot that we could not land.

16. From there too, fear-stricken, we quickly sailed away, and for four days were carried along, beholding the countryside aflame by night and in the midst thereof a heaven-high fire greater than the rest, that seemed to touch the stars. By day this showed as a lofty mountain that was called "The Chariot of the Gods."

17. Two days later, having passed these fiery torrents, we reached a bay called "Horn of the South." In a corner of this there was an island like the former one, enclosing a body of water in which there was a second island. This was full of savages. Far the most of these were women with hairy bodies, whom our interpreters called "Gorillas." Although we pursued the men, we were unable to capture these, as all of them eluded us by climbing cliffs and warding us off with rocks; but we caught three of the women, who bit and scratched their captors and would not come along. So we slew and flayed them and brought their skins back to Carthage.

18. Provisions failing, we sailed no farther.

It will not have escaped notice, even on a cursory reading of this account, that Hanno's expedition had a twofold purpose. Primarily he seems to have been dispatched to transport a large body of colonists and settle them along the Atlantic coast of Morocco. Having accomplished this—and perhaps more on his own initiative than by specific commission of his native city— he proceeded to conduct a much more extensive voyage of exploration, presumably with only one or two of his original fleet of sixty penteconters, heading beyond Morocco far to the south toward equatorial Africa.

The modern literature about his voyage is unexpectedly large. But it is so filled with disagreement that to summarize it with any thoroughness would be to annul its effectiveness, as the variant opinions would cancel each other out. As already indicated, controversy is not directed so much at the identity of Hanno among the numerous Carthaginian nobles of that name, or at the precise date of his expedition, or at the credibility of his narrative, but at its geographical interpretation, in search of convincing solutions to the very natural and seemingly innocuous question: Where did Hanno go?

Sailing times are so frequently recorded and topographical indications are so specific that it might be anticipated that Hanno's voyage could readily be traced on a modern map. Perhaps too many armchair geographers have essayed to do so and, by seeking to impose their own interpretations to the discredit of those advanced by others, have introduced unnecessary complications. On the assumption that Hanno rendered his account in good faith, certain fixed points occur in his itinerary; and between these firm points of attachment other links in the chain can be inserted with negligible chance of falling into serious error.

But before attempting thus to reconstruct Hanno's journey, some more general observations may be helpful:

1. Sailing distances are recorded by Hanno in terms of days, without indication of whether the reference is to daylight hours only, with nights spent in bivouac ashore, or to continuous twenty-four-hour periods. Nor is any mention made of time spent in exploring the various stretches of coastal waters or in landing in hope of acquiring information from inhabitants of the country. Even when the number of hours under sail at sea

seems ascertainable, there is no accompanying information on the direction or strength of the winds and ocean currents, despite the fact that these are factors that would have introduced very great anomalies into the length of the day's run. Thus, on the simplest sort of arithmetical calculation, for a sailing ship traveling with an average speed of four knots, the difference between a twenty-four-hour run in the teeth of a two-knot head-current and one with a favoring one-knot current from directly astern is the difference between 48 and 120 miles! Yet this reflects the contrast between sailing west along the Algerian coast to the Strait of Gibraltar and heading southwest along the Atlantic coast of Morocco after having turned Cape Spartel at the Atlantic end of the Strait. Perhaps, by use of oar, Hanno's penteconters could have lessened this discrepancy; but the forces of wind and current must never be forgotten for the days before ships were propelled by steam.

2. Trouble arises from the varying impression that mountains and hills and shoreland heights may have produced, according as these features were sighted in the midst of otherwise level country, rose close to the shore, or were visible in the distance, were scenically striking, etc. Special uncertainty in interpreting the text is caused by the failure of Greek speech to make our English distinction among hills, mountains, and ranges. The Greek word *oros* was applied indifferently to high mountains and relatively unpretentious hills, so that it may not be translated invariably as either. The tremendous snow-clad range of the Anti-Atlas are termed in #7 "great *orē*" and also simply "*orē*"; in #9 there are "extremely large *orē*" up-river from Kernē, although no high mountains are to be found in the vicinity of the Sahara's coastal strip; in #12 there are "great wooded *orē*" so close to the sea that ships may moor beneath them; and in #16 there is an "extremely large *oros*," upon which the fires at night seemed to "touch the stars."

3. There is a similar lack of precision in the word *limnē*, which may designate a true landlocked lake of any size or a saltwater lagoon or an enclosed bay or gulf of the sea. The strange sequence of landmarks that occurs twice in the narrative —once at the "Horn of the West" and again at the "Horn of the South"—where there is in each case an island in a "lake" inside

an island in a gulf or bay, ceases to be a geographical curiosity on proper interpretation of the kind of *limnē* intended.

4. Only a few commentators have (with Pliny) mistaken the "horns" in #14 and #18 for capes or promontories despite the specific description of them as gulfs of the sea.

Thus armed with precautionary guides to the understanding of the text, we may try to follow Hanno from his native city of Carthage to Morocco and down the Atlantic coast of northwestern Africa to Liberia, on the verge of the Gulf of Guinea:

#1. The distance from Carthage to the Strait of Gibraltar on a course laid within sight of the coast of Tunisia, Algeria, and Morocco is slightly more than a thousand miles. The Greek geographer Scylax (fourth century B.C.?) is our authority for making this a voyage of seven days and seven nights under extremely favorable conditions. (But this must be somewhat of a record; for Polybius makes mention of a ship setting sail from Ostia, the port of Rome, and passing through the Strait of Messina in the course of the fifth day. Keeping always within sight of the Italian coast, the distance thus traveled would have totaled about 370 miles, so that 80 miles a day would appear to have been a more normal rate of fair progress.) Since access to fresh water and meals and fire and sleep were a virtual necessity after the close quarters of a penteconter (and no one has managed to explain how Hanno could have transported 30,000 passengers in sixty ships!), Hanno's fleet should have taken at least a full fortnight to reach and pass out between the "Pillars."

#2. From Gebel Mūsa, or "Monkey Mountain," the African "pillar" of the Strait, as far as Cape Spartel at the Strait's Atlantic end, there would have been slow going against the inward-streaming ocean, with a veering wind more frequently blowing counter from the west. It is a run of slightly less than thirty miles; but it may well have used up a good part of the first of the two days "outside the Pillars." But then at Cape Spartel the African coast turns abruptly south southwest; and with equal suddenness the ocean current should have veered to help instead of hinder Hanno's ships; while, if the season was late spring, the trade wind would already be blowing to favor speed. Even so, the two days' voyage from Gebel Mūsa could hardly have exceeded 130 miles in all.

After turning Cape Spartel, the course at first led along sandy beaches with low hills close behind and higher mountains on the skyline, and thereafter by alternating low cliffs and scrubby sandhills to the mouth of the only sizable river in this stretch of coast. Here, on either side of the river valley, the land is wide and level, forming the broad plain of Hanno's narrative. It was here, quite probably, that the first settlement, Thymiaterion, was planted. The district today ranks among the richest agriculturally in all Morocco. Port Lyautey, a growing city on the south side of the river some eight miles from the ocean, may mark the very site of the Phoenician colony.

#3. "Thereafter we put out to sea toward the west and assembled at Soloeis, an African headland overgrown with trees." A few miles beyond the mouth of the Sebu River, beside which Thymiaterion may have been located, the Moroccan coast trends somewhat more westerly past Casablanca and Cape Blanco to a conspicuous headland that rises precipitously two hundred feet above the sea. For a variety of reasons, taking into account also the references of other ancient writers, this headland (known today as Cape Cantin) has been identified by most of the commentators as ancient Soloeis, despite its present total lack of trees. It was a Greek practice to build temples or set up altars to the sea-god Poseidon on rocky capes that ships had to turn amid possible peril from wind, wave, and current (Cape Sunium on the southernmost promontory of Attica is a famous instance; but there are many other examples); and it would not be in the least remarkable if the Phoenicians entertained a similar superstition.

Here the coast turns sharply south—but not, as Hanno thought, "toward the sunrise." Everyone who has concerned himself much with the geographical notices occurring in the ancient authors has been many times perplexed by their failure to report the points of the compass with even approximate correctness. (A comparable experience that may have its appeal for the reader is our modern tendency to undergo similar confusion whenever we navigate the land in a motor car without benefit of map.) About thirty miles beyond the cape—half a day's journey for Hanno's fleet—the inconspicuous mouth of the Wadi Tensift hides a large inland river that floods its marshes behind the coastal reef in the late spring when the upland snows have melted. Here perhaps is where Hanno saw the elephants and other wild animals feeding. Since none such feed there today, it may be that we have by now lost the track of Hanno's passing along these shores. Neither have any traces yet been discovered of the five cities founded near the sea after a day's journey beyond the elephant's marsh—though it may be guessed that Mogador Island, close offshore, and the highly fertile river valley of the Sus behind Agadir would have attracted the new settlers. But all uncertainty about this sector of the voyage is of no particular importance for Hanno's further itinerary because #6 leads to one of its fixed points, from which to start anew, confident that the track has once more been found.

Near the southern limit of habitability of the Moroccan coastland, the Wadi Dra'a coincides with a striking climatological division of crucial import in the economy of human existence. North of the river there lifts the great mountain range of the Atlas, whose snowy summits are clearly visible from shipboard after Mogador is passed. South of the river an utterly arid country suddenly begins. Here is the oceanward end of the mighty Sahara Desert, extending south from the Dra'a for fully a thousand miles of ill-watered and agriculturally unprofitable coast. Thus the Dra'a marks the division between the high pastoral world of upland Morocco and the low-lying, scarcely habited Sahara. It is Morocco's longest watercourse, and if its lower final stretch were not today diverted into innumerable irrigation channels in a struggle to keep the edge of the desert fertile, it would still be always a great river where it reaches the sea, and not only when it is in spate in late spring from the melting snow near its sources.

It was here that Hanno, after settling his five colonies along the coast, "came to the Lixos, a large river flowing out of Africa." The "nomads pasturing their herds" are still to be found in the seasonally shifting pastoral dwellers of the skirts of the Anti-Atlas range. Upland beyond these, where the Dra'a emerges from a rocky gorge, the land grows wilder—as no doubt its inhabitants once did also. As Hanno remained "for some considerable time" at the Dra'a before undertaking the second part of his project and proceeding to investigate the forbidding country to the south, his crews had opportunity for exploring the interior under guidance of the friendly "Lixites" and for catching at least a glimpse of the high interior country "infested by wild beasts and hemmed in by great mountains, out of which the Lixos is said to flow" and inhabited by more primitive and far less hospitable tribes.

If one wonders how Hanno and his men managed to converse with the natives dwelling beside the Dra'a, the explanation lies in the widespread Berber race with its dialectically little-diversi-fied Berber tongue with which the Phoenician-speaking folk of Carthage were thoroughly familiar through political and com-mercial contact with the natives of the interior of Tunisia. Even if the Berber dialect spoken on the banks of the Dra'a sounded somewhat strange to those who had learned a version of it in the environs of Carthage, it was apparently sufficiently similar to encourage the idea of taking on some of the Lixites as interpreters for the Saharan cruise. But what language or languages the Lixites may have known in addition to their own must remain an open question.

I have never had any opportunity for acquiring a firsthand knowledge of the Atlantic coast of Spanish Sahara and Maure-tania, with its sandstone cliffs and gravelly hills alternating with dunes and sandy beaches backed by an interior where nothing is to be seen except the desert itself; but from the sailing manuals it would appear that for a stretch of more than a thou-sand miles the rollers break heavily against the shore to make landing difficult and dangerous. And even if one succeeds in getting ashore, there is nothing of interest to explore. This sector of Hanno's voyage must have proved dreary and dis-couraging. But there was some measure of compensation in that the northeast trade wind blows almost uninterruptedly down this empty coast and an ocean current generally sets in the same direction as the wind, to add as much as thirty miles to the length of the day's run. With wind and current aiding and nothing to lure the sailor ashore except the need to replenish his supply of drinking water wherever a feeble desert stream broke the shoreline, it may be presumed that Hanno kept his ship (or ships) at sea for the greater part of each day and night. In that case he might have run more than a hundred miles in every twenty-four-hour period; and in consequence, on the ninth day after setting out from the Dra'a, he would have found himself at last clear of the desert zone. Rounding the remarkably long but very narrow tongue of sandy marshland and dunes that separates the Senegal River from the sea, Hanno would have turned east into the great estuary of the Senegal. Exploring this, he would have discovered on the seaward margin of the westernmost branch of the river, ten miles above the mouth whereby he had entered, a narrow sandy island about a mile in length—the same island whereon today is situated the city of Saint-Louis, one-time seat of government for the province of Senegal.

But it should be noted that in this paragraph (but nowhere else in the entire text) it must be assumed that the copyist or translator has introduced a couple of errors in his figures. For the manuscript sets the "voyage southward past the desert" at only two days and gives the circuit of the "small island in the recesses of the gulf" at five, and not fifteen, stades. The latter slip may be corrected without hesitation by consulting Pliny, who states that "Polybius reports that Kernē lies in utmost Mauretania, eight stades [one Roman mile] distant from land; and Cornelius Nepos assigns it a circuit of not more than two miles." Since all later information about Kernē was ultimately derived from Hanno's account, these figures for Kernē's size and its location close to the shore should be accepted.

The correction of the other textual error has no such support from any ancient author; but it is no less mandatory. For the voyage "southward past the desert" could not possibly have lasted only two days. Even at the most favorable rate of speed, two days' voyage southward from the Wadi Dra'a would have left Hanno still in the heart of the Sahara zone—somewhere about Cape Bojador, where there is no river and no opportunity of sailing east. From Bojador it is another 170 miles or so to the Rió de Oro, which has by some been identified as the site of Kernē. But while it is an enormous bay, the Río de Oro despite its name is not a river; and this causes insuperable difficulties in the immediately following paragraphs. With these considerations in mind it has been very plausibly suggested that, somewhere along the line of copying and recopying, the letter *theta* (by which, in default of specific numerical symbols, the Greeks indicated "nine") has been mistakenly read as the very

similarly formed letter *beta* (which was used to signify "two").
Some such correction must in any case be made in order to give
Hanno time to overpass the thousand-mile desert coast of the
Saharan zone. A virtually conclusive confirmation for this
emendation appears to have been overlooked by the commentators. In Arrian's account of India, the so-called *Indica,*
often printed as a supplement to his *Anabasis of Alexander,*
the concluding chapter makes the following reference to Hanno:

> But Hanno the Libyan, starting out from Carthage, traveled
> beyond the Columns of Heracles out into the ocean, keeping
> Africa on his left. On heading eastward his voyage lasted thirty-
> five days; but on turning south he encountered many difficulties
> —want of water, blazing heat, and fiery streams running into the
> sea.

Disregarding the confusion in points of the compass, since
Arrian's source of information was necessarily Hanno's own
account, his figure of thirty-five days must have been drawn
from the *Periplous* by the simple expedient of adding up the
number of days recorded in the text. As the reader may readily
convince himself, a sum total of thirty-five will result only if
the journey past the Sahara in #8 is taken at nine days. But if
Kernē was reached by a nine-day trip from the Dra'a, its only
intelligible location is in the estuary of the Senegal.

Modern Saint-Louis therefore, on this interpretation, marks
the site of Carthaginian Kernē; and the great river Chretes that
was next explored (in #9 and #10) can only be northwestern
Africa's greatest river, the Senegal, more than a thousand miles
in length and navigable at certain seasons of the year for fully
half that distance from the sea. On a secluded little island,
sheltered from the Atlantic surf and not easily accessible from
the nearby land, Hanno constructed some sort of camping place
and cache, to which he might return after exploring the mighty
river inland.

#9 has caused needless confusion among the commentators
through their failure to perceive that the "great river," the
"lake that contained three islands larger than Kernē," and the
"second river, great and wide, swarming with crocodiles and
hippopotamuses" were all parts of one and the same river, the
Senegal, and that this explains the otherwise wholly inexplicable
backtracking to Kernē in the course of the expedition.

A glance at the map will show how Hanno could have spoken of Kernē as an island in the recess of a gulf and distinguished this gulf from the great river that he thereafter investigated. If the season of the year was by now approaching autumn, the Senegal would have been in flood from the summer rains and vast areas would have been under water, converting the level land along the river's lower reaches into immense lakelike marshes. One of these, known nowadays as Lake Cayor, extends for many miles. On reaching the head of such a "lake" or series of inundated plains, and following its upper shore, Hanno would necessarily have rejoined the main rivercourse once more. Up this still "great and wide" stream he could have proceeded a long way, perhaps even to the modern late-summer limit of navigation at the Felu Falls, more than five hundred miles from the sea.

To be sure, there are no "very high hills" adjoining the flood-plain lakes lower down, nor anything more than outcropping rocky ridges higher up; but at least it can hardly be coincidence that the *Encyclopaedia Britannica* reports that "crocodiles swarm in the upper Senegal," [6] whence "the hippopotamus is gradually disappearing," and the official French survey map of the river notes "Crocodiles" on the middle stretch of the main stream.

"So we turned back again and retraced our course to Kernē." What else could Hanno have done?

The return to the island near the mouth of the Senegal sets another fixed point in the itinerary, on which calculations and conjectures may be based for the continuance of the voyage. Whereas exploration of the Senegal had led eastward into the interior, resumption of the coastal route now necessarily led south. Actually, as the map shows, from the mouth of the Senegal the African coast runs southwest to Cape Verde, close to Dakar, then gradually works through south to southeast along the Guinea coast. To Hanno, sailing without chart or compass, all this would have been a journey southward, even as he recounted in #11. In twelve days, with wind still favorable and ocean currents not adverse, he could have made good progress. Once the Sahara is left behind, the land becomes increasingly fertile, but tends to monotony. There are sizable rivers emptying into the sea, and among them one of great size,

[6] *Encyclopaedia Britannica*, 11th ed., *s.v.* "Senegal River."

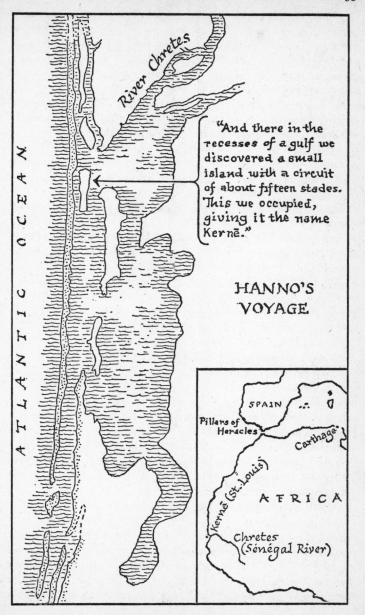

"And there in the recesses of a gulf we discovered a small island with a circuit of about fifteen stades. This we occupied, giving it the name Kernē."

HANNO'S VOYAGE

River Chretes

ATLANTIC OCEAN

SPAIN
Pillars of Heracles
Carthage
Kernē (St. Louis)
AFRICA
Chretes (Sénégal River)

the Gambia. Of this there is no mention in Hanno's narrative, perhaps because its muddy shores lined with mangrove thickets made landing impossible and discouraged exploration. Farther on, the swampy shoreland growth of mangrove becomes an increasingly persistent feature, often obstructing all view of the low-lying land behind.

No mountains fringe this stretch of the Guinea coast and seldom are even hills of any size visible behind the level strips of shore densely covered with bush and leading back to wide featureless plains. Off Conakry a high mountain peak appears inland in clear weather; but it is only where Guinea is succeeded by Sierra Leone that mudflats and shoals along a junglelike monotony of overgrown shore suddenly give place to a very different landscape, with high wooded mountains standing hard above the sea. These are the sierra, from which the country takes its name. The change of scene must have impressed Hanno as forcibly as it does the writers of the modern sailing manuals that describe this subequatorial stretch of coast. This may explain the sudden vividness of #12 in contrast to the laconic brevity of the preceding paragraph, in which twelve days are passed over without comment or mention of other incident than that of the frightened natives who fled uttering "words unintelligible to the Lixite" interpreters.

At the previously calculable rate of progress during the long run past the desolate Sahara, continuous sailing, day and night, for twelve days' time would have accounted for considerably more than a thousand miles. But lower Senegal and Guinea were not Mauretania: there were deep gulfs and bays with numerous islands to be visited and shoreland expeditions to be attempted. If the previous rate of uninterrupted progress is cut in half, and fifty miles is taken for the average day's run, twelve days would pretty closely account for the distance between the mouth of the Senegal River and the Sierra Leone peninsula, which far better than anything else corresponds to the description in #12.

It follows that Hanno must have found the bights and bays and river mouths more interesting than the uninviting Sahara, perhaps breaking journey long enough to navigate the lower stretches of the Gambia despite the mud and the mangroves that must have rendered the trip unexciting; and more than once he may have landed in the hope of gathering information from the dark-skinned "Ethiopians," whose language not even the Lixite interpreters could understand. (No wonder! The native tongues beyond the great barrier of the Sahara belong to totally different linguistic families from Berber speech or any other language of the Atlas uplands.)

The "great forest-clad hills," the wood of whose trees was "odorous sweet and of great variety," below which Hanno moored on his twelfth day from Kernē, deserve fuller description than Hanno chose to give. That they were indeed mountains, at least in comparison with the low and swampy Guinea coast, appears certain from modern descriptions such as the following:

> In the Sierra Leone peninsula the hills come down to the sea, elsewhere a low coast plain extends inland 30 to 50 m. . . . The Sierra Leone peninsula . . . is traversed on its seaward face by hills attaining a height of 1700 ft. in the Sugar Loaf, and nearly as much in Mount Herton farther south. . . . Sugar Loaf is timbered to the top, and the peninsula is verdant with abundant vegetation.[7]

> The southern side of the entrance to the Sierra Leone River, consisting of a peninsula formed of bold forest-clad ranges of mountains terminating in Cape Sierra Leone, presents a striking contrast. . . . The high land of the Sierra Leone Peninsula extends about 22 miles from Cape Sierra Leone to Cape Shilling. . . . Immediately inland from the coast, the land rises to the Sierra Leone Range, many of the peaks of which attain an elevation of over 2,000 feet. The southern part of this range is the higher, and, although the summits are generally clouded over, they can often be seen from as far as 40 or 45 miles seaward. The most conspicuous peak, Mules Ears, rises to an elevation of 2,701 feet about 6 miles northeastward of Cape Shilling.[8]

This was the high land past which Hanno sailed, to reach in two days, about eighty miles beyond the Sierra Leone River, the entrance to Hanno's "enormous inlet of the sea," the Sherbro River, "which can more correctly be described as a sound or strait, extending about thirty miles in an easterly direction and then about ten miles southward." [9] As Hanno correctly ob-

---

[7] *Encyclopaedia Britannica*, 11th ed., *s.v.* "Sierra Leone."

[8] U.S. Hydrographic Office, "Sailing Directions for the West Coasts of . . . Northwest Africa," 1942, pp. 396 and 403.

[9] *Ibid.*, p. 407.

served, "on the landward side was a level plain," the sound being bounded on the south and west by twenty-seven-mile-long Sherbro Island and other smaller islets, but on the north and east by the mainland, which is low and well-cultivated for a considerable distance toward the interior.

It was here that leaping fires began to be seen at night, to the perplexity and, seemingly, the terror of the ship's company. These fires have seemed less mysterious to the modern commentators ever since one of them reproduced a passage (frequently quoted since) from Mungo Park's *Travels in the Interior District of Africa:*

> The burning grass in Manding exhibits a scene of terrific grandeur. In the middle of the night, I could see the plains and mountains, as far as my eye could reach, variegated with lines of fire; and the light reflected on the sky made the heavens appear in a blaze. In the daytime pillars of smoke were seen in every direction; while the birds of prey were observed hovering around the conflagration and pouncing down upon the snakes, lizards, and other reptiles which attempted to escape from the flames. This annual burning is soon followed by a fresh and sweet verdure, and the country is thereby rendered more healthful and pleasant.[10]

If this is the correct explanation of the fires in #13 and #14 and the "blazing country" with its cascading "fiery torrents" in #15, it should follow that Hanno visited the Sierra Leone and Liberia coasts during the autumn of the year. But it has proved impossible to discover how far along this coast he traveled, as the landmarks that are mentioned cannot be convincingly reconciled with any natural features. In particular, the "lofty mountain called 'the Chariot of the Gods,' " from whose summit the fires "seemed to touch the stars" has given rise to great perplexity. If the description is accepted literally, there is the insuperable objection that there exists no great mountain close to the sea anywhere along the West African shore except spectacular Mount Cameroon, rising 13,000 feet almost out of the very sea and crowned with fire and lined with blazing cascades of lava when its volcanic peak is in eruption. But Cameroon lies at the easternmost end of the huge Gulf of Guinea, more than a thousand miles beyond Liberia, the farthest land that any

[10] Mungo Park, *Travels in the Interior District of Africa* (London, 1799).

plausible interpretation of the preceding paragraphs of the text can mean—unless perchance a whole section of the original has been dropped out or been overlooked by the translator of the Punic text! On the other hand, if the "Chariot of the Gods" was only a ridge of high hills that stood out against the sky when viewed from the seaboard, there are several such in Liberia. The two "Horns," with their complicated series of lakes and islands, are readily understood to be long narrow lagoons, such as are especially a feature of the Ivory Coast beyond mountainous Liberia. Commentators have occasionally strayed into supposing that these horns were capes or promontories, perhaps through unconsciously associating them with Cape Horn, which might well rank as a "Horn of the South" *par excellence,* and forgetting the Golden Horn of Constantinople, which is the very opposite of a headland, being a drowned river mouth. The Greek word *keras* means primarily the "horn of an animal," but by transference is applied to various horn-shaped objects, including, as in the present instance, the crooked "arm" of a marine inlet. In #14 the "sea-like body of water" described as being "within" a large island corresponds to a frequent geographical feature of the West African coast, where a long strip of land that may itself be surrounded by the sea shuts off a deep sound or bay in which there may lie numerous smaller islands. Alternatively, the "Horns" may merely have been long lagoons with breaks in the bar at either end, thus converting the bar into an island; but since the translator uses the word *kolpos,* meaning "bay" or "gulf," of each of the two horns, the former identification is perhaps the better one. On either interpretation there are too many possible candidates to lift the doubts that cling to these final paragraphs. But the crowning uncertainty comes at the close of the whole document in the encounter with the savage creatures "whom our interpreters called 'Gorillas.'" At first reading, since everyone knows what gorillas are, there would seem to be no possible dispute about the simian nature of the "women with hairy bodies" who "bit and scratched their captors." But this assumption is too hastily made, because it is specifically this passage in Hanno's *Periplous* that is responsible for our modern application of the word "gorilla" to the huge and fairly formidable "manlike ape, native to West Africa from the Congo to Cameroon" (but apparently *not* found in

Sierra Leone and Liberia!), for which it has been recommended that we should substitute the true native name *pongo*. To say that Hanno's "Gorillas" were gorillas is, therefore, mistaking an assumption for a fact. Richard Lyddeker, himself competent to form an opinion, contented himself with saying that "in the opinion of those best qualified to judge, it is probable that the creatures in question were really baboons." [11] Among baboons the West African representative of the genus is the mandrill, which is said to frequent open rocky ground in large droves and may be exceedingly fierce and difficult to approach. It might be objected that the astonishingly brilliant and bizzare rear coloring of these particular apes must have persuaded Hanno that he was not dealing with "wild men" or savages. Perhaps this consideration has induced others to suggest that the beasts in question were chimpanzees; but these are small, completely arboreal apes and not in the least formidable. Still others have preferred to take Hanno *au pied de la lettre* and insist that he meant what he said when he spoke of "wild men." In this connection it should probably be treated as mere coincidence that the *Encyclopaedia Britannica* remarks that "in the densest forest region between the Mano and the St. Paul's river is the powerful Gora tribe of unknown linguistic affinities."[12]

For myself, not being among "those best qualified to judge," while personally much attracted to gaily colored mandrills, I must leave the reader to choose as he pleases among savages, baboons, and chimpanzees, as well as to believe as he sees fit about the part of western Africa where he thinks that Hanno came ashore and strove with these brutes. With the noncommittal announcement that he slew and flayed the three recalcitrants and brought their skins back to Carthage, and the still briefer and unenlightening final remark that "provisions failing, we sailed no farther," even as Hanno leaves his public, so we, his public, must here leave Hanno.

Until the power of Carthage was broken by Rome at the close of the Second Punic War in 201 B.C., her ships must have maintained communication with her colonies and trading posts on the coasts of southern Spain and western Morocco. But there

[11] Both references to gorillas here are from *Encyclopaedia Britannica*, 11th ed., s.v. "gorilla."
[12] *Op. cit.*, s.v. "Liberia."

is no evidence for any attempt by Carthage to repeat or exceed Hanno's exploit or attempt any further exploration of equatorial Africa. Half a century later, with the utter collapse of Carthaginian empire attending the Roman destruction of the great capital city in 146 B.C., the western seaways were open to all who acknowledged the supremacy of Rome. Yet little or nothing is recorded of any Greek or Roman explorer taking advantage of this opportunity to navigate the open Atlantic. What little is known is quickly stated.

Pliny makes passing reference to a certain Midacritus as being "the first to import lead from the Tin Land," but gives no indication who Midacritus was or when he lived or how he reached "Tin Land" or even whether by "lead" he meant "white lead," a variant Latin name for tin. Pliny's notice of Midacritus occurs in the course of a passage of considerable length devoted to listing First Inventions and Discoveries—such as who first thought of making bricks, who first cast copper tools, who invented the spindle, who the loom, who was the first shoemaker, who first mined gold, who first worked iron, and so on for other items in a catalogue without authority or merit.

Somewhat more light is shed on another Greek, who was named Euthymenes and hailed from the Phocaean city of Massalia—a fellow townsman, therefore, of the famous Pytheas (see Chapter V). Like Pytheas, Euthymenes undertook a voyage of distant exploration along Atlantic shores; but unlike Pytheas, he left no great mark on surviving historical memory to make it possible to determine when he lived or exactly what he did or why he did it. All that can be made out is that, while Pytheas turned north in the Atlantic, Euthymenes must have turned south and, like Hanno, traversed the thousand-mile stretch of arid Saharan coast; for we hear (and this unfortunately is all that we hear!) that he came to a great river whose waters were driven back by an onshore wind, and that in that river—like Hanno on the upper Senegal—he saw crocodiles. This is probably reason enough for supposing that Euthymenes, too, discovered and explored the Senegal River. The presence of crocodiles, taken with the tidal flooding of the huge waterway where, in the season of low river, the ocean's influence extends some two hundred miles inland, led Euthymenes to imagine that he had discovered a distant headwater of the Nile!

History sometimes repeats itself in an unexpected manner. When the Portuguese navigator Diniz Diaz entered the great estuary of the Senegal in A.D. 1445, he too thought that the river must be a branch of the Nile. In consequence, for more than two hundred years thereafter the Senegal continued to be known as "the western Nile" until its upper reaches were finally explored—whereupon it was mistaken for a branch of the Niger. Not until Mungo Park in 1795 ascended the Gambia River and crossed over into the Senegal basin in a search for the headwaters of the Niger was the hydrography of the three great rivers of West Africa correctly established. Needless to say, the Nile had long since ceased to be part of the picture!

Euthymenes' exploit seems to have been repeated—perhaps at about the same period—by a famous Greek historian who is not often thought of as an explorer. Polybius of Megalopolis in Arcadia had been a staunch supporter of the Roman cause at a time when that cause was viewed with suspicion and open hostility by most of the Greek states, understandably alarmed at the prospect of losing their century-old independence. While an enforced resident of Rome, Polybius had the great good fortune of becoming the bosom friend of Publius Cornelius Scipio—the Scipio who was to add to his name the title of "Africanus" after he destroyed Carthage in 146 B.C. Shortly after that momentous event, the Roman commander and the Greek political historian, still devoted friends, were together in southern Spain at the seaport city that had been Punic Gadir and was then Roman Gades. Perhaps in reminiscence of Hanno's adventurous voyage, but more probably moved by political and economic interest in the defunct Carthaginian colonial empire, Polybius was entrusted by Scipio with a detachment of the Roman fleet and set out on this from Gades to explore the Atlantic coast of Morocco. In the course of this enterprise he appears to have sailed beyond Morocco past the great belt of Saharan desert and visited the Punic trading post established by Hanno at Kernē in the estuary of the Senegal; for, like Euthymenes, he is reported to have viewed a river full of crocodiles.

There is no evidence that this ambitious voyage had any enduring consequences. Rome made no immediate attempt to maintain the Carthaginian colonial settlements in Morocco; and when, nearly two hundred years later, she annexed Morocco to her empire, she sent her conquering soldiery overland and afoot without naval cooperation. Meanwhile, with Carthage over-whelmed and the sea gate to the Atlantic open to all who chose to pass, no one from the Mediterranean world seems to have sensed or seized the opportunity for trade derivable from equatorial Africa (unless we consider Euthymenes to have been sent out by Massalia to investigate this very matter). We may safely assume that the thousand-mile barrier of Saharan wasteland was the great deterrent to Mediterranean penetration of the tropics. Only a single Greek of later date than Euthymenes and Polybius is on record as having attempted the passage. His effort was part of a heroic decision to circumnavigate the whole of Africa in order to reach India—an ambition that marks him as the forerunner of the Portuguese navigators so famous in the modern history of maritime exploration.

The story of Eudoxus of Cyzicus is remarkable in many ways. According to the account in the second book of Strabo's *Geography*, he was a Black Sea Greek sea captain who had twice made the Red Sea voyage to India—a notable achievement for the second century before Christ. Although commissioned and equipped for these voyages by the Ptolemaic rulers of Egypt, Eudoxus took it amiss that the royal exchequer claimed for itself the profits from the cargoes that he brought back from the Far East. He determined to make still another Indian voyage, but this time for his own account. In order to escape the exactions of the Egyptian state he decided not to pass through the Red Sea but to take the longer route around Africa, after acquiring a cargo in the western Mediterranean.

Presumably, in common with the Greeks of his time, Eudoxus had no conception of the enormousness of such an undertaking, but supposed that the encircling ocean stream would lead him directly from Atlantic West Africa to Somaliland and Arabia beyond Aden. He had been encouraged in this supposition by his earlier discovery of a carved figurehead that had been cast up on the Somali coast and that he mistakenly believed to have belonged to a Punic ship from Gadir that had been wrecked on the West African shore.

The rest of his story runs in Strabo as follows:

Thus persuaded that the circumnavigation of Africa was possible, Eudoxus went home, put all his property into the venture, and set out. He sailed first to Dicaearchia, next to Massalia, and thence along the coast to Gades, everywhere crying abroad his project and amassing funds. At Gades he rigged out a large sailing vessel and two smaller boats like those that pirates use. On these he embarked dancing-girls and physicians and artisans of various sort, and so with steady breezes blowing sailed for India across the open sea. But when his passengers wearied of the voyage, he unwillingly shifted sail toward the land, being afraid of the rise and fall of the tides. Precisely what he dreaded happened: the ship ran aground. However, the shock was not violent enough to break up the vessel on the instant, so that there was opportunity to convey the cargo safely ashore and bring off most of the ship's timbers. From these Eudoxus constructed a third craft about the size of a penteconter and in this sailed on until he came to people whose speech made use of the same words that he had previously noted down [on Africa's eastern coast]. This convinced him that these people were Ethiopians of the same race [as the East Africans].

Thereafter he gave up the voyage to India and turned back. While coasting along on the return journey he remarked a well-watered and well-wooded, but uninhabited, island. On getting safely back to Morocco he disposed of his ships and proceeded inland on foot to the court of King Bogus, whom he tried to interest in backing his expedition. But the king's advisers prevailed against this by stressing the danger that his kingdom might lay itself open to planned attack, once the way to it had been disclosed to the foreign invader. When Eudoxus got wind of it that he was being ostensibly dispatched on the expedition that he projected, but in reality was to be marooned on a desert island, he fled to Roman territory and thence crossed over to Spain.

Once again he fitted out ships, this time a round merchantman and a long penteconter, the one for the open sea, the other for exploring the coast. Having embarked agricultural tools and seedcorn and carpenters, he set out once more on his previous course, intending if he met with delay to spend the winter on the island which he had noted on his previous voyage, there to sow the seed and reap the harvest and then complete the expedition as planned.

That is as far as I can go in the story of Eudoxus (says Poseidonios). Perhaps those who live in Gades or in Spain may be able to tell what happened to him after that! [13]

[13] Strabo, *Geography*, II.3.4.

Fifteen and a half centuries were to elapse after Eudoxus' unexplained disappearance before anyone again ventured to compete with his attempt to reach India by rounding the Cape; and full sixteen centuries passed before any European navigator actually succeeded in accomplishing the feat.

❦ IV ❦

INNER AFRICA

IT is not in the least remarkable that the exploratory expeditions directed toward Africa and recounted in the preceding chapter were all accomplished by ship, because it was only the sea that offered sure passage of the great natural barrier dividing the Mediterranean world from equatorial Africa. There were two such ocean highways past the desert—the Atlantic on the west and the Red Sea on the east. In addition there was a less easily navigable waterway leading like a narrow corridor through, instead of around, the great Saharan zone. This was the river Nile, which gathers its waters and brings its flood from lofty mountains beyond the desert and, after suffering much diminution on the long rainless traverse through the desert's heart, leads at last to the open Mediterranean. Although it is not, like the Atlantic and the Red Sea, continuously navigable, being obstructed by rock-strewn rapids in Upper Egypt and Nubia and by dense masses of floating vegetation south of the Sudan, the Nile at least offers sure guidance through desert and jungle alike, and everywhere assures the voyager of an unfailing draught of the precious water that is life; whereas elsewhere the Sahara must be traversed over waterless stretches of sunstruck desolation. Even so, there are two journeyable land routes leading across the desert from the Mediterranean coast to the verge of tropical verdure. Neither of these is to be lightly attempted, for well water is scarce and day marches are long. Of the two, the more western route is the longer because it starts from the more northerly western basin of the Mediterranean and consequently must add the belt of Algerian mountainland to its itinerary. This western route, which terminates at Timbuktu on the upper Niger, seems never to have been traveled by Greek or Roman or Carthaginian; in the early history of civilization, the entire western Sahara must be rated as unexplored territory.

Under Roman rule—to be specific, in A.D. 42—a commander of a legion marching in pursuit of rebellious Moroccan native tribes was (so Pliny says) "the first Roman leader to cross the Atlas, advancing quite a distance beyond." According to this legate's report as summarized by Pliny,[1] he found "the summit even in summer under deep drifts of snow." After ten days of bivouacking he managed to cross the main Atlas range and reached "a river known as the Ger[2] by deserts of black dust with here and there projecting burnt-out ridges of rock, places uninhabitable because of heat even though encountered in winter season." However, since he had seen "the nearby woodlands abounding in elephants and wild beasts and every sort of serpent," we may conclude that Caius Suetonius Paulinus (for this was the Roman commander's name) never got very far into the Sahara from the southern foothills of Atlas.

So much for the only recorded ancient pretense of an attempt to penetrate the desert on the west! In contrast to this, the slightly shorter and perhaps a little less arduous eastern passage across the desert, which runs from Tripoli almost due south to Lake Chad on the northeast boundary of Nigeria, although never open to Greek exploration, comes curiously into our narrative through an unexpected lifting of the curtain of obscurity that otherwise hangs heavy over central Africa. Once again it is Herodotus to whom we are indebted for this glimpse beyond civilization into savagery.

In the popular mind the Sahara is often pictured as one huge sea of shifting sand. But sand is only a by-product of the great forces of desiccation that have created the Sahara during the 10,000 years since the ending of the last Ice Age. Although it is true that in certain regions an enormous covering of blown sand has been heaped up, most of the Sahara shows a more normal landscape, whose sole misfortune is its lack of rain. Extending from the Atlantic to the Red Sea across the entire breadth of Africa, this huge, arid belt covers an area greater than the United States. If its eastward prolongation across Arabia is in-

[1] Pliny, *Natural History*, V.14–15.
[2] And called now the Wadi Ghir.

cluded, the desert exceeds in size all Europe west of Asia. Naturally, so vast an area displays the geophysical variety of a full-sized continent. Particularly notable are the high interior mountain ranges running diagonally across the line of the Tropic of Cancer and lifting peaks up to 11,000 feet above sea level in the very heart of the Sahara. On these there is occasional rain in summer, and during the winter some snow has been seen on the higher ridges. But throughout most of the Saharan zone extreme and well-nigh perennial drought has produced wildly broken, rocky uplands, long and more nearly level plateaus of dreary treeless gravel, and, where the wind has accumulated it, mile-long wavelike dunes of sand. Rock, gravel, and sand make up a desolate world that nonetheless is by no means wholly destitute of life or without its widely scattered human inhabitants.

The two previously mentioned routes across the Sahara from north to south succeed in avoiding most of the sand—indeed, it is with this in view that they take their course. But elsewhere the sand may be a formidable obstacle to every sort of intercourse. The extreme instance of its barrier to communication is encountered about two hundred miles west of Egypt, where dunes have been amassed to form the nearly impassable Libyan Desert. Of this forbidding region, the best-informed and most graphic writer on the Sahara, E. F. Gautier, gives the following discouraging account:

> There, in the great Libyan Erg, we find what is probably the most imposing mass of dunes on the whole face of the earth. They cover a vast area, some 750 miles in length by 250 to 300 miles wide. It is a region more unknown than the Antarctic, and unknown because it is impenetrable. . . . Within the confines of the Libyan Desert we find an extreme rarity or even . . . a total absence of wells, pasturage and running water.[3]

This tremendous barrier, as long as the entire length of Egypt from Cairo to the First Cataract and as wide as the breadth of the Red Sea, would have completely prevented any communication between ancient Egypt and the interior of northern Africa to the west, had there not existed a highly peculiar sandfree corridor along the Libyan Desert's northern edge. As this corridor

[3] Émile Félix Gautier, *Sahara, the Great Desert,* translated by Dorothy F. Mayhew (N.Y.: Columbia University Press, 1935), pp. 103 and 106.

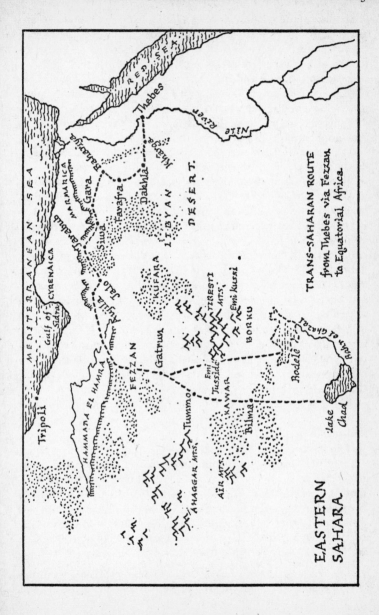

RED SEA

MEDITERRANEAN SEA

Thebes

Nile River

Gulf of Sidra

CYRENAICA

MARMARICA

Bahr Belama

Gara

Siwa

Farafra

Dakhla

Kharga

LIBYAN

DESERT.

Jalo

Aujila

Kufara

TIBESTI MTS.

Emi Kussi

BORKU

Tripoli

HAMMADA EL HAMRA

FEZZAN

Gatrun

Emi Tussidé

Bodelé

Bahr el Ghazal

Tummo

KAWAR

Bilma

Lake Chad

AHAGGAR MTS.

AIR MTS.

TRANS-SAHARAN ROUTE
from Thebes via Fezzan
to Equatorial Africa.

EASTERN
SAHARA

is an important element in the Herodotean story that we are about to tell, some further explanations must be made before the uncommunicative lines of the modern map can be expected to impart any useful information.

Between the Nile and the great waste of sand that constitutes the innermost Libyan Desert, or Erg, all the intervening country, being equally without rain, is also arid land; but it is a desert composed rather of denuded rock and bare limestone hills and empty stretches of gravel, with comparatively little sand. At certain spots in this desolate area, the featureless landscape suddenly gives place to green garden plots and date palms by the thousand, because the subsoil water has in one way or another been brought to the surface. These widely spaced resurgences of fertility are the oases and resemble nothing so much as green islands in the far-horizoned sea. There are several such deep depressions with access to water; and these are situated at almost equal distance between the Nile and the lifeless Erg, affording habitability for an undemanding human population. But five among the number are of outstanding size; and these make a sort of chain laid roughly from southeast to northwest across the desert waste, from the latitude of ancient Thebes (today Luxor) to that of ancient Memphis (now replaced by Cairo). Their names may be unfamiliar, yet have a sort of mysteriously attractive ring—Khârga, Dakhla, Farafra, Baharîya, and Siwa (where once was the famous oracle that was the first to salute Alexander the Great as a god).

But it is not only Siwa with its oracle of Ammon that has a place in ancient history. Once again it is Herodotus who heard and retold the incident:

The Persian king, Cambyses, son of Cyrus, had invaded Egypt with an army made up of Ionian and Aeolian Greeks and other nationalities subject to his rule. Having forced the lower Nile-land into submission, Cambyses conceived still more ambitious projects for the aggrandizement of his empire. Among them was an expedition to be sent into the Libyan Desert to occupy the oases and in particular to seize and destroy the oracle of Ammon in Siwa. Accordingly King Cambyses,

> on reaching Thebes, detached a force of 50,000 men with orders to enslave the Ammonians and burn the god's oracle. . . . So those dispatched on the expedition against the Ammonians set

out from Thebes with [native] guides. They are known to have
reached the settlement of Oasis,[4] distant a seven days' march
from Thebes across the sand; but though their army is reported
to have come thus far, no one has any word to tell about them
thereafter, except what the Ammonians themselves say and
those who learned of it from them. At any rate, they never
arrived at the oracle nor yet came back [to Egypt]. The report
circulated by the Ammonians is this: After the army left Oasis
and was proceeding against them across the sand and had arrived
about midway between Oasis and them, while they were halting
to eat, a south wind of extraordinary violence blew against
them, overwhelming them with sand. In this manner they disappeared utterly from sight.[5]

The great sandstorm may or may not have happened. (The
perennially popular tales of entire caravans buried under blowing sand invariably turn out to be fictitious.) It is at least equally
likely that in order to protect their sacred oracle the native
guides deliberately led the army westward into the waterless Erg
of dunes and left them there to perish. We shall never know
what really happened. But the journeyable route from Thebes
in upper Egypt across the Libyan Desert to Siwa by way of
Khârga and the other oases, as implied in Herodotus' story, was
(and still is) an actuality.

From Siwa this desert route continues into the backland of
Cyrenaica. And about this portion of the route Herodotus has
something more to say. He himself has never been to Siwa or
consulted the oracle there; but at the time of a visit that he paid
to Cyrene in order to gather firsthand information for his
chronicle of the history of that Greek colony in northern Africa
he engaged in conversation "with men of Cyrene who asserted
that they had visited Ammon's oracle and talked with Etearchos,
the Ammonian king."

This gave the wonderful old storyteller an opportunity to di-
gress on one of his most entertaining anecdotes. As this directly
concerns the exploration of the interior of Africa in ancient
times, it has an appropriate place in the present chapter and is
here reproduced in full:

Now the talk somehow turned to the Nile, how nobody knew
its source, and Etearchos said that some Nasamonians had once

[4] El Khârga.
[5] Herodotus, *History*, III.26.

come to his court . . . and being asked if they had any novel information about the desert parts of Libya, they said that some of their own chieftains' sons had become rather out of hand and attempted all sorts of daring deeds and, in particular, had chosen five of their number by lot to explore the wastes of Africa and see whether they could behold something more than those who had hitherto gone farthest.

Now, the region of Africa adjoining our northern sea from Egypt all the way to Cape Soloeis, where Africa ends, is inhabited throughout by Libyans and by many different Libyan tribes, at that. But the region inland from the sea and its seaboard habitants constitutes Wildlife Africa; while inland thereafter, beyond this wild animal zone, all is fearfully sandy and waterless and destitute of life.

So these young men, sent off by their comrades well supplied with water and food, proceeded first through the habitable zone and after passing through this reached the region of wild animals and from that penetrated the desert, taking their way toward the west. Having passed through much sandy territory, after many days they beheld trees growing in a plain; and advancing, they were helping themselves to the fruit on these trees when small men, of less than moderate height, set upon them and took them captive. The Nasamones understood nothing of their speech nor their captors of the Nasamonian. They led them through enormous swamps, beyond which they reached a town where everyone was of the size of their captors and black of color. A great river ran past the town, flowing from the west toward the rising sun, and in it were to be seen crocodiles.

Let this suffice for the story related by Ammonian Etearchos, save that he declared (according to the Cyrenean account) that the Nasamones reached home again and that the people among whom they had been were all sorcerers. Etearchos, too, conjectured that the flowing river was the Nile; and this is indeed reasonable.[6]

Since neither Herodotus nor any of his countrymen was addicted to far-inland exploration (the Greeks being by inherited interests and everyday experience a thoroughly maritime people), no one could have had any definite idea where it was that these Nasamonian youths had gone, except that it was clear that they had crossed the inland desert to a fertile and well-watered land beyond. And yet, by a singular perversity, Herodo-

[6] Ibid., II.32–36.

tus, while he was in Cyrene, had gathered from other conversations with its Greek inhabitants a good deal of information about the very route that the Nasamonian band had taken, but had failed to connect it with the anecdote that he had previously recounted. In consequence, he introduced this material quite independently elsewhere in his *History*. The adventure of the five young Nasamonians appears early in Book II apropos of the Nile and its problematical source, while the itinerary of the caravan track across the Sahara is not reported until near the end of Book IV, where it occurs in connection with a discussion of the history and geography of the region of Cyrene as Herodotus proceeds to "a description of the Libyan tribes in their proper order, beginning from Egypt." After citing a number of tribal names that need not concern us, Herodotus comes to the tribe that had already figured so picturesquely in his narrative, saying:

> Next on the west one comes to the Nasamonians, a numerous people who in summer quit their flocks by the seaboard and go inland to the district of Augila to harvest the date palms which grow there in huge number to great size and all bear fruit.[7]

Perhaps, considering how little this part of the world has undergone change until our own time, it is not a matter for wonder that there is an oasis in the interior of Cyrenaica that bears the name Augila, that it is famous for its date palms, and that still today from regions nearer the sea the pastoral nomads converge on it when the dates are ripe, in order to collect their share of the harvest.

After mentioning the rest of the pastoral tribes along the Libyan seaboard as far as the modern border of Tunisia, Herodotus reverts to the neighborhood of Egypt in order to describe conditions inland, giving a highly picturesque account that comes closer to the literal truth than would at first reading be credited:

> These, the seaboard Libyan nomads, have now been recounted. Behind them in the interior is the Libya of wild animals, and beyond these there runs a sandy crag that extends from Egyptian Thebes to the Pillars of Heracles. Along this crag at roughly ten-day intervals there are mounds of salt in

[7] *Ibid.,* IV.172.

large lumps and from the summit of each of these there spurts cold sweet water from the midst of the salt. Around about there dwell men, the last inhabitants desertward beyond the region of wild animals. . . . Beyond this sandy crag toward the south and the interior of Africa the country is waste and waterless, without animal life or rain or wooded growth; for there is no drop of moisture in it. . . .

First from Thebes, after a ten days' march, come the Ammonians, who took their sanctuary from the god of Thebes. . . . After the Ammonians, by another ten days' march along the sandy crag, there comes a mound of salt similar to the Ammonian, also with water and with men living about it. The name of this place is Augila. This is the place which the Nasamonians frequent for harvesting the date palms. From Augila after another ten days' march there is another salt mound with water and a great many fertile date palms; and the men who live there have the name Garamantes, a mighty tribe who spread earth over the salt and cultivate it. There is a direct route from these to the Lotus-eaters by a journey of thirty days.[8]

Here it is time to pause and take our bearings. We need not feel ourselves lost in the unknown; for the Garamantes are an historical people of the hinterland of Tripoli. And there can be no doubt either about where they lived or about where Herodotus located them. The "sandy crag" may be equally easily identified—though it must be granted that Herodotus was badly astray when he claimed that it ran all the way from Egyptian Thebes to the Pillars of Heracles. At the widely separated termini that Herodotus sets, there is no such formation, either in the vicinity of Egyptian Thebes or the Gibraltar Strait: since these are some 2,500 miles apart, such a geological formation would indeed be a prodigy. And yet, precisely inland from the Cyrenaic headland, there really exists just such a desert escarpment, running unbroken for several hundred miles from the western edge of the Delta to the frontier of Tripoli. Gautier speaks of "the great escarpment which forms the southern boundary of the Marmarica, a very long continuous cliff which extends from Siwa to the delta of the Nile . . . continued westward by the one which forms the southern limit of the Cyrenaica," adding that behind this escarpment there

is a narrow sand-free passage which puts into communication

[8] *Ibid.*, IV.181–83.

two separate portions of the desert otherwise practically sealed
from each other. . . . Southward from this route and coming
into immediate contact with it, extends the worst and most
awesome part of the Libyan Desert.[9]

In this corridor or "sand-free passage" between the escarpment
and the huge sandy waste of the Libyan Erg, there lies a string
of inhabited oases—Aujila, Jalo, Jarabub, Siwa, and Gara—
and these are remarkable for their abundant and excellent
water. All these oases of the Marmarica Depression are limestone sinks or troughs, very little above (and at Siwa actually as
much as eighty feet below) Mediterranean sea level, in which
the groundwater from beneath the long stretches of sand comes
to the surface as artesian springs, only to spread out and evapo-
rate under the desert atmosphere into a saline accretion or crust.
This string of oases, well-known to ancient visitors to Ammon's
Oracle at Siwa, entirely substantiates the Herodotean account—
except that they do not continue westward all the way to
Morocco! In the other direction, east and south from the Oasis
of Ammon, a second string of oases—Baharîya, Farafra, Dakhla,
and Khârga—dots the wide wasteland of the Egyptian Desert
west of the Nile valley, thus connecting, however intermittently,
the Marmarica Depression with Upper Egypt opposite Thebes.
Of the southernmost pair of these oases, the same geographer
observes that

> in the vicinity of Khârga and Dakhla the water sometimes
> gushes from artesian springs whose outlet is the crater-like center
> of a small clay knoll, a form which first captured the attention
> of Herodotus.[10]

What with the saline incrustations and the artesian jets, there
is thus considerable justification for the picturesque description
of mounds of salt from which cold pure water spurts.

Herodotus' sweeping generalization that all the watering
places are about ten days apart agrees very closely with modern
travelers' estimates for the journey between Aujila and Siwa and
that between Siwa and Baharîya. Our author was, however,
flagrantly in error when he stated that the Oasis of Ammon
(i.e., Siwa) could be reached in ten days *from Thebes*. Though

[9] Gautier, *op. cit.*, p. 153.
[10] *Ibid.*, p. 153.

the matter is not of great moment, the mistake is explicable on the supposition that Herodotus' informant told him that the Oasis of Ammon was ten days distant *from Egypt,* and he himself, recalling that Cambyses' ill-fated expedition against the shrine of Ammon had been dispatched from Thebes, confused the situation. As for the next stage onward, still today the caravan-track westward from Siwa follows the arc of the great escarpment through the smaller oases of Jarabub and Jalo to the low-lying and comparatively fertile oasis of Aujila with its luxuriant date palms. The distance is about the same as (or a trifle more than) that from the Baharîya Oasis or the Wadi Natrun to the Oasis of Ammon, some eighty to ninety hours of modern going with a string of camels, or almost exactly ten days' march.

So far there has been no significant error in the wonderful account. But from here on we must watch with great care; for Herodotus' desert route is passing beyond the regions of Greek geographical knowledge and, Herodotus to the contrary, the long escarpment that the caravan route has been following dies out beyond Aujila in the huge but ill-defined depression that seems to be an inland extension of the great Gulf of Sidra. Beyond, to the west of this very decided break, the cliff resumes again in a much modified form as the southern face of the long, arid plateau of the Hammada el Hamra in the Tripolitanian hinterland; and in its western outrunner, the Hammada of Tinghert, it finally dies away in the heart of the Algerian Sahara. From here on there is erg and wasteland aplenty, but no straightaway route or obvious passage "to the Stelae of Heracles." The Herodotean desert road from Thebes to Gibraltar does not exist and never could have existed. In the face of this indubitable discouragement, most commentators dismiss all beyond the third resting stage as mere invention—whether Cyrenaic or Herodotean hardly matters—even though these same commentators have been ready to admit that the third resting place was a reality, since the Garamantes were actual.

If we take Herodotus for our guide and follow his text literally, journeying from Aujila westward for ten days at the previously established rate of progress, we shall discover that we have covered some 250 miles and find ourselves amid the dark rocks of the Jebel-es-Soda or the bleak red upland gravel stretches of the Hammada el Hamra. And since there are neither oases with water here nor settled population, we must suppose that the direction due westward is mistaken and that the route must either have veered northward into Tripolitana or southward toward the Fezzan. And in fact, if we had continued in the direction already followed between the oases of Jarabub and Aujila, slightly west of southwest, we should have been heading straight for the nearest of the long valleylike depressions, well watered and filled with millions of date palms, which are collectively called the "Fezzan" and which constitute the most fertile district to be found anywhere in the heart of the Sahara. That Herodotus was correctly informed that this was where the Garamantes lived is fortunately proved by his seemingly casual and gratuitous remark that this third resting stage among the Garamantes "is the nearest point to the Lotos-eaters, from whom it is a thirty-day journey." Now, as far as Herodotus is concerned, there can be no dispute about the habitat of the Lotos-eaters; for in Chapter 177 of this same book he set them upon "a foreland projecting into the sea" in the land of the Gindanes; and anyone who checks the geographic detail of the periplus in this section of Herodotus will discover that the dense groves of date palms that cover the projecting foreland just east of the town of Tripoli must be the spot where the Lotos-eaters led the indolent and self-contented existence of those who partake of the sweet fruit of the African date. A thirty-day trek inland from Tripoli should represent (through broken upland and desert country) a distance of somewhat more than five hundred miles. Perhaps it is partly coincidence, but Gustav Nachtigal, the intrepid first European penetrator of the Tibesti mountainland of the hostile Tibbus, on the start of his expedition in 1869 took precisely thirty days of marching time from Tripoli to reach Murzuk, the modern chief town of the Fezzan. Since Pliny and other Roman writers refer to the district thus reached as "Phazania," and to its inhabitants as "Garamantes," it would be unreasonable to refuse the conclusion that this conspicuous group of oases forms the third step in Herodotus' desert route; and I do not believe that any student who has seriously and competently considered the evidence has ever reached any other decision. But not enough consideration has been given to the corollary observation that, in swinging southwestward into the Fezzan, this route has deviated from its original direction (dictated by the need of skirting the huge Libyan dunes) and is no longer headed for the Gibraltar Straits and the "Stelae of Heracles" as Herodotus supposed.

His mention of the Lotos-eaters in this connection may have been intended to tie this inland track with his preceding coastal description of Libya; but the form in which this remark is introduced suggests that it was known to his informants that the Fezzan oases were a junction point for two caravan routes, one from the Nile, the other from the Mediterranean, uniting here for joint continuance into the desert. No modern geographer, if asked whither that continuation led, would for a moment be in doubt of the proper answer: during uncounted centuries the Sahara has been crossed by heading south from the Fezzan over the high barren upland that stretches like a saddle between the great peaks of the Ahaggar and the Tibesti ranges. Within hundreds of miles east and west, there is no other practicable passage to equatorial Africa. That this was indeed its course in Herodotus' account (even though he himself was unaware of it) will become apparent from internal evidence.

The modern commentator who hopes to assure greater accuracy by transferring data gleaned from ancient sources to modern survey maps, noting the consequent mileage and compass directions, may often be harming rather than helping his chances for uncovering the truth, because he has introduced concepts and criteria unfamiliar to antiquity. Though recorded in stades, distances were seldom measured, but roughly computed from time elapsed in travel. How inaccurate the result might be is apparent to anyone who considers Herodotus' account [11] of how he calculated the length and breadth of the Black Sea. Similarly, directions did not derive from compass or chart, but were deduced from the general trend of routes and the relative location of regions. Thus Herodotus supposed [12] that the coast road through Thermopylae ran north and south because he knew that by it one journeyed from northern into central Greece. More specifically, east and west in a fifth-century writer never mean the cardinal axes but are only vaguely oriented on the

[11] Herodotus, *op. cit.*, IV.86.
[12] *Ibid.*, VII.176.

range of shifting points on the horizon where the sun rises and sets. "West," therefore, since it could not be precise within fifty degrees, was obviously not an accurate indication of direction at all. When traveling, one went from landmark to landmark along a general course vaguely fixed in relation to the moving sun. On such a system, the direction in which one starts is apt to be mistaken for the direction in which one continues. So Herodotus, having been informed that the great inland escarpment which he calls a "ridge of sand" ran westward from Egypt behind Cyrene, argued that on this account it must ultimately reach the Atlantic. Just because there never was such a road of communication between the Nile and Morocco, it is not sensible nor good scholarship to refuse all credence to Herodotus' report: the rational and proper procedure is to accept the route as actual and try to discover where it went.

As for the ten-day intervals and the marvelous regularity with which the mound of salt and the fresh water and men dwelling around repeat themselves through two months of travel, one must remember that fifth-century Greece ascribed to the Creator its own love of symmetry and geometrical form. Oases amid the waterless waste are in themselves so miraculous that their orderly arrangement behind a straight-ruled line of desert cliff demanded little more of Greek credulity.

But we have not yet finished with the Garamantes, who occupied the third resting place on the route.

"They sow crops by spreading earth on the salt." [13] This can only mean—and be intended to mean—that the inhabitants of these oases neutralized the salinity of the soil, due to continuous evaporation of the undrained surface water in the landlocked *wadis*, by digging and spreading fresh alluvium from the *wadi* floors and stagnant pools. Precisely in this way the inhabitants of the Fezzan today succeed in cultivating various kinds of grain and even a small amount of cotton to supplement the magnificent staple harvest from their date palms.

Among them are found the backward-grazing cattle. These are so called because they have their horns bent so far in front that they cannot graze if they move forward because they strike their horns against the ground. In other respects they do not differ

[13] *Ibid.*, IV.183.

from ordinary cattle except that their hide is abnormally thick and harsh.[14]

It is of course possible that Herodotus or some informant of his has here been the victim of a pleasantry; and I dare say that it is not only the English schoolboy who has chuckled at the absurdity of this yarn and the gullibility of its recorder. However, as so often elsewhere in the *History,* the facts substantiate Herodotus:

The lateral valleys of the once-active river courses in the higher regions west of the Fezzan preserve numerous ancient rock-carvings on their smooth walls; and similar records from the past have been found in the Ahaggar and Tibesti mountains. Their date is difficult to establish, but there is reason to believe that the majority are not very old, as such drawings go. Because they include representations of crocodiles, giraffes, and hippopotamuses, these do not automatically relegate them to a remote geologic past. Among the animals thus represented there are cattle with long horns curving forward in front of their eyes of a species that is now extinct in northern Africa, having succumbed to the ever-increasing desiccation of the Sahara. This same climatic process has exterminated the other animals mentioned, with the exception of such stray survivals as the stunted crocodiles discovered by modern explorers in rare upland pools. Whether this strikingly fine bovine is the *bos ibericus* with which it has been identified, is beyond my competence to say; but it closely resembles some of the curved-longhorn cattle in the Spanish rock-shelter drawings, animals that presumably were brought over from northern Africa by the mesolithic invaders of the Iberian peninsula at some period near 6000 B.C. That such an animal could have given rise to the report of "backward-grazing" cattle is evident; and that it may still have been common as late as the fifth century B.C. is suggested by other drawings, such as the one next to be discussed, which occur in the same region and are executed in the same technique.

"These Garamantes hunt the cave-dwelling Ethiopians with four-horse cars." The spectacular archeological confirmation of this thoroughly implausible statement is sufficiently familiar in

[14] *Ibid.*

certain quarters; but it is not widely known. Since the horse-drawn car did not reach Egypt until it was introduced by the Hyksos, it could hardly have reached the inner Sahara except through the coastal Libyans and hence not until the New King-dom was well established. Consequently such a drawing cannot be older than Herodotus by more than a millennium at the utmost and may well have been made only shortly before his lifetime. In the light of such evidence it is impermissible to deny credence to his explicit statement that the Garamantes drove chariots in their desert biding place.

Like the long-horned cattle, horses apparently disappeared from the Sahara with the increased desiccation of the entire area. Since camels, which were previously unknown in the Sahara district, were introduced there on a considerable scale during late Roman imperial times, it is likely that they sup-planted horses at about that period. With a more favorable turn to the climate shortly before A.D. 1000, the horse seems to have been reintroduced into the desert by the Arabs at about the time of their great penetration into the hitherto exclusively Berber world during the eleventh century of our era. More re-cently they have again lost ground; and today, horse and camel alike are being shouldered out by the jeep and the half-track car.

Herodotus continues:

> These cave-dwelling Ethiopians are the swiftest footed of all men of whom we have knowledge. They live on snakes and similar reptiles. They use a language unlike any other, much like the twitter of bats.[15]

The ancient Libyans were of white Berber stock (i.e., they were a non-Negroid Hamitic race). Berber dialects may still be heard in most of the northern African oases, including Siwa, Aujila, and parts of the Fezzan; and the vast area southwest of the Fezzan, all the way to the great bend of the Niger, belongs almost exclusively to the Tuareg, who have been dubbed "the men of the blue veil" because of the colored facecloth with which they protect themselves against dust, wind, and sun. These Tuareg are as nearly pure-blooded Berbers as exist any-where in Africa. We may safely assume that the Garamantes who hunted the cave-dwelling black men were themselves white Berbers.

[15] *Ibid.*, IV.183.4.

Ever since its formation at the close of the last Ice Age the Sahara has set a tremendous barrier between the equatorial Negro races and European man, a barrier that only the recent facilities of transportation have broken down. But the three breaches in the great desert rampart—namely, the Nile valley and the two caravan routes, one leading from Lake Chad to the Mediterranean Gulf of Sidra, the other from Timbuktu on the Niger to Algeria and Morocco—have always permitted a certain amount of infiltration. Until the Arab from farther east joined the contest, the history of the Sahara might be presented as an unending conflict between the Libyan Berber working southward and the equatorial Negro filtering northward. More recently for several centuries the Tuareg, as well as the Arabs in certain districts, have harried, plundered, and enslaved the southern Negroes without truce or mercy. It is in terms of this racial antagonism that we may interpret the Garamantian chariot-hunting of the horseless but fleet-footed Ethiopian.

There is, however, a third ethnic factor, besides Berber and Negro, in the central Sahara. South of the Fezzan, there rises the great triangular mountain mass of Tibesti, whose volcanic peaks are the highest points of the desert, with summits more than 10,000 feet above the Mediterranean level. Here today dwell the aloof Tibbus, maintaining an isolation of custom, language, and race that is truly remarkable. Though darker-skinned than the Berbers, they are said to be no more than modified by Negroid admixture; and in the build of their bodies and their unbelievable hardiness, endurance, and agility are set apart from other Saharan people. Nachtigal suggested that these Tibbus of the Tibesti are descendants of the fleet-foot, reptile-eating rock-dwelling "Ethiops" whom the Garamantes pursued in Herodotus' narrative. And if the Tibbus are the remnants of a more widespread indigenous Central Saharan folk, Nachtigal may have been entirely correct in his surmise. In any event, it is toward their remote and barely accessible mountains that Herodotus' caravan route next led. According to his account,

From the Garamantes after another ten days' journey there is again a salt mound with water, and around it there dwell men called Atarantes who are the only nameless people known;

for although, taken all together, they are called Atarantes, no individual one of them bears a name.[16]

Herodotus does not mean that there are no tribal names, or names for racial subdivisions, but quite specifically that the individual members of this people make no use of any distinguishing personal appellation. And if this is so, once again we are led to the Tibbus of the mountain stronghold of the desolate Tibesti massif. In *Sahara und Sudan* [17] Nachtigal relates the strange attitude of the modern Tibbus in regard to individual personal names. A Tibbu married woman (who, like the Carian women in Herodotus, may not eat with her husband) turns her face away when she speaks to her man and will not utter his name in the presence of others. Save in direst emergencies, the woman's sisters and parents will not allow the man's name to pass their lips. In consequence, when a young man marries, his name is thenceforth so seldom uttered that it virtually disappears, to be replaced by some circumlocution. When his children are referred to, he himself may be mentioned as So-and-So's father; but when these children in their turn marry, the males must join their sire in anonymity. If such a practice obtained in antiquity among the ancestors of this people, it is easy to understand how neighboring races might say of them that they had no individual names.

As for Herodotus' final comment that these Atarantes "execrate the sun overhead and foully reproach him for afflicting them and their land with his burning heat," [18] it should be observed that the caravan track is at this point crossing the tropic line in approaching the long descent into the southern Sahara and that there are today no oases and scarcely any well water in the waste upland; for this is the most exposed and exhausting portion of the whole passage through the desert, as is attested by the skeletons of animals and wayfarers who have succumbed to the rigor of sun and drought.

The next station on the route has been a major crux for the commentators, although actually it furnishes the most decisive evidence on the direction and objective of this seemingly purposeless wandering in the wilderness. That Herodotus himself

[16] *Ibid.*, IV.184.
[17] Gustav Nachtigal, *Sahara und Sudan* (3 vols., London, 1879–89), p. 450 ff.
[18] Herodotus, *History*, IV.184.2.

wholly misapprehended the geographical situation does not invalidate the information that he gathered and wrote down in his *History*. We may well believe that he was told something very like the following:

> After another journey of ten days there is again a salt mound with water and with men inhabiting.[19] In the neighborhood of this salt mound [20] there is a mountain with the name Atlas. This is slender and perfectly round and so high that its summit cannot be seen because neither in summer nor winter is it free of cloud. The natives call this the Pillar of the Sky; and the men at this mountain take their name from it, being known as Atlantes.[21]

If we have any faith at all in Herodotus' account, we should expect that at some three weeks' journey south from the Fezzan there should be a conspicuous and impressively lofty volcanic peak—though whether it was always capped with cloud because it was an active volcano or because its isolated altitude made it a cloud-gatherer, and whether its local name much resembled the Greek proper name "Atlas," must be left undecided.

The peak itself is indubitably there. Nachtigal was apparently the first modern European to behold it. Shortly before sunset of July 11, 1869, from a stony wasteland rather less than two thousand feet above sea level, he suddenly caught sight of the huge mass of the Tarso heights, which he judged to be "several thousand metres" above him, filling the eastern horizon, and rising over this the "giant cone" of Emi Tussidé. Actually, the peak was still more than thirty miles away with its isolated, round volcanic top clearing its wildly rifted shoulders by fully two thousand feet and the desert to its west by nearly nine thousand feet. Perfectly symmetrical in form, alone on its distant horizon, after the featureless monotony of weeklong plodding over dreary gravel and rock up to the southward watershed, the sight of Emi Tussidé must be the most memorable landmark of the Sahara crossing. If the oasis dwellers with whom the Cyrenean Greeks came into contact knew anything to tell of the great caravan route that passed through their stations, the great mountain would certainly have been included. And as we shall

[19] In other words, another oasis.
[20] I.e., oasis.
[21] *Ibid.*, IV.184.3.

see, the five young Nasamonians must have passed this way on
their adventurous journey into the tropics. So it is not in the
least surprising that Herodotus heard of the great mountain.
But because his oasis road had set out from Aujila by heading
west toward the Fezzan, he mistakenly supposed that it continued in that direction. He would therefore have imagined the
great mountain as located a thirty-day journey *west* of the Aujila
oasis, which would have brought it in his opinion in the vicinity
of the Gibraltar Strait.

It is strange to reflect that Herodotus may have been the first
to identify the mid-Saharan "Pillar of the Sky" with the giant of
Greek mythology who, in Homer,

> Knows all the depths of the sea and holds
> Tall columns keeping earth and sky asunder

and at the same time, by completely mistaking its location and
placing it near the Gibraltar Strait, have been responsible for
wrongly attaching to the Moroccan mountain range the name
by which we still call it.

However, there is a pertinent objection to identifying the
peak of Tussidé in the Tibesti with the Pillar of the Sky in
Herodotus because the present caravan track between the Fezzan
and Lake Chad, by which alone the eastern Sahara is regularly
crossed from north to south, leads from the halting place called
Tummo over the high shoulder that connects the Ahaggar with
the Tibesti peaks and passes too far to the west of these latter
to allow any sight of them.

To this objection the reply might be made that Herodotus
does not say that the great mountain was actually on the caravan
route but that it adjoined it, and that, whether Tussidé were
visible or not, the existence of the great Tibesti peak must have
been known to every wayfarer in the Sahara. So, in Nachtigal's
experience, the inhabitants of the Fezzan were able to tell him
a great deal about the Tibbus and Tibesti, even while they
refused to accompany the explorer thither. But I do not think
that this is the correct solution of the difficulty.

It is here that the five Nasamonians may be made to come
to the rescue. For if the anecdote of their adventure is read over,
it will become fairly evident that what these enterprising youths
set out to discover, and what they succeeded in exploring, was

nothing else than the travel route to the south across the breadth of the Sahara, which their Nasamonian compatriots and elders, content with their flocks and herds and date palms, had never felt any compulsion to investigate.

It will be recalled that the youthful band, according to Herodotus, set out "to explore the wastes of Africa and see whether they could behold something more than those who had hitherto gone farthest" and that they "penetrated the desert, taking their way to the west"—a course that would have brought them from the Aujila oasis into the Fezzan. Therafter they passed "through much sandy territory" and "after many days beheld trees growing in a plain." Here, while replenishing their exhausted supplies by helping themselves to the fruit on the trees, they were captured by little black men who "led them through enormous swamps" to one of their towns on the bank of "a great river, flowing from west to east," in which there were crocodiles. They took this river to be the Nile (mainly, one supposes, because of the crocodiles).

The tree-clad plain, the huge swamps, the great river with its crocodiles, all combine to prove that the youths must have penetrated the subequatorial rain forest south of the Sahara. But where was the scene of their encounter with the little black men? The suggestion, occasionally made, that the town was Timbuktu and the river flowing "from the evening toward the rising sun" was the Niger is ill-considered and betrays little familiarity with the Sahara as revealed in the abundant and readily accessible modern geographical literature. It is true that it would have been physically possible to cross from the Fezzan southwest to the great elbow of the Niger, since the Tuareg today occasionally do so; but it would have involved a journey of considerably more than a thousand miles diagonally across the desert through difficult gorges and broken mountainland; and the geographical setting does not correspond with the narrative, because the Niger at Timbuktu is still on the desert verge and is not preceded by a "plain covered with trees," its inundations do not constitute "enormous swamps," and it is extremely unlikely that Negrilloes, the "little black men of less than medium height," were ever found so far to the west of their present haunts in the Congo and French Equatorial Africa. But the trouble is that, except for the Niger, there seems to be no great eastward-

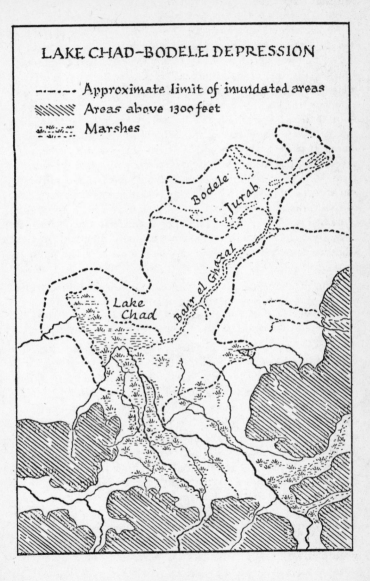

LAKE CHAD—BODELE DEPRESSION

—·—·— Approximate limit of inundated areas

Areas above 1300 feet

Marshes

Bodele

Jurab

Lake Chad

Bahr el Ghazal

running river at the southern edge of the Sahara, large enough to be mistaken for the Nile.

Yet the river is there—or at least it *was* there in Herodotus' day. Not many centuries ago, the whole territory northeast of Lake Chad was a great shallow and swampy sea, covering an area roughly the size of Belgium and Holland together. This was maintained by the overflow from Lake Chad (then much more extensive than at present) through the long river valley of the Bahr el Ghazal—not the better known "Gazelle River," which is the chief western affluent of the Nile, but a homonymous watercourse that is today only a dry depression extending for some three hundred miles, but that was erstwhile a great tropical river. The scant surplus waters of Lake Chad in the rainy season are still supposed to flow along it beneath the surface of the soil. Less than a century ago, Nachtigal saw the first eighty miles of its bed flooded and heard on every hand that, only a few generations earlier, boats could travel its entire length from Lake Chad to the lowlands of Bodele. In the words of the latest investigator:

> One may conclude that until the early centuries of the Christian era this low-lying and now completely waterless region of the lowlands of the Chad may have been a great zone of lakes and marshes dotted with sandy or rocky archipelagos.[22]

The countless unfossilized skeletons of fish that still strew the vast Bodele basin, the occasional skeletons of elephants in a region where neither grass nor water is any longer to be found, the rock-drawings of Yarda where hippopotamuses are represented, and the numerous ruins of settled villages, especially where the Bahr el Ghazal falls into the Jurab (to quote the same authority), all testify to the remarkable change that has overtaken this huge landlocked sink at the southern edge of the great desert. A modern geographer estimates that in the not too remote past the inundated area of the Chad-Bodele depression was not far short of 100,000 square miles.

Accordingly, since there is excellent reason for supposing that in antiquity a great tropical river ran northeast into Borku, south of the great Tibesti mountains, spreading out into a vast swampland, I suggest that it was here that the Nasamonian

[22] Jean Tilho in *Geographical Journal*, LVI (1920), p. 258. Cf. also Nachtigal, *op. cit.*, p. 77 ff.

youths were captured by the little black men and taken through the intricate tropical marsh to some settlement on the bank of the river, whence they beheld crocodiles in the stream (and to judge by the archeological and paleological evidence, also hippopotamuses in the water and elephants on the shoreland).

Such a conclusion is tantamount to the assertion—in itself entirely reasonable—that the Nasamonian band merely followed the same trans-Saharan route that we have been tracing; but it supplies the interesting modification of supplying a reason for supposing that in antiquity, when the Bodele basin was still fertile, this much nearer exit from the desert was the terminus of the Saharan crossing, rather than (as in modern times) Lake Chad. But such a course would have skirted the Tibesti massif close to the west of it, using Emi Tussidé as its guiding landmark. And this brings us back to the caravan route in Herodotus, in which this consideration of the Nasamonian adventure among the Negrilloes has been a very pertinent interlude.

Two stages, each of the routine ten days' journey, have led from the Garamantes of the Fezzan to "Mount Atlas," identifiable with Tussidé of the Tibesti mountains. Up to this point, Herodotus records,

> I have been able to list the names of the tribes inhabiting the sand belt, but not farther on beyond these. However, the band extends as far as the Pillars of Heracles and the region outside them. In it, after [another] ten days' journey, there is a salt-mine with men dwelling there, all of whose houses are built of blocks of salt. Accordingly, this region of Africa must be without rain, since otherwise, if it rained, the house walls, being made of salt, would not endure. The salt that is dug out in this place is of two kinds, white and bluish.[23]

I have nowhere noted any observation that this highly peculiar description of the final desert station on the caravan route is, in itself alone, proof positive that we must discount Herodotus' belief that the route continued westward to Morocco, and that in reality it had an equatorial trend. What is equally important, the picturesque and improbable detail, perhaps hardly credited by the writer himself, supplies a touchstone for the accuracy of his information. Just as dates are the prime object of trade

[23] Herodotus, *History*, IV.185.

and export from the North-Saharan oases, so salt has always
been the staple product of commerce in the southern Sahara
to furnish subequatorial Africa with the vital commodity that
Nature has denied to it. To quote a French geographer's description of interior Africa:

> Deposits of salt are common in the Sahara but wholly lacking in
> the Sudan; and the inhabitants of the desert derive from these
> deposits the wherewithal to purchase their food. Entire tribes
> are engaged in the transport of salt, much as dates are trans-
> ported in the northern desert.[24]

On the present trans-Saharan route from the Fezzan to Lake
Chad the next halt after crossing the great shoulder between
the Ahaggar and the Tibesti mountains is the little string of
oases of Kawar, among which are the extensive salt works of
Bilma. Nachtigal speaks [25] of "inexhaustible salt-mines" here,
from which "almost all of Bornu and the Haussa states" are
supplied, and describes the salt-laden caravans "with some 3,000
camels in each" that travel thrice a year; while Heinrich Barth
supplies an even more detailed and impressive account of this
rather surprising industry. The salt is produced in two grades,
the finer being snow-white, the poorer of a greyish or grey-green
cast. Gautier writes of the Bilma mines that "the salt is found
here in a very pure state and is carefully prepared by traditional
methods. These salt works, situated on the finest caravan route
of the Sahara contribute much to its traffic."

Although the salt at Bilma is cut into slabs and blocks, neither
Nachtigal nor Barth reported any houses constructed out of
these. But much farther to the west, where the salt for Nigerian
trade is mined and transported to Timbuktu on what I have
been calling the "West Saharan crossing," the Arab traveler
ibn-Batuta in the fourteenth century beheld the walls of a town
that he calls "Teghazza" entirely made of slabs of salt. And much
farther to the east, in the Danakil Desert of Ethiopia near the
Red Sea and on about the same latitude as Lake Chad, a recent
writer reports huts built entirely of salt and gives the following
description:

[24] Auguste Bernard, *Afrique Septentrionale et Occidentale: Sahara,* in Vidal de la
Blache and Gallois, *Géographie Universelle* (Paris, 1939), vol. xi, Part 2.
[25] *Ibid.,* 533–5.

The roof of each circular hut was constructed of large slabs of the salt, stretching entirely across its diameter. All these blocks and slabs were well squared, for the men used serviceable hatchets in their hewing. These refuges were probably very similar in appearance to the ice huts which the Esquimaux build.[26]

Not only does the story in Herodotus correspond to actuality, but proves beyond objection that his Greek informants in Cyrene were familiar with details of the great Saharan caravan route such as could not have been known to them except from the reports of travelers who—like the Nasamonian youths— had actually crossed the desert.

If in antiquity the eastern route through the desert was not directed toward the more distant Lake Chad but the much nearer Bodele basin, its course would necessarily have skirted the Tibesti massif along its western edge and passed close under Tussidé, the cloud-hung peak "that natives call the Pillar of the Sky" and to which the name of "Atlas" was attached by Herodotus. (I have suggested elsewhere that "Atlas" was a Greek version of *adrar*, the universal Berber word for "mountain uplands.")

It is true that this more easterly track would entirely miss the salt mines of Bilma. But this does not in any way invalidate the suggested interpretation of Herodotus' account; for salt abounds almost everywhere in the huge territory south of Tibesti, being merely the product resulting from the desicca- tion of all the vanished watercourses that, in the remoter past, descended from the central Saharan upland. And actually, at Budu in the region known as Borku, through which the track from Tussidé to Bodele passes, Nachtigal saw salt being ex- tracted, much as at Bilma, and spoke of enormous deposits from which the lands of Wadai and Kanem were even then being supplied. As at Bilma and as in Herodotus, there were two grades of the salt, the better pure white, the poorer greenish grey.

At the houses built of blocks of salt the itinerary in Herodotus abruptly concludes; but it can be continued by interpolating the account given by the young Nasamonian explorers, who "after having passed through much sandy territory, after many

[26] L. M. Nesbitt, *Desert and Forest* (London, 1934), p. 439 ff.

days beheld trees growing in a plain" and were taken prisoner and conducted "through enormous swamps" to a town on the bank of "a great river, flowing from the west toward the rising sun." There could hardly be a more fitting description of the great Bodele basin, as modern geographers imagine it, two to three thousand years ago.

It was in this roundabout way that Greece got word of an equatorial world of growing trees and running rivers beyond the great African desert. But there is no evidence for any further Greek interest in the Sahara. To the Greeks the sea and not the land was the explorer's highroad: if the camel is the Arab's "ship of the desert," the ship was the Greek's "camel of the sea." So it may be asserted with every assurance of certainty that no Greek trader or explorer ever set foot far inland in Africa, remote from any Mediterranean shore. In contrast, the Latin tribes of Italy were landsmen by natural inclination. Although Rome was forced to build and man ships of war in order to defeat Carthage in the Punic wars and her sailors gave a good account of themselves at sea, by tradition and by preference the Romans were neither sea lovers nor seafarers like the Aegean-cradled Greeks. They did not share the Greek dread of losing sight of the sea, and did not hesitate to march their armies far inland on the three continents. But their objectives were military and political; so that they became explorers more by accident than of set intention.

So it was that the first Mediterranean people to follow in the track of the Nasamonian adventurers across the Sahara were not Greeks but legionaries of Rome, dispatched for the subjugation of rebellious (or perhaps merely uninterested and otherwise oriented) foreign tribes. Five centuries after Herodotus, a detachment of the Roman army of occupation of the Tripoli shoreland moved into the northern Sahara. In 19 B.C. the proconsul governing Tunisia, Cornelius Balbus by name, occupied the chief settlement of the Garamantes. Later, during the emperorship of Vespasian, a punitive expedition of three months' duration, under the command of a certain Septimius Flaccus, seems to have secured Roman occupation of the entire Fezzan. And finally, though the precise date of the event is not recorded, a commander named Julius Maternus is reported as having set out from Garama (which should be one of the Fezzan oases) and led a force southward (and therefore into the central Sahara) till he reached "Agisymba, where the rhinoceros foregather." Agisymba is otherwise unknown. But it is difficult to suggest any other plausible objective or course for such an expedition out of the Fezzan into tropical Africa except the age-old trans-Saharan track over the high saddle between the Ahaggar and Tibesti ranges to the flooded Bodele lowlands leading to the marshy lake district of Chad. Where else, better than here, might the tropical rhinoceros "foregather"?!

The third great passageway across the North African desert is the river Nile. Since this road stands always open, in the sense that the river flows through its valley year in, year out, opposing no mountain ridges to be crossed and (with one exception) no long waterless marches to be made, one might suppose the Nile to have been from remotest times a heavily traveled route linking the Mediterranean with equatorial Africa. Contrary to expectation, the Nile does not seem ever to have played much of a role as a corridor of communication between these two racially distinct regions. Through the three thousand years of ancient Egyptian civilization no one in Egypt could have told whence the Nile came, from what sources it drew its flood, or through what countries it passed before entering Nubia, the nearest land south of Egypt. When Herodotus with typical Greek curiosity inquired where it was that the great river rose, his Egyptian informant told him a nonsensical story about "two sharp-peaked mountains whose names were Krophi and Mophi, situated between the Thebaid city of Syene and Elephantine" (which in modern terms would be at Aswan by the First Cataract). The informant went on to say:

> Between these two mountains flow up the bottomless fountains of the Nile; and half of the water flows northward into Egypt, and the other half southward into Ethiopa.[27]

Herodotus was intelligent enough to perceive that this was merely a misinterpretation of the behavior of the river at the rapids of the Cataract and did not help him to find an answer to his query. What particularly puzzled him was the contrariness of the Nile in going into flood during the summer months and

[27] Herodotus, *History*, II.28.

subsiding through the winter, when all the Greek rivers with
which he was familiar always behaved in just the opposite
manner, dwindling in the summer drought and swelling with
the autumnal and winter rains. The only explanation of this
phenomenon that he could suggest was altogether wide of the
truth.

It was thoroughly characteristic of Herodotus to have traveled
upstream as far as the barrier to navigation would allow (which
was the very spot where "Krophi and Mophi" were to be), in
order to see, what he could with his own eyes. It was equally
characteristic of his Greek attitude of mind that he never entertained any project of exploring the river further, but contented
himself with remarking that, as to the source of the Nile, he
was unable to learn anything more from anyone, "though I did
get some hearsay answers to my questions about the land beyond." What he thus managed to learn was accurate enough as
far as it went:

> If you proceed upstream from the city of Elephantine, the
> country rises sharply, so that the boat has to be tied with ropes
> on either side and dragged along by oxen.[28] After four days
> journey . . . you come to level land. Here the Nile flows
> around an island and [widens into] a large lake. Thereafter you
> will have to disembark and proceed [on foot] for forty days,
> since it is not possible to navigate the Nile there because of
> the many jagged rocks and reefs. But after forty days when
> this stretch is past, you may again take to the river and after
> twelve more days reach a large city named Meroë. This is re-
> ported to be the chief town of the [local] Ethiopians. . . .
> From this city by another voyage of equal length with that
> [already made] from Elephantine you will come to the metrop-
> olis of the [upriver] Ethiopians. . . . On this wise the course
> of the Nile is known through a journey of four months by river
> and road above its flowing through Egypt. But beyond this,
> nobody has anything certain to report; for the country is a desert
> on account of the heat.[29]

All in all, this is not an inaccurate description of the course
of the great river from the First Cataract upstream to Khartum
in the Sudan. The chief point is correctly taken, in that the

[28] This, of course, would be true only for the comparatively brief passage through
the rapids.
[29] Herodotus, *History*, II.29–31.

river is not navigated above its widening around the many islands that dot the Second Cataract and that at this point the traveler lands for a long overland journey before once more embarking on the river. But what Herodotus apparently did not understand is that it is not only because cataracts are frequent above Wadi Halfa, but because an enormous bend of the river may be shortened by cutting straight overland through the Nubian Desert, that the upriver route reaches Nubia in this manner. Still today the traveler from Cairo to Khartum, who does not overpass all difficulties by taking to the air, follows the Herodotean track, ascending by steamer as far as Wadi Halfa, short of the Second Cataract, and thence crossing the Nubian Desert by rail for nearly 250 miles, to rejoin the river at the head of its long circuitous loop. In antiquity an unmanageable stretch of river and a perilously hostile desert crossing combined to keep Egypt out of easy communication with upper Nubia. If traversed on foot instead of by rail, the passage across the desert would have been far from easy. It was here that the Persian king Cambyses, who lost his Siwa expeditionary force in the Libyan Desert, met with equally ill success in attempting to invade Nubia with the rest of his army. Herodotus tells the story with his usual vividness:

> When Cambyses reached Thebes on his march, he chose about 50,000 men from his army with orders to take the Ammonians captive and burn their oracle of God, while he himself set off with the rest of his forces against the Ethiopians. But before the army had covered a fifth of the way, all the provisions that they had with them were exhausted; and after that their animals failed them, as they ate them up. [Still they went on, as Cambyses obstinately refused to abandon his enterprise.] . . . And as long as the soldiers could gather anything from the soil, they ate grasses and stayed alive. But when they came to the sand, some of them committed a dreadful deed: choosing by lot one man in every ten, they devoured him. When Cambyses learned this, in dread of such cannibalism he abandoned the expedition. Advancing no farther, he returned to Thebes after having lost much of his army.[30]

Where Persian Cambyses failed so miserably, the earlier Egyptian kings had often succeeded in marching their armies

[30] *Ibid.*, III.25.

into Nubia, which during the New Kingdom had become virtually an Egyptian province. But none of these invaders seems to
have exerted any effort to carry his conquests farther up the
river or explore its various tributaries, such as the Atbara and
Blue Nile, major streams that descend steeply from the high
mountainland of Abyssinia, or the fan-shaped network of tropical watercourses that spread out westward of the Sudan over
an enormous area. Least of all were they able to track the chief
head current of the White Nile, which brings down out of
equatorial uplands the gathered water of the great Victoria
Nyanza lake. One might imagine that this intricacy of far-flung
river courses would have acted as an irresistible lure to draw
Egyptian and Mediterranean men alike into the heart of Africa.
Yet both of these races remained content to let hearsay take the
place of exploration and personal investigation. And this is not
difficult to understand, for there are formidable obstacles to
tracing the multifarious sources of the Nile.

Taking the river for their highroad, Egyptians and Nubians
were habituated to travel by water instead of by land. But upstream beyond Nubia the Nile and its chief tributaries soon
become unnavigable, and the country through which they run
discourages journey afoot. A brief description will make this
clear.

In upper Nubia the Abyssinian tributaries of the Nile—the
Atbara and the Blue Nile with their confluents—swell the river's
main stream, bringing down from the high mountainous plateau
of Ethiopia the flooding waters that keep Egypt fertile. These
floods are literally cataclysmic as the heavy summer rain on the
uplands drains down through tremendous clefts and gorges.
The main feeder of the Atbara is known locally as the Takazze,
said to be a native word for "terrible." It is described as taking
a drop of nearly five thousand feet over waterfalls and rapids
through a gigantic crevasse that cannot be crossed or entered
when the stream is in flood. The other great tributary, the Blue
Nile, has an even longer and more tortuous career, originating
on the Ethiopian plateau, where it issues from the thousand-
square-mile lake called Tana and descends in an almost complete
circle through rifts and gorges to the lowland of the Sudan, to
join the much longer mainstream of the White Nile at Khartum.
Although this latter stream held to comparatively level land, free

of rapids and reefs, yet after some six hundred miles of unobstructed waterway all further travel was blocked by enormous masses of floating and decaying water plants forming a huge swampland through which no ship could steer or be propelled. Beyond, there were still a thousand miles of river to be traveled before anyone could claim to have discovered the ultimate source of the Nile.

It was this combination of formidable natural barriers that made the Nile's origin a mystery to the riverfolk of Egypt and Nubia alike and deprived them of every reliable answer to give to the curious Greek visitor when he asked them whence came the water of their astounding river.

Not that the superintelligent Greek did not take it on himself to invent a variety of more or less plausible explanations for the phenomenon of the Nile's annual summer flood. Early in the sixth century B.C. Thales of Ionian Miletus, who had visited Egypt, thought flooding was due to the constantly blowing summer trade wind holding the river water back. Around the close of the sixth century Hecataeus (also of Miletus) suggested that the water came from the earth-encircling stream of ocean, on which (he thought) the Nile drew. Herodotus' guess was much wider of the mark. He argued that when the sun went south in winter it dried up the usual sources of the river, thus causing low water during that season of the year. In the fourth century, Ephorus, author of the first universal history of Greece, advanced an even wilder notion. He maintained that the inundation was a sort of exudation, as of sweat, from the superheated earth! Before his time, Anaxagoras, an Ionian philospher and physicist residing in Athens, had hit upon a better, though still erroneous, explanation. He held that the inundation was due to melting snow on the mountains of Ethiopia. But this idea was very generally rejected (among others by Herodotus) on the very reasonable ground that the farther south one went the hotter the climate became, and hence there could not be any snow in Ethiopia. A contemporary thinker, Democritus of Abdera, improved on this theory by suggesting that the summer trade wind, on striking the high Ethiopian mountains, brought torrential rains there. This is part of the true explanation (though most of the heavy Abyssinian summer rain appears to be brought by an equatorial airstream from the southwest).

Diodorus, writing much later, records the erroneous counter-objection to this that the seasonal date of the Nile's flooding of its banks does not agree with such a theory because the trade wind does not begin to blow until midsummer (this was judging by its behavior much farther north in Greece), and anyway the Ethiopian mountains are not "the highest on earth," as Democritus had asserted. So the debate continued; and even when the correct explanation was divined at last, it was by no means universally accepted.

As far as can be made out, it was Nearchus, who served under Alexander in India (and about whom there will be much to be said in a later chapter of this book), who finally hit upon the correct explanation through recognizing that the flooding of the great Indian rivers presented a situation exactly comparable to that of the Egyptian Nile. Arrian, writing in the second century of our era but drawing his material directly from Nearchus, states the case succinctly and correctly:

> On the analogy of the Indian rivers we may conclude that there are rains on the mountains of Ethiopia during the summer and that therefore the Nile, swollen by these, overflows its banks in the Egyptian land.[31]

So the great mystery was a mystery no longer—even though everyone did not agree about the right solution. But while the annual inundation of Egypt by the sudden increase of the Atbara and the Blue Nile was at last correctly explained, this knowledge threw no light on the source of the Nile's main stream, the White Nile.

About this question even the all-knowing Aristotle was as much in the dark as everyone else. Apparently, word had somehow reached him of the existence of great marshlands far up the river in Upper Sudan, for he speaks of "the marshes south of Egypt where the Nile has its source"; but in another passage he betrays his ignorance in supposing that the Nile and the river Chremetes (which seems to be the modern Senegal and the Chretes of Hanno's famous exploration) had a common origin in the "so-called Silver Mountain." (The two rivers never come within 2,500 miles of each other!) And while every intelligent Greek considered himself entitled to an opinion, no one enter-

[31] Arrian, *Indica*, 6.6.

tained any idea of actually going to see whether there was snow on the Abyssinian mountains or torrential rain in summer, or whence it was that the main stream of the mighty Nile first gathered its water. Not until the Greeks took over the rule of Egypt was any progress made toward serious exploration of the upper Nile. The second Ptolemy, on whom the byname of Philadelphus was conferred, dispatched an expedition, the importance of which is not to be measured so much by the information that it may have gained as by the fact that here at last was an instance of Greek exploration undertaken with no other motive than a desire for increasing geographical knowledge.

When finally Rome replaced the last of the Ptolemies with her imperial rule, ambitions of political conquest and commercial gain gave African exploration new impetus. We have already noted how Julius Maternus (whoever he may have been) marched a legionary detachment through the eastern Sahara Desert all the way to the Bodele depression and perhaps beyond. Pliny records a comparable expedition up the Nile into further Nubia, which—to judge only from his account—would seem to have accomplished little or nothing. All that he says is that

> some pretorian guardsmen under command of a tribune were sent exploring by the emperor Nero, who was contemplating an Ethiopian war. They reported everything utterly desolate.[32]

But the philosopher Seneca, who was Nero's tutor and counsellor, gives a much more enlightening account of this expedition. In the course of his *Physical Inquiries* he introduces the following passage:

> I myself have heard two centurions whom Emperor Nero had sent to investigate the source of the Nile tell how they accomplished a long journey, for which the king of Ethiopia provided them with an escort and commended them to the next nearest kings, by which means they penetrated far beyond his realm.
>
> As they themselves said, "We came to tremendous marshes, from which the natives knew no way out, nor could anyone hope for one, so entangled were plants in the water and so impassable were these waters whether on foot or by ship, because the muddy and obstructing marsh will not permit passage to any but a tiny one-man craft. There" (said one of them) "we be-

[32] Pliny, *Natural History*, VI.181. .

held two rocks from which there tumbled the vast might of
the river." But whether that was the true source or merely
some sort of supplement to the river . . .[33]

and here Seneca concludes by reiterating his own belief that the
Nile is ejected from a huge subterranean reservoir (perhaps
clinging in his mind to the Egyptian story in Herodotus—which
Herodotus himself did not credit—about the gulf between the
rocks Mophi and Krophi, from which the Nile comes out of
the earth).

If the great waterfall was not merely a picturesque invention,
the centurions must have adapted for themselves a faraway
feature, about which they had learned from native informants;
for they admitted that the dense, floating *sudd* had stopped
them, and there are no rocky falls anywhere in that region.
Nonetheless it was no slight achievement to have explored the
White Nile all the way from Khartum to Lake No, where the
Bahr el Ghazal joins the Bahr el Gebel, uniting all the waters of
the southwest Sudan with those from the equatorial highland
of Uganda.

So, little by little, the curtain of ignorance was lifted. Travelers down the Red Sea, landing on the coast of Eritrea, seem to
have gathered rumors of the Blue Nile's rising on the vast inland plateau of Ethiopia to the west of them, perhaps had even
learned of Lake Tana, named to them as Lake Coloē.

But the great discovery that finally resolved the secret of
centuries of idle wonderment came about in a most extraordinary and unexpected manner. Strange as the story reads, the
geographical knowledge with which it is informed makes it
impossible to impugn its veracity. Unfortunately, the account
comes to us only at third hand in the works of Ptolemy (not
one of the Macedonian kings of Egypt, but the great mathe-
matician, astronomer, and physical geographer of the second
century of our era), who drew on his almost contemporary predecessor Marinus of Tyre, who in turn had access to the original
narrative. What can be put together amounts to this:

At some unspecified date in the early Roman Empire, a Greek
of unknown lineage, occupation, and accomplishments, who
bore the not uncommon name of Diogenes, was forced into an
unintentional voyage down the East African coast by being

[33] Seneca, *Naturales Quaestiones*, VI.8.3–5.

blown for twenty-five days before the northeast monsoon of the Indian Ocean. It is thought that he came ashore in Africa opposite the island of Zanzibar, which is to say in northern Tanganyika, whence, for reasons unknown to us, he decided to journey inland. Heading into the interior, perhaps up the valley of the Pangani River, Diogenes appears to have sighted Africa's highest peak, Mount Kilimanjaro, and probably also the equally conspicuous but considerably lower peak of Mount Meru. If he persisted on his northwest course, he could not have failed to come eventually to the shore of Africa's greatest lake, Victoria Nyanza, one of the largest bodies of fresh water in the world. Still more surprising than his arrival at Victoria Nyanza, five hundred miles inland from his starting point on the coast, is Diogenes' apparent realization that in this great inland sea he had chanced upon the main source of the water of the faraway Egyptian Nile. Yet Ptolemy's specific statement (which must derive from Diogenes' account) that the Nile originates in two lakes, from each of which there issues a river that unites with the other to form the mainstream, comes too close to the truth to permit doubt of the genuineness of Diogenes' investigations. It cannot be objected that Ptolemy's two lakes are Victoria Nyanza and Tana and that the union of the two streams from these lakes is merely the junction of the White Nile and the Blue Nile at Khartum, because the account continues that both the lakes are replenished by the snow melting from a vast range called the Mountains of the Moon. Diogenes therefore knew of Lake Albert as well as Lake Victoria, since it is entirely true that the collected waters of Lake Albert run together with those from Lake Victoria to send the Nile on its way. The further remark that the Mountains of the Moon run east and west for five hundred miles is altogether erroneous, as no such extensive snowclad range exists. Yet if we ignore the false orientation and drastically trim the mileage down, it would seem unreasonable to deny that Diogenes' Mountains of the Moon are the Ruwenzori range of extremely lofty, snowcapped and glacier-lined equatorial mountains that run for some 60 miles north and south and send their melted snows through the Semliki River into Lake Albert.

There is no way of ascertaining how much of all that has here been set forth was actually visited by Diogenes and seen with his own eyes, as opposed to what he may have learned from natives conversant with the interior of their country. But if he ever really beheld the high Mount Kilimanjaro peak and the huge Lake Victoria and the snow-mantled Ruwenzori range, then he must take rank as the Stanley of Antiquity and be given a worthy place among History's Great Explorers.

PYTHEAS OF MASSALIA

IN an earlier chapter Herodotus was cited as authority for the statement that the earliest Greek explorers of the western Mediterranean were Ionian mariners from the town of Phocaea at the mouth of the Gulf of Smyrna, and that they followed up their discoveries by establishing maritime trade with the Mediterranean coast of Spain, extending their voyages even into the Atlantic beyond the Gibraltar Strait to take advantage of the wealth of the region of Tartessos.

The main base of operation for this western trade was the colonial town that the Phocaeans had founded a few miles east of the mouth of the Rhone in southern France on a magnificent harbor still greatly frequented today. To their (probably very modest) settlement on this site they gave the name "Massalia"; the famous city of Marseilles perpetuates both the name and the situation of their tiny colony.

The exact foundation date of Massalia is uncertain, but is very generally held to be close to the year 600 B.C. For at least a century after the event, Massaliote ships traveled the coastal route between their home port and the silver-rich Andalusian district on the Atlantic beyond Gibraltar. But then, in the early decades of the fifth century, while the Persian War diverted Greek attention from the West, Phoenician Carthage, Persia's ally, closed the Gibraltar Strait to Greek shipping and cut off all Greek trade with Tartessos by fortifying a small offshore island in a large landlocked bay near the mouth of the Guadalquivir, to serve her as a naval base and trading center for her own ships. To this strategic vantage point the name "Gadir" was attached, signifying "stronghold" in the Phoenician tongue.

"Gadir" later became "Gades" in Roman speech, and "Gades" in turn survives as Spanish "Cádiz"—although the city is no longer surrounded by sea but has become attached by a narrow spit of sand to a much larger island, divided by only a narrow channel from the Spanish mainland.

When access to the Atlantic thus became denied to all Greek shipping by the inimical hostility of its Punic rival, the traders of Massalia were forced to discontinue their calls along Spain's southern shore. Yet they maintained commercial contact with the native Iberians as far down the eastern coast as they could sail without encountering opposition. This meant that they could travel at least as far as the modern port of Almería and possibly farther west, to the vicinity of modern Málaga. Thereby, Massalia was able to keep alive her traditions of seamanship, maintaining an intimate knowledge of nearly a thousand miles of western Mediterranean coastal waters, from the Gulf of Genoa almost to Gibraltar.

In this Greek colonial town on the verge of a generally bright and sunny, but at times very stormy sea, some three hundred years after the town was first settled and while its seagoing reputation was still at its height, Pytheas was born and grew to manhood.

Nothing whatever is known of his birth or ancestry, nor yet about his financial condition or the extent of his education, except that it is clear from various references by ancient writers that he enjoyed a considerable reputation as a geophysicist. Further, it may be presumed that he was a person of distinction in his native town, to have been entrusted by his fellow citizens with the command of so ambitious a voyage of exploration as he is known to have accomplished. To be sure, the Greek historian Polybius (as reported by the geographer Strabo) found it

> altogether unbelievable that a private citizen, and a poor man at that, could ever have traversed such vast distances either by sea or land.[1]

With this remark Polybius intended to cast a slur on Pytheas' veracity, about which he entertained very considerable doubts. But it would be an obvious reply to this unpleasant innuendo to point out that, if Pytheas himself lacked the necessary funds,

[1] Strabo, *Geography*, II.iv.2.

the expedition must have been organized as a communal venture and financed by the authorities of his native town. It will be apparent in due course why Massalia took so great interest in this particular voyage of exploration.

So little is known about the circumstances attendant on this undertaking that it has not proved possible to determine, with any approach to certainty, in what year Pytheas set out on his voyage, how long he was gone, or in consequence when it was that he returned safely to Massalia—to write out that account of his extraordinary experience which we know to have once existed, but which unfortunately has not survived.

Nevertheless certain inferences may be drawn from references to Pytheas by other ancient writers. Thus, inasmuch as the historian Polybius attacked his credibility, Pytheas must have been either a near contemporary or a predecessor of Polybius. Similarly, since the geographer Eratosthenes is reported to have made use of information gathered by Pytheas in his account of Britain, Pytheas must necessarily have been either a contemporary or a predecessor of Eratosthenes. As the literary activity of both Polybius and Eratosthenes can be dated with near certainty, it follows that the closing decade of the third century B.C. is the latest possible period in which Pytheas could have made his voyage (though, of course, his expedition may have taken place much earlier).

Counter inferences may be made, not from mention but from failure to find mention of Pytheas in writers who would undoubtedly have incorporated the results of his explorations and discoveries if they had known of them. Thus, it is clear that neither Plato nor Aristotle had any knowledge of the far-northern latitudes visited and described by Pytheas. Hence his expedition is to be dated later than Aristotle's death in 322 B.C.

In order to narrow the gap of more than a hundred years resulting from these considerations, it may be argued that the appropriate place for Pytheas in the development of Greek scientific thought on matters of a geophysical nature sets him closer to Eratosthenes than to Aristotle or his immediate followers. This line of argument would bring Pytheas' expedition toward the middle (rather than in the opening decade) of the third century B.C.

Finally there is the inference from political history. From

the scant notices in ancient authors and the inconclusive evidence of archeological discovery it would seem that Pytheas was the first Greek navigator to pass through the Gibraltar Strait and put in at Gadir after Carthage closed the Atlantic to all Mediterranean shipping except her own. There is nowhere any suggestion that Pytheas had to run a hostile blockade or elude observation in order to reach the outer sea; and, although it is not expressly so stated, he appears to have touched at Gadir, which more than once is mentioned as a fixed point on the itinerary of his voyage. It is extremely unlikely that a Greek ship would have been permitted to travel west of Málaga or would have been given friendly entry to Gadir as long as Carthaginian naval power dominated the western basin of the Mediterranean. The suggestion has been advanced that, in the brief period between 310 and 306 B.C., Carthage was too heavily engaged in her struggle with Sicilian Syracuse to maintain her Atlantic blockade and that this would have given Pytheas an opportunity to elude Punic vigilance both on his outward and again on his return voyage. But this is a gratuitous assumption, which might be true only because it cannot be categorically proved false. It was not until Rome, which had hitherto been a military power only on land, became also a naval power when she saw no other way to defeat Carthage in the First Punic War that the situation was drastically altered. After many reverses and heavy losses in naval engagements, Rome finally succeeded in gaining unchallenged command of the sea. By the peace treaty of 241 B.C. Carthage relinquished all claim to the Sicilian side of the Tunisian Strait. In the following year she was further crippled by the savage mutiny of her mercenary army on African soil; and a year later she found herself debarred from the island of Sardinia in consequence of a gross breach of treaty on the part of Rome. But then, after some five years of complete demoralization threatening her western Mediterranean empire with disintegration, Carthage made a determined and highly successful attempt to reestablish herself as a military power by concentrating attention on her Spanish possessions with their native Iberian connections. Her brief phase of extreme helplessness on land and sea in the years between 242 and 236 B.C. constitutes the only period during the third century that afforded Massalia, the close ally of Rome, a feasible opportunity for

sending out an expedition whose purpose could not possibly
have been approved by Carthage.

In this manner a combination of inferences from different
types of evidence seems to narrow the chronological range for
Pytheas' voyage of exploration to the third quarter of the third
century B.C., with 240–38 B.C. as the most likely choice for a
precise dating.

Unfortunately, this rather elegant demonstration of chronological bracketing, to restrict an elusive target to a fixed location in time, is very generally judged to have badly missed its
aim because proved completely mistaken by the following
remark in Strabo:

> Polybius says . . . that Eratosthenes . . . believes Pytheas;
> and that, too, though Dicaearchus does not believe him.[2]

Now, Dicaearchus was one of the pupils and followers of Aristotle who outlived his great master's death by a considerable
span of years. Obviously, if Dicaearchus disbelieved Pytheas,
Dicaearchus must have read or heard about the latter's voyage; and as Dicaearchus does not appear to have survived the
year 285 B.C., that year becomes the latest admissible date for
Pytheas' return from his expedition. Those who, for one reason
or another, are inclined to put Pytheas as late as possible, have
set 285 B.C. as the hypothetical date of his voyage; while those
who have been more concerned with the obstacle of the Phoenician blockade to the Atlantic have opted for 310–6, considerably earlier in Dicaearchus' lifetime and not long after Aristotle's death; whereas those who have not been influenced by
special considerations, historical, philosophical, or otherwise,
have contented themselves with assigning Pytheas' expedition
to the late fourth or early third century without attempting a
closer reckoning.

While freely granting the apparent validity of the foregoing
argument, I am led to reject it. Since it necessitates a conclusion completely at variance with other indications, it must be
under suspicion as based somehow on unsound interpretation
of the supposed evidence. The problem thus raised is too involved for detailed examination; but a brief summary may
properly be included here.

[2] *Ibid.*

When Polybius observed that Eratosthenes believed Pytheas "and that, too, though Dicaearchus did not," he was not making a sweeping statement about the credibility of the explorer's report on his expedition, but taking issue with certain estimates on sailing distances in the western Mediterranean that had no connection whatever with northern Europe, Britain, or the Atlantic. Dicaearchus, in his lost treatise on the geography of the known world, had estimated the sailing distance from the Strait of Messina at one end of the western Mediterranean to the Pillars of Heracles (i.e., the Strait of Gibraltar) at the other end to be a journey of seven thousand stades—obviously a round number, perhaps calculated on seven sailing days, but in any case very far short of the actual distance, whether measured on the direct route over open water by way of Sardinia or by following the European coast all the way. Strabo, our authority for this piece of information, proceeds to tell us that Eratosthenes gave this same figure of seven thousand stades for only the part of the voyage that lay between Massalia and Gibraltar—and adds that Eratosthenes' estimate was close to the truth. It has been very generally conceded that the fact that Eratosthenes cited Massalia as a point from which to measure a sailing distance to the Atlantic end of the Mediterranean strongly suggests that he took his data from Pytheas' account of his voyage. In this sense, Eratosthenes "believed" Pytheas (the Greek word may equally correctly be translated "relied on"!) and rejected the previous estimate given by Dicaearchus, who consequently was in disagreement with Pytheas. Strabo either misunderstood or deliberately distorted the situation in saying that Dicaearchus did not accept Pytheas' estimate: it would have been nearer the truth to have said that Pytheas did not accept Dicaearchus. If Dicaearchus had seen Pytheas' report, he would have realized that a Massaliote could not fail to be accurately informed on sailing distances in his own sector of the Mediterranean, and would have revised his estimates accordingly.

A much more serious objection to the proposed date for Pytheas' voyage is the apparent use of Pytheas as a source of information by the Greek historian Timaeus, whose great historical work (preserved only in scattered fragments) is held to have been completed before 250 B.C.

In the fourth book of his *Natural History* [3] Pliny relates that

> inward [4] from Britain by six days' voyage there is an island called Mictis, which is the source of tin. To this the Britons consort in wicker craft sewn about with leather.

This notice may seem to have been drawn from Pytheas' account of his visit to the tin mines of Cornwall.

Again, in another portion of his encyclopedic compendium,[5] Pliny asserts that

> Pytheas says that the Gutons,[6] a people of Germany, inhabit an inlet of the ocean, called Metuonis, that extends six thousand stades; [7] and that at a day's voyage from this there is an island called Abalus. There in springtime the waves wash up a marine concretion that the natives use for fuel and sell to their Teuton neighbors. Timaeus ˙concurs with this, but gives the name of the island as Basilia.

The reference here can only be to amber; and Pliny's specific mention of Pytheas seems to imply that Timaeus was familiar with that navigator's visit to the amber island.

Those who maintain that in these two items Timaeus' source was Pytheas will have to explain why Timaeus fails to agree with what Pytheas must be assumed to have written. In one case a wholly different name is given the amber island, and in the other an island trading post, Mictis, six days distant from Britain and totally unidentifiable, is substituted for the detailed and accurate account of Saint Michael's Mount in Cornwall that is given by Diodorus and can only have been derived from Pytheas' report on his visit to the Cornish tin mines (as narrated on a later page of the present chapter).

I suggest that, instead of proving that Timaeus was acquainted with Pytheas' account of his voyage, these discrepancies indicate that he did *not* have knowledge of it. In that case there is reason to assume that Pytheas made his great voyage of exploration after Timaeus' lifetime. There is therefore no objection derivable from these passages in Pliny to the suggested

[3] IV.30.
[4] I.e., toward the Mediterranean?
[5] XXXVII.11.
[6] Goths?
[7] *Ca.* 700 miles.

date of 240–38 B.C. for Pytheas' expedition. The statements attributed to Timaeus presumably were derived from rumors that were reaching the Mediterranean during his lifetime—reports that would have heightened Massalian interests in tracking them to their source.

Viewed across an interval of more than two thousand years, it may seem thoroughly unimportant to discover whether Pytheas set out from Marseilles about the year 308 B.C., as is most frequently stated, or some seventy years later, *ca.* 238 B.C., as seems to me much more likely. But it is actually very important indeed, because on the decision between these two dates depends fundamentally our judgment of the purpose for which the expedition was undertaken and, in accord with that purpose, our reconstruction of the course that was followed and the regions toward which it was laid.

Ever since Charles Darwin published his account of the *Voyage of the Beagle,* on which he functioned as "naturalist" attached to a geographical survey expedition, the concept of exploration for purely scientific purposes, with professionally trained and equipped specialists on the staff, has become so familiar that it is not often realized that, prior to modern times, exploratory expeditions were never exclusively motivated by intellectual interest, but sent out for material aims, such as the extension of political empire, the increase of commerce, or the acquisition of wealth.

None of these three motives could have been operative for Massalia so long as Carthage prohibited Greek access to the Atlantic. And we may dismiss the notion that Pytheas, even though he was a learned scientist, might have organized, equipped, and personally financed his expedition solely to satisfy his own intellectual curiosity and further his career as an authority on geography. Quite rightly, Polybius objected that "it is unbelievable that a private citizen, and a poor man at that, could ever have traversed such vast distances either by sea or land."

But when Carthaginian dominion over the western Mediterranean and its Atlantic approaches was shattered by Rome's victory in the First Punic War, there suddenly opened up the alluring prospect of securing for Greek ships and the Greco-Roman market the immensely profitable Atlantic trade, over which Carthage had hitherto exercised an unchallengeable monopoly. It was this prospect which Pytheas was commissioned to investigate, with instructions to proceed beyond Cádiz for the express purpose of discovering the sources from which Cádiz had been drawing its cargoes, and inquiring into the practicability of substituting Massalian for Carthaginian interests in those regions.

The origin and significance of this Atlantic commerce will be discussed in greater detail later on. For the moment, it is being advanced as the prime objective of Pytheas' expedition and the only one that adequately explains its inception. But if this was indeed the quest on which Pytheas set out from Massalia and headed for the Gibraltar Strait, we must somehow dismiss Dicaearchus as evidence and settle on the final years of the First Punic War as the earliest appropriate date for this unprecedented voyage.

Although we today have every reason for crediting the truth of Pytheas' account of his explorations insofar as we can manage to reconstruct its content, many (and possibly most) of his own contemporaries categorically refused to believe it. It is a curious human trait to delight in listening to fantastic yarns of faraway places with their unfamiliar marvels, and yet whenever a returning traveler from distant regions gives an eyewitness account of whatever he has actually seen that is strange and wonderful, he is not believed but is branded as an impostor and a liar. So Marco Polo, on his return to his native Venice after a long sojourn at the court of Kublai Khan in China, was nicknamed *Marco Millioni* by his townsmen in mockery of his innumerable tales, none of which was credited. In much the same vein, Polybius, the Greek historian of the Punic Wars, refused to believe that Pytheas had ever seen Britain or visited the North Atlantic islands and the amber coast; and Strabo, the Greek-speaking geographer of early imperial Roman times, outdid Polybius in his refutation of Pytheas' pretensions, contemptuously comparing his "lies" to the deceptions of mountebank magicians and mentioning his achievements only to dismiss them as ridiculous. The modern world has treated him better than did his contemporaries; for we know that their doubts were mistaken and that Pytheas really traveled "to the very ends of the habitable world."

We have no information on the number or type of ships that

took part in Pytheas' expedition. But nothing encourages the assumption that more than a single vessel set out. As for its type, a former president of the Royal Geographical Society made the following suggestion:

> A large Massilian ship was a good sea-boat and well able to make a voyage into the northern Ocean. She would be from 150 to 170 feet long, with a depth of 25 or 26 feet and a draught of 10 to 12. Her tonnage would be 400 to 500, so that the ship of Pytheas was larger and more seaworthy than the crazy little Santa-Maria with which eighteen hundred years afterwards Columbus discovered the New World.[8]

Ancient Greek ships were generically of three classes—triremes, penteconters, and merchantmen. The arrangement of the oars and the disposition of the oarsmen in the "three-banked" trireme have been endlessly discussed and disputed; but there is no disagreement that triremes were warships. As such, one would hardly have been chosen for a voyage of exploration in foreign and distant waters. The penteconters were swift cruisers, capable of long voyages; but their narrow build and crowded quarters left little room for supplies and equipment, and their traditional complement of a 50-man crew would be difficult to feed and maintain and unnecessarily large for an exploratory mission. The little information about the rate at which Pytheas completed various stretches of his itinerary suggests very leisurely progress. This may have been due to his interest in exploring unfamiliar regions in careful detail; but it also tends to favor the supposition that his ship was a slow trading vessel such as Massalia used in her traffic with Spain.

To summarize the foregoing discussion of probabilites, it may be reasonably surmised that it was in or about the year 240 B.C. that the authorities of the Greek trading town of Massalia decided to take advantage of the Roman destruction of Carthaginian naval power in order to explore the resources from which Carthage had been deriving the enormous profits of her Atlantic trade, centered on the fortified island of Gadir off the Spanish coast beyond the Gibraltar Strait. A private citizen of the town, Pytheas by name, a geographer and physicist of renown, was entrusted with the overall command of the expedition; and

[8] C. R. Markham, "Pytheas the Discoverer of Britain," in *Geographic Journal*, June, 1893.

SHETLAND IS.

ORKNEY IS.

NORTH SEA

BALTIC SEA

BRITISH ISLES

Elbe R.

Rhine R.

Nantes
St. Nazaire
Loire R.

BAY OF BISCAY
Bordeaux

Narbonne
Marseille
PYRENEES
ITALY

Ebro R.
Ampurias
Tarragona
CORSICA

SPAIN
SARDINIA

Guadiana R.
BALEARIC IS.
SICILY

Guadalquivir R.
Malaga
Cadix
Almeria

A F R I C A

WESTERN EUROPE

one of the Massaliote trading ships was suitably manned and equipped for a voyage that promised to be of long duration.

It is not recorded at what time of year the ship put out from Massalia, but presumably it was late spring, which was the season when navigation of the Mediterranean was normally resumed after winter's interruption by stormy weather.

Despite the untoward accident that Pytheas' own published account of the voyage has perished completely, surviving ancient references to it, of one sort or another, make it possible to reconstruct most of its course with remarkable assurance.

There can, of course, be no uncertainty about the first week or two of the voyage, since Massaliote seamen were intimately familiar with the Mediterranean coast of France and Spain as far as the approach to the Gibraltar Strait. Since the reader may not be equally familiar with that sector, it may be helpful to his mental picture of Pytheas' voyage to have some of its salient landmarks noted.

East of Marseilles the Alps descend to the sea to form the picturesquely rocky coast of the Riviera; but in the other direction, in which Pytheas headed, the great river Rhone has built a level valleyland and dropped soil into the sea to make a broken shoreline of sandbars and lagoons stretching for miles. There were no Greek settlements on this shifting and swampy coast. But beyond the last lagoon, shortly before the whole continental shoreline turns south toward the headlands of the Pyrenees, there was a tiny Greek settlement called *Agathē* ("The Good") apparently founded for trading with an important nearby Celtic town, whose ancient name of Narbo still survives as "Narbonne." Today it is a sleepy provincial French town of no great size, lying five miles inland from the sea; but in Roman times it had antedated Lyons as the chief city of Transalpine Gaul and was then a seaport on a Mediterranean bay. Not only then, but for several centuries before the advent of Roman power, Narbo was important as the terminus of the shortest and the only easy trade route overland between the Atlantic and the Mediterranean. Its name will appear again more than once in the course of the present chapter.

From here, on laying his course due south, Pytheas would have seen off his starboard bow the hard, clear line of mountains on the sky. These are the high eastern outrunners of the chain

of the Pyrenees, whose western end, 270 miles away, descends
with almost equal abruptness to the Atlantic. On reaching their
rocky headlands Pytheas would have been passing from Gaul to
Iberia—or in more recent terms, from France to Spain—and
thereat the whole character of the landscape changes from sandy
beaches backed by green lowland to rockbound and precipitous
shores rising toward a background of high mountains. Even so,
there is no unbroken line of cliffs along this coast; but a succession of tiny bays and harbors gives way to a large fertile basin
watered by small streams. And here Pytheas would have turned
in to the sheltered harbor of a walled Greek town, at which he
would have received a cordial welcome inasmuch as it had been
founded by the same Ionian Greeks from Phocaea who had
settled Massalia, and its inhabitants must have been of close kin
to many in Pytheas' crew. Named *Emporion* ("The Trading-
post"), it had grown from a mere port of call for Massalian ships
on their way to southern Spain and Tartessos to become a typical
Greek town, with streets running at right angles to enclose
blocks of small patioed houses, and a central market square, and
a tiny temple to Asiatic Artemis. An interesting feature was a
large native quarter shut off from the Greek sector of the town
by a dividing wall—a barrier that might be interpreted as due
to distrust of the local Iberians, yet must also be taken as an
indication that relations between Greek and "barbarian" were
cordial enough to permit a double settlement on a single site.
Emporion (whose name has survived almost unchanged as "Ampurias" and has given the title of "Ampurdan" to the whole
surrounding plain) has been extensively excavated by Spanish
archeologists, to become the most interesting relic of the ephemeral Greek colonization of Spain.

Leaving Emporion, Pytheas continued southwest along the
Spanish coast, passing the site of the great modern city of Bar-
celona without encountering any signs of his countrymen. At
Iberian Tarragona he might have found friendly reception.
Then came the sandy delta of the Ebro, the only important river
on the entire Mediterranean coast of Spain; and then, on the
second following day, the marvelous landmark sighted by the
first Greek explorers of the far-western Mediterranean nearly
four full centuries earlier when they crossed by the island bridge
of the Balearics and caught their first glimpse of the Spanish

mainland in the towerlike thousand-foot headland today called "Ifach," but named "The Lookout" by the Greeks. Here there was some sort of Greek settlement—though it is not possible to say how large it was or how it was planned and built, because the Spanish archeologists have not yet dug the narrow neck of land behind the towering rock, where the Greek town lay.

At this point the coast, which has been trending southeast, abruptly turns southwest again, continuing for close on two hundred miles, until it takes another sudden change of direction, to run due west below the lofty snowclad chain of the Sierra Nevada mountains. From their crest, some twenty miles inland from the coast, one can at times sight the rugged coastal hills of North Africa; for here the broad western basin of the Mediterranean narrows to a corridor with an average width of barely a hundred miles, extending for nearly three times as great a length, only to contract suddenly to an open passage less than ten miles wide—the Pillars of Heracles of the ancients, the Gibraltar Strait of more recent times.

Pytheas, hugging the Spanish shore, would have seen only open water on his left and caught no glimpse of nearby Africa until the high sentinel headland of Gibraltar Rock, like a second and even greater "Lookout" mountain, came into view and he beheld behind across the strait the answering sentinel rock of Jebel Musa in Morocco. These two guardians of the Atlantic gateway are the famous "Pillars of Heracles" of ancient lore—though why they were called pillars is far from clear. Perhaps they were thought of as the two upright piers that line a gateway, carrying the sky for lintel overhead. But more probably "pillars" is a mistranslation (encouraged by the Latin mistaken version, *columnae*) of the Greek word *stelai* intended in its sense of "marker" or "boundary stone"; so that the twin mountains were conceived as marking the limits of the Inner Sea that, for the Greeks, was the navigable world. Heracles, their national hero, had so identified them when he came west to Spain on one of his mythical adventures. Thanks to the Phoenician merchants from Carthage, they had indeed marked the limit of seafaring for Greek ships in the fifth and fourth and first half of the third centuries B.C. Yet Pytheas passed between them undeterred and seemingly unchallenged—an event that, as previously suggested, calls for explanation. More than that, he seems to have put in at

Gadir, to rest and take on provisions before his great advance into the unknown.

From Gibraltar to Cádiz by sea past Cape Trafalgar is a distance of only some seventy miles. But a strong head-current sets eastward through the strait, the oceanic tides run unusually high along the Andalusian coast, and there are many reefs and hidden sandbanks offshore. Besides, there is every warrant for believing that no Greek vessel had passed that way for centuries. To this extent, even though he was pursuing a route once thoroughly familiar to his ancestors, Pytheas was entering an unknown ocean that had to be tested and explored anew.

Beyond Cádiz-Gadir it was only a half-day's voyage to the mouth of the "Great River" (for this is the sense of the Arabic words concealed in the modern name "Guadalquivir"), which was the "silver-rooted Tartessos" of the older Greek poets and the goal of the earliest Greek sea journeys to the west. Beyond it the Andalusian shoreline continues along a thirty-mile stretch of sand dunes and unfertile coastal hills with little sign of life to the deep estuary of the Río Tinto (Columbus' starting point for *his* Atlantic exploration!), and beyond, along a coast still sandy and unpromising, to the mouth of a second great river, today called the "Guadiana" and now serving as part of the boundary between Spain and Portugal. Here, for sure, Pytheas had reached a land unknown to the Greeks except by such hearsay rumor as had inspired Herodotus to write:

> The Celts are outside the Pillars of Heracles and border upon the Cynesians, who are the dwellers farthest to the West of all that inhabit Europe.[9]

Still the coast led west, until it turned abruptly north at the final headland where the unbroken 175-foot cliffs of Cape St. Vincent front the open Atlantic. Strabo informs us that the geographer Eratosthenes quoted Pytheas as making it a five-day journey from Gadir to the Sacred Headland, as the ancients called it (in the language of our times, from Cádiz to Cape St. Vincent); and the late-second-century-B.C. geographer Artemidorus claimed that this was one more instance of Pytheas' lying. Actually, even following all the ins and outs of bays and headlands, the distance between these two points does not exceed two

[9] Herodotus, *History*, II.33.3.

hundred miles at the very most; and we should have to agree that an average of only forty miles a day was poor running even for a clumsy Greek merchantman. But Pytheas is also quoted as having had to contend with powerful tides along this stretch of coast; and the U.S. Hydrographic Office in its *Sailing Directions* for the coast of Portugal confirms Pytheas, adding the comment that harbor shelter from ocean gales is almost entirely lacking, while dangerous shoals and shifting sandbanks fringe the shore. I think that we should give Pytheas credit for recording his log honestly and accurately.

This scanty notice on Pytheas' rate of travel and his experience of oceanic tidal currents may serve as a typical example of the fragmentary state of our information about the course and character of his voyage and illustrate how dependent we are on indirect accounts transmitted at second and even third hand.

From here on, all the way from Cape St. Vincent to the head of the Bay of Biscay, there is nothing to tell us how Pytheas fared or how long he took to pass the four-hundred-mile shore of Portugal, to round the deep bays and dangerous precipitous headlands fringing the northwestern extremity of peninsular Spain, and thence to follow its rocky northern coast to the point where the Pyrenees again come down to the sea and the harsh mountainlands of Spain give way to the pleasant green lowlands of France. Indeed, it is only by a combination of two unconnected notices in Strabo that we can be sure that Pytheas took this course and continued to follow the continental shore instead of cutting out into open sea to cross the wide and often very stormy mouth of the Bay of Biscay directly from Cape Ortegal in northwest Spain to Land's End in northwest Brittany, a point-to-point passage of more than three hundred miles.

On reaching what is today France's Atlantic Riviera of the *Côte d'Argent,* Pytheas' familiarity with the constellations of the stars made him aware that he must now have reached the very same latitude on which he had set out from Massalia. To be sure, he could not similarly have calculated his *longitude* by consulting the starry map of heaven. But despite the fact that he had no chart for his voyage and could not have constructed even the semblance of a geographic map of its course, he could not have failed to realize from his calculation of directions and distances that, in circumnavigating the Iberian peninsula, he had virtu-

ally completed the four sides of a great square; so that he now
not only had returned to the same latitude as his home port but
could not be situated at any very great distance from it on a
direct line overland from sea to sea. His appreciation of this fact
is reflected in a remark attributed to him, to the effect that

> the northern part of Iberia is more readily accessible by way of
> the Celtic land than in sailing by way of the Atlantic.[10]

According to Strabo, Eratosthenes accepted this statement as
correct, whereas Artemidorus (a somewhat later Greek geographer) attacked Eratosthenes on this point, maintaining that
the statement was false. Of course, it was Artemidorus who was
in the wrong—very flagrantly so, since Pytheas had journeyed by
sea some 1,700 miles, more or less, to reach a sector of the Atlantic coast to which he could have traveled overland, if he had
left ship at Narbonne, in a third of the time for a sixth of the
distance. But we may be content to have had Artemidorus air
his ignorance, since, ironically, it is only because he disbelieved
the truth of Pytheas' pronouncement that we know that Pytheas
ever made it; and it is largely on the strength of it that we are
entitled to conclude that Pytheas sailed around, instead of across,
the Bay of Biscay.

Confirmation comes from a rather longer citation in Strabo,
which Strabo himself unfortunately failed to understand, with
the result that many modern commentators on Pytheas have
missed its significance. The passage reads as follows:

> Hereto should be added the bulge of Europe outside the
> Heraclean Pillars, situated opposite Iberia and projecting to-
> ward the west for more than three thousand stades; likewise
> the various headlands, particularly that of the Ostimians which
> is called Kabaion, and also the islands there along, the last of
> which, Uxisamē, Pytheas says is distant three days' sailing.[11]

Except that Strabo omits to name the point from which
Uxisamē was three days distant, everything is as clear and accurate as could be desired. But Strabo raised the objection that

> all these places lie in the north, being Celtic and not Iberian—
> or rather, they are mere inventions of Pytheas! [12]

[10] Strabo, *Geography*, III.2.11.
[11] *Ibid.*, I.4.5.
[12] *Ibid.*

But Pytheas never said that the places named here were Iberian, i.e., located on the coast of Spain or Portugal. Strabo misunderstood the connotation of the phrase "outside the Pillars of Heracles," which he took to refer exclusively to the Spanish coast outside the Gibraltar Straits. But to the Mediterranean mind all the Atlantic coastal regions that were reached through the Gibraltar passage lay "outside the Pillars." Once this is appreciated, it becomes perfectly clear that "the bulge of Europe," lying opposite Spain and projecting westward for "more than three thousand stades" to Cape Kabaion and, last of the islands there along, Uxisamē, succinctly and accurately describes the Atlantic coast of France; for France in just this manner curves out in a long arc westward to the projecting nose of Brittany, lies opposite Spain, across the Bay of Biscay, and terminates in a series of headlands, off which there is a number of small islands, the last of which is the Île d'Ouessant.

Despite the fact that modern authorities tend to disagree on almost everything connected with Pytheas' voyage, there seems to be virtual unanimity of opinion that Cape Kabaion is the spectacular headland called the *Pointe du Raz,* Brittany's end-rock below the Bay of Brest, and Uxisamē is the rugged little island of Ouessant, some fourteen miles out at sea above the same bay. Pytheas' estimate of three thousand stades (probably about 350 miles) is somewhat, but not very greatly, short of the mark. On the contrary, a glance at the modern map will confirm one's faith in Pytheas' veracity and oblige one to admire his intelligence as a practical geographer in a mapless world.

Thanks to the hostile skepticism of his contemporaries and successors, as evinced in the "refutation" of his claims by writers such as Polybius and Strabo, it has been possible to reconstruct from his critics' citations the course that he must have taken, continuing along the continental shoreline of the Bay of Biscay past the deep estuary of the Gironde—at whose head a Celtic town already marked the site that was to become the great modern seaport of Bordeaux—and farther up the coast, within a second deep river mouth, that of the Loire, putting in at Celtic Corbilo, the station for Atlantic seaborne trade that functioned then as St. Nazaire and Nantes in the same location do today. And so, after "three days' sailing," he passed Cape Kabaion and reached Uxisamē, outermost of the islands. Here, on the four-thousand-acre rampart of granite cliffs in a fogbound sea without other sight of land, Pytheas and his crew must have felt themselves "at the very ends of the habitable world." Yet the ocean still stretched on ahead; while behind them the mainland, as once before at land's end of Spain, bent abruptly eastward, having now completed "the bulge of Europe" facing Spain.

Since ancient mariners, lacking chart and compass and chronometer, relied on the land for guidance through the sea and avoided wide-open water as much as possible, even when its extent and farther shore were already known, Pytheas would naturally have continued to follow the European coast, steering east into the Gulf of St. Malo and then due north (perhaps sighting the Channel Islands) to round the Cherbourg headland and thereafter alter course again to east and south of east until he had crossed the mouth of the river Seine and skirted the Normandy shore to the Strait of Dover to get his first sight of the white chalk cliffs of Britain.

In this way Pytheas would naturally and in due course have discovered England. Yet actually he appears not to have kept to this continental route at all, from the isle of Uxisamē, but to have put out into the open sea to cross the English Channel at its mouth, steering direct from Land's End of Brittany to Land's End of Cornwall.

How did Pytheas come to choose this course, and how did he dare venture upon it? Possessing neither chart nor pilot's handbook, how could he have known that there was land a hundred miles to the north in the great encircling ocean of the world?

These questions are not always asked and even less often answered. Yet they raise a most interesting issue. However, in order to make this issue clear it will be necessary to desert Pytheas at this point and delve into the unwritten history of the Atlantic world "beyond the Pillars" to sketch in shadowy outline against doubtful dates and among seafaring peoples of uncertain race a most mysterious episode.

Some five thousand years before our present time, Mesopotamia and Anatolia had developed urban civilizations and attained a knowledge of metallurgy. But throughout most of the European continent during that period, an earlier phase of culture persisted or even, in many regions, was only just being introduced. This was the agricultural mode of settled village life that archeologists and ethnologists call the neolithic phase. Replacing the century-old manner of subsistence by hunting, fishing, and gathering fruits and herbs, the new economy of farming and herding and communal living spread over the whole of Europe, to reach finally its western fringes and be carried oversea to the islands off its Atlantic shore.

Those who have closely studied this neolithic diffusion have concluded that there were two mainstreams of transmission of this agricultural and communal way of living, one moving along the Mediterranean shorelands, the other working inland through central Europe by way of the Danube River system. This is, of course, an oversimplified description of a highly complex sequence of events. Nonetheless, the two major streams are so sharply distinguishable that it has been possible to trace the southern or Mediterranean current of neolithic culture westward to southern Spain and thence northward through western France into Brittany and oversea to western England, Ireland, and the west coast of Scotland, with its adjacent isles; while the other, or midcontinental, neolithic advance can in turn be tracked beyond the Danube through the Rhine and other north European river valleys to the Baltic and North Sea. This second current also passed oversea to Britain, approaching its eastern instead of its western shores. Quite dramatically, the prehistoric archeologists who have dug neolithic burials in Scotland have found the two streams still distinguishable, with the Mediterranean stream represented on the west and the central European stream on the east of the country.

From all this there follows an important consequence:

Somewhere in the course of the westward advance of the Mediterranean neolithic stream—most probably in southeast Spain—a knowledge of mining, smelting, and casting copper ore was acquired and transmitted farther along the travel route of neolithic expansion. This experience with the metallurgy of copper was either accompanied or soon supplemented by the further knowledge that the addition of a comparatively small amount of tin ore would transform molten copper into a much harder kind of metal—the alloy we call "bronze." Thus there was repeated, several thousand miles away from its earlier sphere of activity, a second Bronze Age epoch, in no sense Anatolian, but independently Atlantic.

There were huge deposits of copper lying ready to be mined in Andalusian Spain. (The copper of the Río Tinto mines is not yet exhausted and still remains Europe's richest source of that metal.) But whereas there was copper aplenty—as well as silver, though this did not seem to have been especially prized at that time—tin appears to have been much harder to come by. And without tin there could be no bronze.

But elsewhere along the course of neolithic advance—in the mountains of Spain's northern coast, in France's Atlantic headland of Brittany, and most abundantly of all across the mouth of the English Channel in British Cornwall—there was river tin in the beds of streams and tinstone (cassiterite) to be mined directly from veins of rock. Rumor of this supply traveled back to southern Spain; and in the wake of rumor came the tin ore itself. Return payment may have been made in finished bronze. The traffic, in either direction, was seaborne, since metals are readily transportable in ships but discouragingly bulky and weighty for portage by land.

Out of this commerce and industry there evolved an Atlantic Bronze Age civilization, of which written history knows nothing whatever because it left no readable records of itself for posterity. However, it did not vanish so utterly as to leave no discernible trace of its onetime, long-ago existence. Where history has been mute, archeology has managed to extract a wordless chronicle that might well be termed sensational.

Along Europe's Atlantic coastlands and on its adjoining islands, closely adhering to the metal route from Andalusian Spain to Brittany, western England, Ireland, Scotland, and the Scottish islands, even as far as the Orkneys beyond Britain's northernmost head, there still stand burial chambers and ritualistic markers and monuments in gigantic blocks of generally shapeless, but on occasion well hewn and fitted, stone. These are the megaliths of archeological lore, the mysterious witnesses to some otherwise unrecorded intercourse between Europe's westernmost communities, probably as much as thirty centuries before the present.

In professional language, megaliths are classed as menhirs, cromlechs, and dolmens—picturesque modern Breton or Welsh words signifying "long stones," "crooked stones," and "stone tables."

Dolmens are the inner chambers of ancient burial mounds. The mounds themselves, whether of heaped earth or piled stones, have long since been rolled or carted or washed away, leaving exposed (and therefore empty of all content) the burial chamber once concealed beneath them. The blocks with which these chambers were built, to serve for walls and ceiling, were too massive for later human hands or natural forces such as earthquake or flood water to displace. In consequence they still stand, although stripped of their erstwhile corpses and burial gifts, outliving their human need by centuries of time.

Menhirs are single, upended stones, rudely shaped and often set in rows to line apparently purposeless avenues ("alignments" is the technical term) or arranged to mark out closed circles or ovals (in which case they are cromlechs). Not infrequently, menhirs are found standing alone, when they may be of remarkable height and almost incredible weight. Thus, near Locmariaquer in southern Brittany, hard by the shore where Pytheas must have passed, there lie prostrate the four pieces of what must haves been the largest menhir in the world until a bolt of lightning shattered it a couple of hundred years ago. Reassembled, it would stand seventy-five feet tall, with an average girth of nearly forty feet and an estimated total weight of more than three hundred tons. Since the granite of which it consists does not occur locally, it must somehow have been transported from a distance, in a single piece despite its enormous mass, and then erected vertically in place. Although "standing stones" are especially numerous in Brittany (where dolmens too abound, not infrequently of huge dimensions), they also occur in considerable number in England, Wales, Ireland, Scotland, and the Scottish isles. Not all of these "standing stones" are so ancient as the dolmens; but the finest of them are indubitably of great antiquity.

Among the menhirs set on circular plan to form cromlechs, by far the most extraordinary is also the most widely famous of all megalithic structures—Stonehenge on the Salisbury plain in southern England, now proved to have been constructed shortly before the year 1500 B.C.

To the archeologist, one of the most interesting aspects of the Atlantic megalithic monuments is their geographical distribution. They are hardly ever encountered at any considerable distance from the sea; and if their occurrence is plotted on a map, it will be seen to be roughly coincident with the course of the previously mentioned Mediterranean stream of neolithic diffusion, with a significant supplementary area of expansion across the North Sea into Denmark and closely adjoining territory. They are not, however, of strictly neolithic construction. Until quite recently, even an approximate dating for these extraordinary relics of prehistoric technical ability could not be established, but continued to be debated without much prospect of any firm decision. It was natural to class Stonehenge as a neolithic structure, because even the unprofessional eye could see that the great upright piers and lintel slabs had been shaped and dressed with bone antler picks and stone sledges and handballs of harder stone, without use of metal tools. But this might mean either that metal was still too scarce and valuable to be expended on such work or that (as in Egypt into late dynastic periods) the tradition of dressing stone with stone continued to be the accepted procedure long after metal was in common use for other needs. But an extremely ingenious astronomical calculation, based on the orientation of the axis on which Stonehenge was laid out, pointed to 1750 B.C. as the apparent date of construction (within a century or so, either way). Most recently, the novel technique of radiocarbon dating, on being applied to antler picks dug up on the site, further restricted probabilities to the lower margin of the astronomically indicated range, not much earlier than 1500 B.C. But by 1500 B.C. the knowledge of metallurgy must have been rather thoroughly diffused along the Atlantic seaboard of Europe.

Current opinion therefore tends to equate the incidence of megalithic construction with the spread of metallurgic knowledge, reinforcing this hypothesis with the interesting and surely very significant observation that the geographic distribution of the European megalithic monuments coincides very closely with the regions from which certain much prized metals and other substances could be obtained. If the track along which the megalithic monuments are found is combined with a map showing deposits of metallic ores, there is a highly suggestive agreement between the two series; for we shall find copper and silver most abundant in southern Spain and Portugal, tin in Brittany and

Cornwall, gold in Ireland, and discover across the North Sea in Denmark a center for amber.

There is no historic record of a flourishing maritime connection among the above listed countries during the second millennium before Christ; but there are no written records of any kind for that part of the world from that remote period. Only the mute megaliths testify to the existence of a seaborne trade route running from Denmark around the tip of Scotland through the Irish Sea to Cornwall and thence across the mouth of the English Channel to Brittany and along the French and Iberian coast to southern Spain. Along this route in either direction traveled raw metal (rather than crude unsmelted ore) and perhaps finished metalwork, each country supplying what the others lacked.

Toward the end of the second millennium B.C. this Atlantic coastal traffic appears to have declined and even to have lapsed entirely during the centuries of profound cultural and economic recession in the Mediterranean that intervened between the Minoan-Mycenaean Age and the Classical Greek civilization. But when the Mediterranean lands stirred to new activity and ships once more plied the sea-lanes in the eighth and seventh centuries, trade and shipping seem to have been resumed at the other end of the ancient world also, and the Atlantic metal-route became operative once more. By this time the megalithic traditions for burial places and religious sanctuaries had long since died out and lost their hold on human minds. In addition, there seem to have been important racial changes along the Atlantic seaboard, with a dominating influx of Celtic blood bringing a new and characteristically Celtic revival of interest in mining and metallurgy. And now, thanks to Greek discovery of Tartessos and Phoenician competition for the Spanish trade, Gadir became the point of connection between North Atlantic and Mediterranean commerce, with metals the chief objective of the ships from Phocaean Massalia and Phoenician Carthage.

Amid a great deal of uncertainty about so many far-off things in the long ago, there should be certainty about one cardinal point: the Carthaginian seizure and fortification of the island site of modern Cádiz and the consequent Punic blockade of the Gibraltar passage to the Atlantic were expressly designed to secure for Carthage (to the exclusion of all competitors) the highly profitable Atlantic shipments of metal and amber. At Gadir the Phoenician cargo ships loaded the silver brought down from the nearby Tartessian mines on the upper Guadalquivir beyond modern Seville and, from far greater distances, the tin from Brittany and Cornwall, perhaps gold from Ireland, and certainly amber from Jutland.

It is very frequently asserted that Carthaginian ships (and even before Carthage was founded, Phoenician ships of yet earlier times) traversed the Atlantic route all the way to Brittany and Cornwall and did not depend on foreign shipments of cargo to Spain. No archeological attestation of this widely held belief has turned up anywhere on the Atlantic coast farther north than the region of the mouth of the Tagus River, where Lisbon is situated. For somewhat later Roman times there is sound evidence that Mediterranean ships voyaged as far as southern Portugal; and it is of course possible that ships from the Carthaginian ports of the western Mediterranean ventured even farther beyond Gadir in the days of Carthaginian greatness as a maritime power. But there seems to be no historical evidence in support of this claim—unless such is to be found in Pytheas' own expedition to the very regions where the Phoenician ships are presumed to have been sailing before him.

For, by now, the purpose of Pytheas' exploration of the European Atlantic must be thoroughly apparent. If he set his course along the age-old "megalithic seaway" from Spain to Scotland and beyond, he did so (needless to say!) not because of any archeological interest in megalithic monuments (one wonders whether he so much as noticed any of them?), nor yet from sheer love of exploring or curiosity about foreign lands and unfamiliar people, even though as a Greek man of science with especial interest in cosmography he could not have failed to be attentive to everything new and strange in the shape of the land and the behavior of sea and sky. Rather, having been dispatched by the maritime merchant city of Massalia, his motive must have been commercial, for increase of trade to benefit his native town. Witnessing the collapse of the hitherto hostile Carthaginian domination of the sea-lanes to the west, and aspiring to take advantage of a situation that might not long endure despite the ascendancy of her powerful Roman ally, Massalia with her long tradition of commercial intercourse with Spain was eager to discover whether the enormously profitable Atlantic trade that Carthage had monopolized might not now be diverted to her own merchant marine.

The occasion of this long digression was the query why Pytheas, having reached the westernmost tip of France, did not continue to explore the European coast but struck out northward into open water and crossed the hundred-mile-wide mouth of the English Channel to Britain's Land's End of Cornwall. And further, we asked, how did Pytheas, without chart or compass to guide him, know what course to steer? The answer to the first of these two questions must now be obvious: Pytheas was following the Atlantic trade route to the chief source of metallic tin, the Cornish mines. To the second question, how he knew the proper course from Brittany to western Britain, there can be only one plausible reply: he must have talked with native traders along his route and either have been instructed verbally by them or have taken on board a pilot for the channel crossing.

But this only raises a further question. How could Pytheas communicate with the native inhabitants along his route? That question, also, is not too difficult to answer—though it can be done only by introducing still another digression into my narrative of Pytheas' great adventure.

The story runs that when Massalia was first settled by the Greeks of Phocaea not long before or after the year 600 B.C., one of the two leaders of the colony married the daughter of the local native chieftain. The incident is embellished with romantic touches by its late Roman narrator; but this is no reason for challenging its truth or for doubting the existence of the very friendly relations between Greek immigrant and Gallo-Celtic native that it underscores. Mention has already been made of the dual nature, part Greek and part native Celto-Iberian, of Emporion, Massalia's chief port of call on the Pyrenean coast of Spain. Where contact was so intimate, Greek and Celt could not have failed to acquire some knowledge of each other's speech. Even if Pytheas himself did not speak or understand the Celtic of the region in southern Gaul where he lived, there would surely have been some in his crew who did. To be sure, the Celtic language was not everywhere uniform, but had already developed dialectical variety on the European continent. But these differences were not nearly so great in Pytheas' day as they have since become in the various branches of Celtic speech. There is good reason for believing that, in the classical Greek period, a Celt from southern Gaul could have understood others of his race, and in turn made himself intelligible to them, anywhere in western and southwestern Europe—which is to say, from Gades to Cornwall wherever on the Atlantic shorelands metal was being mined.

For it should be added that, whatever may have been the racial affinities of the megalithic monument makers, in classical times the Celts, by then widely distributed over Europe, were the master metalworkers and engaged in mining and smelting wherever opportunity offered. In consequence the Atlantic metal trade, whose Mediterranean distribution had been jealously kept as a Carthaginian monopoly, must have relied largely on the Celts for its sources of supply.

It is this which makes intelligible—and therewith imparts an especial significance for the present narrative—the following passage from the Sicilian Greek historian Diodorus, who wrote in the time of the first Roman emperor, Augustus, but must have based his account of the Cornish miners on Pytheas' narrative of his voyage. That Pytheas was the ultimate source of information may be accepted for the sufficient reason that it has not been possible to suggest anyone else from whom it could have been derived. From Julius Caesar's account of his two cross-channel raids on Britain in 55 and 54 B.C., it is clear that he had no knowledge of the island beyond his own penetration into the lower valley of the Thames. He knew Kent, but not Cornwall. And there is no evidence of any sort that, prior to Caesar, either Greek or Latin had ever set foot on English soil —except Pytheas and his crew.

This is the passage from Diodorus:

> The natives of Britain near the headland of Belerion are unusually friendly and through intercourse with foreign traders have become very mannerly. They have a clever process for extracting tin from its bed, which is of rock with earthy veins. Along these veins they dig galleries. . . . After they have smelted and refined the tin they hammer it into the shape of knucklebones and transport it to an adjoining island named

Iktis. Having waited until the ebb-tide lays bare the intervening channel, they bring entire loads of tin across on wagons.[13]

We can be certain that in this account Belerion refers to
Cornwall because Diodorus has just previously described the
island of Britain as triangular in shape and assigned to the
apices of this triangle the names Kantion, Belerion, and Orka.
Inasmuch as Kantion can be shown to be Kent, and Orka the
northern tip of Scotland opposite the Orkney Islands, by elimi-
nation Belerion must be the ancient native name for Land's
End in Cornwall.

As for Iktis, the adjoining island that could be reached by
wagon at low tide, this description precisely fits a picturesque
feature of the Cornish coast only a few miles east of Land's
End. There, just offshore from the head of the bay on which
the seaport of Penzance is situated, stands the rocky islet of
Saint Michael's Mount. The modern guidebook describes it as
"rising precipitously to a height of 230 feet and connected
with the shore by a natural causeway, ½ mile long, which is
uncovered for about 3 hours at low water." [14] Whoever today,
having read of Pytheas, visits St. Michael's Mount must feel (as
the present writer did) a curious thrill at the haunting mental
vision of a Greek-rigged and Greek-manned merchant ship
drawn up stern-first upon the sands 2,200 years ago.

It may be added that Diodorus concludes his account by stating that the ingots of tin were shipped across to France (perhaps
to the Gaulish town of Corbilo in lower Brittany at the mouth of
the Loire, near the site of the modern seaport of St-Nazaire).
Thence the tin was transported overland by pack animal to the
mouth of the Rhone near Marseilles. But here Diodorus was
supplementing Pytheas' report with his own contemporary
knowledge of the tin trade as practiced in Roman times when
Gaul was a Roman province with good Roman roads.

It is high time to return to Pytheas, whom we left crossing
the mouth of the English Channel to the "tinland" of Cornwall.

It might perhaps have been anticipated that this was the
ultimate goal of his voyage; but it is clear that this was far from
being the case. Strabo cites Polybius as recording Pytheas' claim

[13] Diodorus, *Historical Library*, V.22.2.
[14] Baedeker's *Great Britain*, 8th ed., p. 157.

to have explored the whole of Britain; but unfortunately it is disputable whether Polybius (who had little use for Pytheas) was making fun of him for pretending to "have walked over all Britain" or merely repeating a statement that he had landed everywhere on the British coast. On either interpretation, it would seem that Pytheas thoroughly explored the shoreland reaches with their deep estuaries along the west coast of England, as well as the tortuous island channels off the west coast of Scotland all the way to the Pentland Firth close under the Orkneys. There is no positive record that he visited Ireland in the course of this voyage; yet he could not fail to have sighted it, since he had to pass through the North Channel where southern Scotland and northern Ireland come within thirteen miles of each other. And if I am right in claiming that Pytheas was exploring the sources of the Atlantic metals, he would scarcely have left Ireland unvisited. It is true that there is practically no gold to be mined there today. But gold ornaments of Irish make have been found in many graves in western Europe. Perhaps the raw gold came from elsewhere; but it seems to have passed through Irish hands. And further, it surely must be assumed that Pytheas had the explorer's typical temperament of curiosity and love of adventure. That he sighted another unknown western isle without turning his ship's bow toward it is to the highest degree unlikely. But against this natural supposition, there is the undoubted fact that the Greek geographers after his time knew little more about Ireland than its ancient name and its approximate location. Diodorus thought its inhabitants cannibals. Strabo agreed with him on this, remarking that they were "less civilized than the Britons" and had the disagreeable custom of devouring their own parents when they died and of holding open intercourse "with other women and with their own mothers and daughters"—but adds that there is no credible authority for these reports. Pomponius Mela, a Roman geographer born in Spain a generation or two after Strabo, was better informed than his predecessor about the Atlantic coast of Spain and France and knew about Britain as far north as the Orkneys; but he too has practically nothing to record about Ireland except "its uncouth inhabitants, more than other people ignorant of every virtue"—from all of which it looks as though he had read Pytheas, but that Pytheas had heard only rumors of the "wild Irish" from unsympathetic British Celts.

Perhaps we are entitled to make a different inference. The Celts who had migrated from western Europe into Britain had penetrated the eastern coast of Ireland several centuries before Pytheas reached the Irish Sea (at least, this is what the archeological evidence suggests). The disagreeable propensities to cannibalism and public incest that Strabo imputes to the inhabitants of the island are not in the least characteristic of Celtic communities. Consequently, it must be the aboriginal natives (whom the Celts dislodged toward the interior of the land, and of whom we otherwise know nothing whatever) that Pytheas heard about and recorded in his account of his voyage.

But whether he touched Irish land or was dissuaded by his Celtic informants from venturing among so barbarous a folk, Pytheas continued northward to the "very ends of the habitable world." For we have a description of the stormy strait between the tip of Scotland and the Orkneys such as could never have been invented by a Mediterranean mariner who had not himself beheld it. Whoever has never heard of the terrific conflict of gale winds with ocean currents in the Pentland Firth will be tempted to agree with ancient skepticism about the reliability of Pytheas' account of his expedition and be somewhat surprised that Pliny should have reported without further comment that "Massilian Pytheas is the author of the statement that the tides north of Britain swell to eighty cubits." Of course, there cannot be 120-foot tides anywhere on the earth. Perhaps Pliny did not translate Pytheas' Greek quite accurately. But even if he did, the following testimony from our own times should be taken into account before we dismiss Pytheas as an ancient "Marco Millioni":

The British *North Sea Pilot* [15] speaks of waves 60 feet high in the Pentland Firth with columns of spray "hundreds of feet" above them when gales blow counter to the tidal race. And the *Encyclopaedia Britannica*,[16] referring to the same narrow ocean passage, asserts "the tidal wave races at a speed from 6 to 12 miles an hour. At the meeting of the western and eastern currents the waves at times rise into the air like a waterspout, but the cur-

[15] British Admiralty, *North Sea Pilot*. Vol. I, p. 19.
[16] *Encyclopaedia Britannica*, 11th ed., *s.v.* "Caithness."

rent does not always nor everywhere flow at a uniform rate, being broken up at places into eddies as perilous as itself." A few sentences later, in speaking of the tiny island of Stroma in the Firth, a mile and a half off the Scottish mainland, the same authority records that "in 1862 a remarkable tide climbed the cliffs (200 ft.) and swept across the island." Whether this is properly called a "tide" may be questioned; but it more than matches the 120-foot *"aestus,"* or tidal flood, in Pliny's text.

Can anyone, after reading these accounts, doubt for a moment that Pytheas must have reached the immediate neighborhood of these waters in order to have learned of this formidable encounter of the Atlantic with the North Sea? But Pliny's notice is not the only bit of evidence that Pytheas visited this hitherto wholly unexplored region ("unexplored," that is to say, by Mediterranean mariners). It must be Pytheas who communicated to Greek geographers the place-name "Orka"; and this cannot be disassociated from the present title of the Orkney Islands (-*ey* being the old Norse word for "island"). In addition there is the report, definitely traceable to Pytheas, of an island six days' voyage still farther to the north, whose name became a word of wonder in Latin speech and still is occasionally met with in English writings—*"ultimate Thule"*—and which became a synonym for "world's end." Finally, and perhaps most conclusively, there is Pytheas' report of midsummer days with twenty hours of sunlight—a phenomenon, in truth, to be met with in the North Atlantic, but only still farther north than the Orkneys and the Shetlands, approximately at the latitude of the "Sheep Islands" of the Faeroes. This group of a score of clustered little islands lies in the open Atlantic nearly two hundred miles northwest of the Shetlands. An ancient sailing ship approaching by way of the Shetlands might well have taken six days to reach the Faeroes from northern Scotland. It is not entirely certain that Pytheas claimed to have personally visited Thule, since he is quoted as having acquired some of his information about the still farther north from native sources. What thus reached his ears could not fail to have struck him as extravagantly strange: his Mediterranean audience for the most part had no hesitation in deciding what to think of so preposterous a story!

The following are the most important ancient texts relative to Thule and the seas beyond:

[1] Relying on Pytheas, he [the geographer Hipparchus] locates a position in the more northern part of Britain where he says that the longest day is nineteen equinoctial hours in length.[17]

[2] Now, Thule has a longest day of twenty equinoctial hours.[18]

[3] Thule: a large island in the ocean under the northern zone; there the sun makes the midsummer day twenty hours long, and the night four. At midwinter, the opposite [holds good].[19]

[4] Concerning the island called Thule, which Pytheas the Massaliote scientist is said to have visited, the report is that the course of the summer sun is wholly above the horizon there, being identical with the Arctic Circle; and daylight lasts an entire month.[20]

[5] Pytheas the Massaliote says in his book about the Ocean that when he was farthest north the natives pointed to "the sleeping place of the sun," meaning that there the nights were continuous.[21]

[6] However, Pytheas the Massaliote calls the region around Thule, which is the northernmost of the British isles, the "ultimate," where the course of the summer sun coincides with the Arctic Circle.[22]

[7] Thule. There the summer nights are bright because at that season the sun keeps higher, so that even when it is not itself visible it nevertheless illuminates its immediate neighborhood. Indeed, at the actual solstice there is no night because then the sun, becoming still more visible, shines not merely by reflection but shows the greater portion of its disk.[23]

[8] Thule is an island of the Ocean, between the north and the west quadrant beyond Britain, near the Orkneys and Ireland.[24]

---

[17] Strabo, *Geography*, II.1.18.
[18] Ptolemy, *Geographical Treatise*, VIII.2.
[19] Stephanus Byzantius, *Ethnika, s.v.* Thoule.
[20] Cleomedes, *De motu circulari*, I.7.
[21] Cosmas Indicopleustes, *Topographia Christiana* (ed. E. O. Winsteat, Cambridge 1909), 117A.
[22] Strabo, *Geography*, II.5.8.
[23] Pomponius Mela, *De situ orbis*, III.6.57.
[24] Servius, in his commentary on Vergil, *Georgics*, I.30.

[9] Pytheas says that Thule is distant six days' sail north from Britain, near the Frozen Sea.[25]

[10] From the Orkneys as far as Thule is a sea voyage of five days and nights. From the headland of Caledonia it is a two-day voyage for those seeking Thule.[26]

[11] The farthest of all known islands, Thule.[27]

[12] From Thule it is a day's voyage to the Frozen Sea, which is by some called Cronium.[28]

[13] Pytheas, by whom many have been misled . . . proceeding to narrate about Thule and those regions in which there was neither land properly so-called nor sea nor sky, but a sort of mixture of all three, like a jellyfish, in which (he says) earth and sea and everything are held suspended in a sort of compound of all the elements, upon which one can neither walk nor sail.[29]

Where, then, was "ultima Thule"? This question has been long debated, but without reaching an answer satisfactory to all inquirers.

It will be seen at once that much of the evidence is contradictory.

From [1], [2] and [3] it appears that Thule lay sufficiently far north of the latitude of northern Britain to ensure it an extra hour of daylight at the summer solstice. Actually, the solstitial day of twenty hours occurs at the latitude of the Faeroes, and the nineteen-hour day between Orkney and the Shetlands. But daylight in these northern regions outlasts the actual rising and setting of the sun by so considerable a margin —as [7] correctly records—that it might well be that Pytheas' estimate is not to be construed as an astronomically exact measurement of the sun's course on June 21 or 22, but interpreted in terms of daylight illumination. It must be remembered that there were no mechanical clocks in Pytheas' age nor any other devices for measuring the passing of time in terms of an hour of fixed duration. Perhaps, therefore, we are entitled to conclude from the first three texts cited above only that Thule

[25] Strabo, *Geography*, I.4.2.
[26] Solinus, *Collectanea Rerum Memorabilium* (ed. Th. Mommsen, 2d ed., Berlin, 1958), 22(12) and 22(17).
[27] Pliny, *Historia Naturalis*, IV.16.
[28] *Ibid.*, IV.30.
[29] Strabo, *Geography*, II.4.1.

lay well to the north of Britain, even as [9] and [10] specify. Yet [4] and [6] set Thule on the Arctic Circle, which is the region of "midnight sun" even farther north than Iceland! The discrepancies seem irreconcilable.

If the expression "equinoctial hours" seems peculiar, it should be explained that in classical times the period between sunrise and sunset was conventionally divided into twelve equal parts, each of which was called an "hour." Since the length of day as so defined varies continuously according to the season of the year, the "hour" necessarily did the same, expanding as the days grew longer and contracting as they shortened. Such a fluctuating unit of temporal measurement was useless for astronomical purposes. The Greek physicists therefore introduced an hour of constant value, based on the equality of day and night at the equinox. (This, of course, approximates our own standard hour.) Appropriately, this was called an "equinoctial hour." It is not known who first proposed this standard unit. Some have suggested that Pytheas himself may have been responsible. Certainly, his interest in measuring the variation in the day's quota of sunlight as he altered his latitude would have necessitated some such fixed scale for recording time. But how could he have made use of this standard unless he carried with him on his voyage some sort of unvarying clock such as an hourglass adjusted to run for an "equinoctial hour"? Might it not have been that his reckoning of the varying length of daylight at different stations along the route were purely mathematical calculations derived from preascertained latitudes? In his role of astronomical physicist, Pytheas would have been entirely capable of working out such problems.

However that may be, Thule could not have enjoyed a solstitial day of twenty hours, as [2] and [3] assert, and also have been situated within the Arctic Circle, as [4] and [6] maintain. On the basis of Pomponius Mela's report in [7], which speaks of the sun's disk as showing continuously above the horizon instead of setting fully, Thule should have lain in the latitude of Iceland or of Norway north of Trondhjem. The latter alternative would seem to be excluded for Thule by [8], because Pytheas, with his accurate knowledge of the compass points as indicated by the constellations, could not possibly have considered Norway as lying "between the north and the west quadrant beyond Britain." The objection that Norway is not an island would have less force, because the Scandinavian peninsula is visibly separated from the main European continent by the Baltic Sea and the Danish straits, so that Pytheas would have had no means of discovering that it was not wholly surrounded by salt water.

If we are to accept the description of Thule in [3] as "a large island," the group of twenty-odd small islands making up the Faeroes would have to be eliminated. This would leave only Iceland as Thule, since there is no other large island in the far-northern Atlantic—in which case, however, Strabo was very wide of the mark in speaking of it as "the northernmost of the British isles"! But is it conceivable that a Mediterranean navigator could have found his way to Iceland (situated as it is far out and alone in the northern ocean close to the Arctic Circle) more than a thousand years before the Viking Norsemen discovered it?

Those who reject the identification argue that the six-day voyage mentioned in [9] and implied in [10] is insufficient for covering the seven hundred miles of sea from the Orkneys to Iceland by way of the Shetlands and the Faeroes, as the course would necessarily have been laid. The prevailing winds and currents would favor a northeast crossing to the Norwegian coast, but make sailing toward the northwest much more difficult. More serious is the objection that Pytheas could not have known of the existence and location of Iceland unless these were already known to the inhabitants of the islands that he visited close to Britain—and such knowledge is a very unlikely supposition. There is a further objection that is often brought into the controversy on the score that a certain passage in Strabo cannot be reconciled with known conditions in Iceland today. This passage was not included among the previously cited texts on Thule because I am not persuaded that it is pertinent to the problem. But since it has often been quoted as evidence, it is here reproduced for what its testimony may be worth. It occurs in Strabo immediately following an attack on Pytheas as a fabricator of imaginary geographical matters, and may be translated as follows:

> However, in regard to celestial phenomena and in mathematical speculation Pytheas appears to have treated the facts correctly . . . [as also in saying that] among those who dwell

near the frigid zone there is either complete absence or very
considerable shortage of cultivated crops and domestic animals,
and nourishment consists mainly of millet, wild fruits, herbs,
grasses, and roots. Those who manage to raise cereals have also
honey and the mead made from it. But not having enough
clear weather, they convey the ripened grain into large buildings
and thresh it there indoors, since otherwise the lack of sun and
the abundance of rain would ruin the harvest.[30]

Such a description of agricultural conditions might have
applied to northern Ireland or the Hebrides and would have
served especially well for the Shetlands; but it has been held to
be signally inappropriate to Iceland, where (it is claimed) no
grain can at present be cultivated, fruit trees will not thrive, and
bees cannot subsist. But even if all this is true, it is irrelevant
to the problem under discussion, as it cannot be shown that the
passage was intended to apply specifically to Thule. It could
equally well have been taken from some other section of Pytheas'
report on his voyage.

A decision whether or not Pytheas may be credited with having made the crossing to Iceland and therewith penetrating the
fringe of the Arctic zone depends almost entirely on the interpretation to be given to the final pair of texts, [12] and [13], the
one taken from Pliny's *Natural History,* the other from Strabo's
Geography, and both explicitly connected with Pytheas' discovery of Thule.

Strabo's "Frozen Sea" and Pliny's "Solid Sea" cannot possibly be interpreted as anything other than the icebound Arctic
Ocean. An apparently qualified modern authority explains
Pliny's phrase *mare Cronium* as a Latinization of Celtic *muir-
croinn,* meaning "frozen sea." Attractive as this etymology is, it
assumes that some form of Celtic speech was current in the
extreme north of Britain in Pytheas' time. However, it seems
that this may well have been the case. It is the opinion of
virtually all recent scholars that the Picts of Scotland spoke a
Celtic tongue and presumably were at that period already installed in their northern habitat.

But the reference to a "frozen sea" occasions very great difficulties. It seems geographically impossible that it could refer
to the solid *pack ice* beyond the Arctic Circle, because (if con-

[30] Strabo, *Geography,* IV.5.5.

ditions were at all comparable to those of the present time) this "frozen sea" lay close to Greenland on the American side of the Atlantic and on the European side was confined by the Gulf Stream far to the north of Norway. At most, therefore, only the broken *drift ice* could represent the frozen sea; and this (if we except stray icebergs) barely touches Iceland's northern shore and, again because of the Gulf Stream, veers away from the Faeroes without even distantly approaching the coast of Norway. Consequently, judging by present conditions, a "frozen sea" of dense drift ice at only a single day's voyage beyond Thule obliges us to identify Thule with Iceland and makes even the Faeroes (which do not constitute "a large island") unlikely. And—unless in Pytheas' time the Gulf Stream was diverted to a very different course from its present one—Norway would have to be excluded as quite impossible.

However, although the Faeroe Islands are today ice-free the whole year round, allowance must be made for the possibility that heavy drift ice may formerly have approached them more closely. Most climatologists agree that the climate of Europe underwent a marked change to colder and wetter conditions during a period that commenced toward the end of the ninth century B.C. and certainly was in full career by the fifth century B.C. Such a deterioration in the continental climate would inevitably have been marked (if not actually caused) by greatly increased glaciation. In consequence, the true Frozen Sea of pack ice might conceivably have extended its southern boundary almost to today's frontier of drift ice. And if that were so, the ancient inhabitants of the Faeroes could have known of its existence.

What, then, are we to make of the weird comparison of the northernmost Atlantic to a gigantic jellyfish?

The well-known Arctic explorer Fridtjof Nansen made the following suggestion based on his own experience:

> What Pytheas saw may have been the ice sludge in the sea which is formed over a great extent along the edge of the drift ice, when this has been ground to a pulp by the action of the waves. The expression "can neither be traversed on foot nor by boat" is exactly applicable to this ice sludge. If we add to this the thick fog, which is often found near drift ice, then the description that the air is also involved in the mixture, and that

land and sea and everything is merged in it, will appear very
graphic.[31]

If we interpret the "sleeping place of the sun" as the region
within the Arctic Circle where the nights are continuous in
winter, [5] would encourage us to revert to the identification of
Thule with the great island of Iceland.

And yet, apart from the fact that the "longest day" of twenty
hours does not apply to Iceland, whose northernmost headland
actually touches the Arctic Circle with its 24-hour solstitial day,
there is still another objection that seems decisive: we have no
reason for thinking that Iceland was inhabited before the
Christian era! It may be accepted as certain that, in any case,
there were no natives there with whom Pytheas could have
communicated or from whom he could have gathered any information. Nor is it in the least likely that Pytheas would have
abandoned his investigation of the Atlantic trade route in order
to steer out across the open north Atlantic on the chance of
striking land somewhere in that great waste of water.

Considerations such as these have induced most commentators
to the opinion that Pytheas' imaginative picture of an impassable concentration of the elements was intended to describe the
dense fog that so often blankets the north Atlantic with its un-
voyageable mixture of wind-whipped spray and water-dripping
air, within which it becomes impossible to distinguish land from
sea. Familiar as these tremendous fogs are to inhabitants of the
Scottish islands, they are unknown on the Mediterranean in
any comparable intensity. Pytheas could never before have encountered their like. The passage from Strabo in which they
are described—[13] of the previously cited texts—further informs the reader that Pytheas claimed to have personally encountered this "jellyfish-like" condition of the sea, whereas he
reported "the other matters" from hearsay only; but this does
not offer any additional clue to interpretation, it being wholly
unclear to what the "other matters" referred.

The conflicting evidence thus far presented seems to pre-
clude any clearcut decision. But there is a line of argument,
not represented in the preceding collection of *testimonia*, that
may be more nearly decisive. In the gazetteer compiled by the

[31]Fridtjof Nansen, *In Northern Mists*, Vol. I, p. 67.

celebrated geographer of the second century of our era, Claudius
Ptolemaeus, generally referred to as Ptolemy, the latitude and
longitude of the headlands, river mouths, and inhabited sites
of the world known to the ancients are systematically recorded.
Admittedly Ptolemy's *Geographike Syntaxis* (or *Compendium of
Geography*) is replete with inaccuracies and even serious errors;
but these tend at least to be mutually consistent within the
general framework of his conception of the inhabited world. In
particular, while his record of latitudes is accurate within a
couple of degrees, his longitudes are often very mistaken. This
is due to the obvious difficulty that, whereas the latitude of any
given locality in the northern hemisphere could be determined
by celestial observation, there was no corresponding means for
discovering its longitude for lack of any chronometric instru-
ment to record east-west displacement in relation to the constellations visible in the heavens.

Book Two of Ptolemy's *Compendium* devotes its second
chapter to the "Albion Island of Britain" and closes with the
following entry:

> The islands located near the isle of Albion and the headland
> of Orkas are
>
> Sketis   long. 32° 40′, lat. 60° 45′,
> Dumna   long. 30°,   lat. 61° 20′,
> and above these are the Orkades, about thirty in number;
> their center is located   long. 30°,   lat. 61° 40′.
> Well beyond these is the island of Thule. The portion of this
> that extends farthest west is   long. 29°,   lat. 63°,
> its easternmost point is   long. 31° 10′, lat. 63°,
> its northernmost point is   long. 30° 20′, lat. 63° 15′,
> its southernmost point is   long. 30° 20′, lat. 62° 40′,
> and its mean position is   long. 30° 20′, lat. 63°.[32]

There are two other entries in Ptolemy that refer to Thule.
These are

> [1] Marinus places Thule as the final parallel of latitude that
> cuts the northernmost portion of the known world. This parallel
> he shows with utmost clarity lies at a distance of 63 degrees
> from the equator, with the complete meridian circle comprising
> 360 such degrees.[33]

[32] Ptolemy, *Compendium of Geography*, II.ii.
[33] *Ibid.*, I.vii.

[2] The northernmost parallel of latitude is 63 degrees north of the equator and is called the parallel passing through the island of Thule. . . . The length of the longest day or night on the northernmost parallel through Thule is 20 hours.[34]

In order to harmonize these data with our modern system of recording geographic location, a subtraction of from two to three degrees from Ptolemy's indicated latitudes will often be demanded; whereas his cited longitudes must all be converted by subtracting 11½ degrees to bring their prime meridian in line with ours—Ptolemy's being taken at the supposedly western-most island of the world (corresponding very inaccurately to one of the Canaries) with an assigned location of 2° 30′ west of Cape Saint Vincent. But even after this conversion has been made, it will be found that Ptolemy's indications for longitude are often grossly inaccurate. Thus if Thule in Ptolemy is located at 62° 40′ N. to 63° 15′ N. by 17° W. to 19° 40′ W., this would appear to place it at *ca.* 61° N. by 5° 30′ to 8° 10′ W., which is to say in the open Atlantic rather less than 100 miles due south of the Faeroe Islands. But to identify Ptolemy's Thule with the Faeroes would be to misinterpret the evidence, since his localization of Thule must be taken in connection with his other data for Britain and its adjoining islands. These have been entered on the accompanying sketch map to outline the British Isles as Ptolemy conceived them.

A glance at the sketch will show that (1) although England is reasonably accurately presented, Scotland is seriously deformed with a north shore of greatly exaggerated west-east extension, and (2) Thule has been set slightly northwest of Cape Orkas and due north of the Orkneys at a distance of about one degree of latitude (or approximately 70 statute miles). Although the orientation of Thule in Ptolemy is wrong by well-nigh ninety degrees, the dimensions given to it by latitude and longitude reckoning (equivalent to about forty by eighty statute miles) do not differ greatly from the overall size of the Shetlands group, which may be set at roughly thirty by seventy statute miles. (Contrast this with the comparatively enormous size of Iceland, some three hundred miles in length and up to two hundred miles in breadth!)

When all these elements are taken into account, it is clear

34 *Ibid.,* VII.v.

that Ptolemy's Thule must be the Shetland group of islands and cannot possibly be equated with Iceland. But Ptolemy states that he has based his gazetteer on the work of Marinus of Tyre, "the latest of the geographers of our time" and one who "has searched most diligently the works of virtually all the historians who preceded him." [35] It is an unchallengeable inference that Ptolemy's data for the location of Thule must go back to Pytheas, since no one else in antiquity ever claimed to have visited that

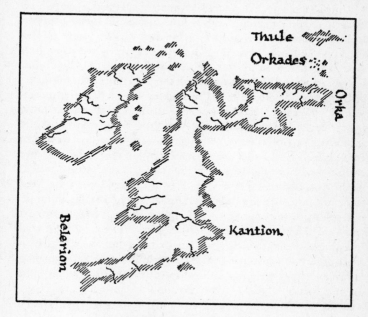

THE BRITISH ISLES
Sketch Map showing Ptolemy's Conception

remote region. The unavoidable conclusion is that Pytheas voyaged as far north as the Shetland Islands, but no farther. Disappointing as this may be to those who would like to think of Pytheas as the first European to have crossed to the American side of the Atlantic, it still remains remarkable enough if

[35] *Ibid.*, I.vi.

Pytheas, navigating only by sun and star and point-to-point local instruction, ever got as far the Shetlands from Mediterranean Marseilles and returned home without mishap or misadventure.

Yet he did more than this. Thule may have been his northernmost port of call, but it was not his turning point for the voyage home. If he was to investigate thoroughly the Atlantic trade route, there was still the source of amber to be sought.

Long, long ago, when the Mycenaean Greeks voyaged the eastern Mediterranean, amber had come to them overland from the southeastern corner of the Baltic Sea. There in East Prussian Samland, beyond modern Danzig and close to modern Königsberg, the sandy shoreland is still known as the Amber Coast (*Bernsteinküste*) because of the unparalleled abundance of fossil resin beneath its shallow waters and within its meagre soil. In view of the fact that amber is still mined there profitably, it can hardly be maintained that the supply was ever exhausted in antiquity. But when direct overland trade to the Aegean by way of the Vistula and lower Danube river valleys became precarious and was interrupted at the close of the second millennium B.C., Baltic amber ceased to be a commodity in the Mediterranean market. Several centuries later, when traffic in amber was resumed, the route by which it reached the Mediterranean was shifted more to the west, terminating at the important trading post of Atria (or Adria) on the delta of the Po, not far from the head of the Adriatic Sea. The curious Greek myth of hapless Phaethon's weeping sisters transformed into poplar trees on the banks of the Eridanus, dropping amber tears, proves that the Greeks were aware that amber was an arboreal distillation; but they were not agreed whether the Eridanus was the Italian river Po or (as Herodotus had heard) "a river thus named by barbarians, emptying into the northern ocean"—surely a distant rumor of the Polish Vistula, which empties into the Gulf of Danzig beside the Amber Coast of Samland. By the time of Diodorus (mid-first century B.C.) more details had become known:

> Off the coast of Scythia beyond Gaul there is an island in the open sea. It is called Basileia and on this the surf casts out abundantly the material known as electron [amber] which is found nowhere else in the world. . . . Now the electron is

collected on the aforementioned island and conveyed by the
natives to the adjoining mainland, whence it is transported to
our part of the world.[36]

This agrees quite closely with what Pliny has to say, drawing
his information from Timaeus and Pytheas:

> Pytheas says that an estuary of the Ocean, Metuonis [?] by
> name, is inhabited by the Gutones, a people of Germany, for a
> distance of six thousand stades and that the island of Abalus is
> distant a day's navigation therefrom. There the spring floods
> throw up amber, a sort of excretion of solidified sea-water. The
> natives use this for fuel and also sell it to their German neigh-
> bors. Timaeus concurs in this, but calls the island Basilia.[37]

What Timaeus' concurrence with Pytheas signified may be
inferred from a second passage in Pliny:

> A great many nameless islands are reported in this region.
> Among these, fronting Scythia, under the name of Raunonia,
> there is distant one day's journey an island upon which in
> springtime amber is cast up by the waves. So Timaeus relates.[38]

On comparing and combining these various passages it would
seem that Diodorus derived his information from Timaeus
(from whom it is thought that he drew much of his material)
and that Timaeus had learned that amber was brought overland
from an island in the ocean north of Europe. To this island he
attached the name Basilia ("royal"). Pytheas seems to have added
more specific data—that the Baltic was an inlet of the outer
ocean, seven hundred miles long, and that its shore was inhabited by a Germanic people, the Gutones, that there was an
offshore island there known as Abalus, on which amber was
washed up by the sea, and that the natives used it for fuel (either
because they did not prize it highly or because it was so
abundant?).

The Gutones of Pytheas' account have been identified as the
Goths, who were a Teutonic race and are thought to have dwelt
in the lower basin of the Vistula before they spread south
through central Europe to the ultimate discomfiture of the late
Roman empire. But the Vistula is the river that empties into
the Gulf of Danzig, whose eastern shore is the Amber Coast.

[36] Diodorus, *Historical Library*, V.23.
[37] Pliny, *Natural History*, XXXVI.11.
[38] *Ibid.*, IV.13.

And the distance between the Danish passage into the Baltic along that sea's southern shore to Samland may be estimated as almost exactly the seven hundred miles that Pytheas reported.

It is difficult (and hardly reasonable) to resist the conclusion that Pytheas, on crossing the North Sea from the tip of Scotland, had made his way through the Danish islands lying between the North Sea inlet of the Kattegat and the East Sea, and visited the Amber Isle. That Samland is not an island but a part of the European continent will not greatly disturb those who have observed how the great headland of Samland is flanked on either side by mile-long lido-like sandbars, behind which broad lagoons extend to the almost invisible mainland, so that when approached by ship it has every appearance of being a seagirt island. As for being a day's voyage from the mainland, the sailing distance from the Vistula past the long bar of the Frische Nehrung is very nearly one hundred miles. There seems therefore no valid objection to identifying Samland with the Amber Island or claiming that Pytheas reached it in the course of his remarkable voyage of exploration.

The account of the Amber Island attributed to Timaeus has so many features in common with that which Pliny ascribes to Pytheas that it may seem that both must derive from a common source; and this source, necessarily, would have been Pytheas. In that case the date of 238–7 B.C. for Pytheas' voyage would be invalidated, inasmuch as Timaeus is reliably held to have died in or shortly before the year 250. However, there are several good reasons for denying that Timaeus had knowledge of Pytheas' voyage: (1) he gives a different name to the Amber Island; (2) he knows nothing of the Cornish miners and their use of Saint Michael's Mount; (3) he subscribed to Aristotle's theory that the ebb and flow of the tide is due to the action of the rivers in their estuaries—an error impossible to anyone who had cognizance of Pytheas' fully correct explanation of tidal phenomena.

A less readily resolvable difficulty arises from quite another quarter. Strabo quotes a gibe by Polybius against Pytheas for having said that "on his return journey [from Thule] he voyaged along the entire ocean coast of Europe from Gadir to Tanais." [39] If this was meant seriously, it is indeed a puzzling

[39] Strabo, *Geography*, II.iv.1.

remark; for "Tanais" was the ancient Greek name of the great Russian river Don, which empties into the Sea of Azov at the head of the Black Sea, nearly a thousand miles farther east than Samland, without any possible connection or communication with the Baltic!

When Strabo (or Polybius) spoke of covering the entire coast of Europe from Gadir to Tanais he was viewing his geography from the Mediterranean end, since Pytheas obviously moved in the opposite direction. I cannot imagine that anyone will find a difficulty here. The trouble is that even if Pytheas had penetrated the Baltic and journeyed to the mouth of the Vistula or the Memel, how could he possibly have imagined either of these to be a branch of a river situated at the very opposite end of the navigable world? To be sure (as we shall see later) Alexander the Great, on reaching the banks of the Indus, supposed that he was viewing the upper reaches of the African Nile! But Pytheas' scientific knowledge of geography was too exact to permit him to have made a comparable mistake about the Vistula.

I shall venture a possible clarification of this seemingly impossible error a little later on, and content myself for the moment with asserting that it can hardly be cited in evidence either for or against the thesis that Pytheas sailed to Samland.

It should be remarked, however, that there have been several among the commentators on Pytheas' expedition who have thought that he never penetrated the Baltic but merely crossed the North Sea to the Danish province of Jutland, arguing that amber was carried by ship as well as by land to the Mediterranean market and that some North Sea island, such as perhaps Helgoland, was the trading point for oversea shipment of amber from the Baltic. But I know of no evidence in support of this view.

In any event, by crossing the North Sea from Orka to Denmark and discovering (whether in the recesses of the Baltic or on the Atlantic coast) the source of the amber that the Mediterranean world prized, Pytheas had completed his assignment. If we assume that he had set sail from Massalia about the beginning of May, it would probably by now have been late September, high time to quit the outer ocean before the onset of stormy autumn weather.

Had he possessed a modern map of Europe he would have seen at a glance that his shortest way back to Spain and the Gibraltar Strait lay along the continental coast past Holland and Belgium to the Strait of Dover. But there are indications that, instead, he recrossed the North Sea to complete his exploration of the seacoast of Britain. That he did so seems to follow from a passage in Pliny to the effect that

> the perimeter of Britain as reported by Pytheas and Isidorus is 3,875 miles—our Roman armies not having extended our knowledge of the island any farther than the neighborhood of the Caledonian woodlands.[40]

On the reasonable supposition that Pytheas' calculation included the major ins and outs of Britain's deeply indented shoreline, his estimate is so close to the correct figure that it must have depended on actual inspection from the sea. Diodorus,[41] presumably taking his information from Pytheas, gives a more specific description of Britain as "being triangular in shape, much like Sicily, with its sides of unequal length," and proceeds to give the dimensions of the three sides, taking the headlands of Kantion, Belerion, and Orka as apices. Disconcertingly, he greatly exaggerates these measurements, so that his disagreement with the total perimeter as recorded by Pliny is difficult to reconcile.

Whether what immediately follows these listed dimensions in Diodorus was likewise taken from Pytheas cannot be determined with any degree of certainty. On the chance that this, the earliest surviving notice of the inhabitants of England, was based on Pytheas' impressions, it may be added here to the ancient sources of information on the great explorer:

> The inhabitants of Britain are said to be autochthonous. They make use of war-chariots . . . and their houses are crudely built of wattles or logs. They harvest their grain by severing the ears from the stalks and stowing them in covered storerooms, from which they always draw out the oldest in preparing their food. Their behavior is simple and forthright, far removed from the knavish cunning of civilized man. . . . The island is densely inhabited, but has a very cold climate, as might be expected in

[40] Pliny, *Natural History*, IV.16(30).
[41] Diodorus, *Historical Library*, V.21.

a far-northern region. There are many chieftains and rulers;
but these for the most part live in peace with one another.[42]

To judge from these accounts, Pytheas considered the exploration of Britain one of the chief attainments of his voyage. Yet
it seems to have aroused no further interest among his Mediterranean countrymen, who left the north Atlantic as unvisited as
ever and learned no more about the British Isles and the Baltic
shorelands than Pytheas had chosen to tell them.

Having completed his *periplous* of Britain's east coast Pytheas would have crossed the Dover Strait and followed the coast
of France back to the headland of Finistère in Brittany, whence
he had crossed to Cornwall on his outward voyage—correctly
arguing that if he persisted along the European shore he must
ultimately rejoin his previous course from Gadir and thus make
certain of reaching the Mediterranean passage to his own
familiar sea.

Is it too hazardous a guess that the phrase that has caused so
much dissension among the commentators in its transmitted
wording, "from Gadir to Tanais," conceals the simple and
entirely correct statement by Pytheas that on his return voyage
he passed along the entire European coast from the Tamesis to
Gadir? It is known from Caesar's *Commentaries* that "Tamesis"
was the native name for the river Thames. Pytheas may not
have heard or remembered the name correctly and have connected it in his mind with the familiar river name "Tanais";
or the error may have crept in later among the copyists of
ancient authors, substituting a familiar for an unfamiliar name.
Or, on another suggestion, "Tanais" may conceal the ancient
name of the present Isle of Thanet (which seems to have been
Tanat), the northeasternmost end of Kent, marking the entry
to the Strait of Dover. On any score, "Tanais," if taken as referring to the Russian river, makes no possible geographic
sense.

This is the last that we hear of Pytheas. It is certain, however,
that he came safely home to Massalia. Even if he never reached
Iceland or cruised the Baltic to the Russian border, he had on
any reckoning voyaged more than seven thousand miles on the
sea and had been the first Mediterranean mariner to sail the

[42] *Ibid.,* V.21.

north Atlantic. He had looked on lands hitherto totally unknown to the Greeks, such as neither Greek nor Roman eyes
were again to behold for many hundred years.

Very justly, Cary and Warmington in their classic predecessor
to the present volume on the Ancient Explorers wrote:

> If the achievement of Pytheas, who hardly ever lost sight of
> land, cannot be compared for boldness with that of Columbus,
> yet in point of distance traversed it exceeded the memorable
> voyage of A.D. 1492. But the very magnitude of Pytheas' dis-
> coveries prevented their due appreciation among his country-
> men. Moreover Pytheas, unlike Columbus, had no successors.
> No other Greek interloper followed in his wake, for after him
> the gates of the Atlantic were again held closed. . . .[43]

What, then, had he accomplished, other than a daring feat of
navigating unknown distant seas? To this query there are two
replies—one based on material considerations, such as the spread
of trade and commerce; the other drawn from the immaterial
realm of scientific knowledge.

It is the latter that deserves emphasis.

Long before Pytheas' day the rotundity of the earth had been
accepted by Greek physicists as an established fact. Aristotle had
advanced adequate proof that the earth was round, but had not
succeeded in calculating the size of its sphere with any approach
to correctness. Even with this crucial factor wrongly evaluated
or left undetermined, it was possible to calculate latitudes in
the Mediterranean zone quite accurately by geometrical methods. The relative north-south location of any given spot could
be determined by measuring the exactly horizontal shadow cast
by an exactly vertical marker at precise noon of the year's longest
day. By simple triangulation, the sun's position relative to the
observer's location could be calculated; and from this the
latitude of the spot followed directly. Pytheas won considerable
notoriety for the precision with which he fixed the latitude of
his native town of Massalia. But it is not recorded by what
method this was accomplished. For there is another equally
simple and much more readily available way by which latitude
can be determined.

[43] M. Cary, and E. H. Warmington, *The Ancient Explorers* (Baltimore, Md.:
Penguin Books, Inc., 1963), p. 40.

This consists in sighting on the north star, Polaris, and determining the angle at which it stands above the level horizon.
The obvious advantage of this method over that of the solstitial
observation of the sun is its applicability to any cloudless night
in the year. That Pytheas employed this method may be confidently inferred from the following statement attributed to
Hipparchus, the most famous astronomer of the succeeding
century:

> In regard to the north pole, Eudoxus is mistaken when he
> says that there is a certain star which remains always in the
> same spot and that this star is the axis of the universe. For
> there is no one single star located at the pole. On the contrary,
> that spot is unoccupied. But there are three stars adjacent to it
> that define an almost perfect rectangle when combined with
> the [empty] spot that marks the pole—exactly as Pytheas of
> Massalia asserts.[44]

Pytheas' discovery of this otherwise not very noticeable discrepancy between Polaris and the true celestial pole (amounting
to a fraction more than one degree) would have resulted from
his use of that star for determining latitudes. As previously
pointed out, the estimates of the maximum length of daylight
for various stations in the north Atlantic, ascribed to Pytheas,
need not have been based on direct clocking of the time between
sunrise and sunset but might have been arrived at by mathematical calculation from the astronomically established latitude.
Some modern commentators have naively argued that Pytheas
must have spent several summers in northern waters or made
more than one journey, in order to have recorded the length of
the summer's longest day in a number of different localities.
We are so accustomed to consult our watches and clocks to
measure the passage of time that we are prone to overlook the
fact that neither Pytheas nor the native inhabitants whom he
may have consulted had any such convenient way of discovering
the number of "equinoctial hours" in a solstitial day. If we
examine more thoughtfully Strabo's statement that

> Hipparchus . . . relying on Pytheas about the more northern
> regions of Britain says that the longest day there is of nineteen

[44] Hipparchus, *Commentary on the Phainomena of Aratus and Eudoxus*, ed. C.
Manitius (Teubner, 1894), I.iv.1.

equinoctial hours, but of eighteen where the winter sun mounts [only] four cubits,[45] being distant from Massalia 9,100 stades.[46]

it should be apparent that all these are mathematically derived values, interdependent among themselves, proving very little about the course or duration of Pytheas' voyage, but affording notable testimony for his excellent understanding of celestial mechanics.

It is extremely improbable that he could have made the necessary observations from shipboard; but on land with very simple apparatus he could have established a level horizon and calculated with near approach to accuracy the angle between this and the pole star at night or the midday sun by day. On basically much the same principle as that of the modern sextant, he could have determined the latitude of his position. But lacking a chronometer to give him his moment of high noon in terms of some other parallel of longitude, he had no way of determining his east-west displacement (or longitude) except by the roughest sort of dead reckoning of distance traveled. It is this impossibility of fixing his ship's *longitude* by celestial observation that has inclined commentators occasionally to credit him with believing that in navigating the Baltic he had reached a point as far east as the Sea of Azov—though how he could have imagined that any river that he there encountered could have been a mouth of the Russian Don defies explanation.

Pytheas' long sojourn in Atlantic waters afforded him abundant opportunity to study a phenomenon virtually unobservable in the Mediterranean—the strangely recurrent ebb and flow of the ocean tide. Since tidal changes of level are of little magnitude in the open reaches of the Mediterranean and are erratically timed where they build up in narrow channels or at the head of long inlets, it would not be surprising if no Greek scientist before Pytheas devoted serious attention to the problem of tidal recurrence. He, however, had much to contribute. It is symptomatic of his scientific bent of mind and his intelligence that he correctly grasped the connection between the rise and fall of the tide and the position of the moon in the heavens. It may be that he was the first Greek ever to have done so. He

[45] I.e., eight degrees above the horizon.
[46] Strabo, *Geography*, II.1.18. 9,100 stades = 13 degrees of latitude according to Eratosthenes' standard of measurement.

is further credited with noting that the tides became higher than normal with the waxing and lower than normal with the waning of the moon—a statement that is not strictly true, but may rest on ancient misunderstanding of Pytheas' observation of spring and neap tides in the Atlantic. Perhaps it does not imply any great alertness of mind to notice that high tide occurs later each day by the same delay that accompanies the rising of the moon, or any extraordinary scientific endowment to argue that the two events must be causally connected. Yet it would be interesting to know whether any of the Celtic dwellers on Atlantic shores had ever grasped this coincidence, which Pytheas may have been the first human being to formulate correctly.

The reader of Strabo and Polybius gains the impression that Pytheas' scientific attainments were belittled or openly ridiculed by his contemporaries and by succeeding generations of his countrymen; but this is clearly a distortion of his reputation, due to the perversity of chance. Both of the two leading geographical physicists of the Hellenistic age—Eratosthenes and Hipparchus—accepted Pytheas' findings and made use of them for their calculations on the size of our planet as well as for the distribution, configuration, and meteorological conditions of its northern regions. Eratosthenes' successful solution of the problem of assigning a precise numerical value to the distance comprised in a degree of latitude not only made it possible for him to calculate the circumference of the earth with close approach to accuracy, but also to convert the latitude readings reported by Pytheas into mileage distances that gave the ancient world its first intelligible conception of north Atlantic geography and the configuration of western Europe. In regard to Pytheas' study of tidal phenomena it should be noted that (according to Strabo) a fully correct formulation of these in their conjunction with lunar phases was given by Posidonius, reputed to be "the most learned man alive" in the time of Cicero and Caesar. It is recorded of him that he spent some time at Cádiz, where he would have had ample opportunity to make tidal observations on his own account. But inasmuch as Posidonius for all his learning seems to have had no particular scientific training or ability, it is a thoroughly plausible suggestion that his theoretical ideas were taken from Pytheas.

No estimate of Pytheas' magnificent venture into the far-northern Atlantic is fairly made if it disregards his scientific accomplishments and intellectual curiosity. This aspect of his character must have been amplified by that sense of fascination for strange lands and unfamiliar ways of life which is the explorer's lure toward the ever retreating horizon of the known world into the unknown beyond. Yet if this may seem sufficient reason for believing that Pytheas extended his voyage across the north Atlantic to Iceland and the verge of the Arctic Circle, it should be recognized that such an excursion would have greatly exceeded his sailing orders and original commission. There can be no doubt that Pytheas' ship was equipped and sent out on a commercial expedition for the express purpose of investigating the hitherto inaccessible and presumptively highly remunerative Atlantic tin and amber market for the benefit of Massalia's foreign trade. As Polybius pointed out, it is unbelievable that "a private citizen, and a poor man at that, could ever have traversed such vast distances."

It is typical of the enduring quality of scientific knowledge and the ephemeral nature of commercial interests that Pytheas' contribution to science survived, whereas nothing seems to have come of the professed purpose of the expedition. There are two apparent reasons for this failure. The first and most immediate was the recovery of Carthage from her defeat by Rome in the First Punic War. With her hold on the western tip of Sicily and the southern portion of Sardinia lost to her, Carthage could no longer control the passage of the Tunisian Strait or prevent foreign shipping from sailing at will in the western basin of the Mediterranean. Nevertheless she succeeded in reestablishing her blockade of the Gibraltar Strait by strengthening her naval base at Gadir and reinforcing her colonial centers in southern Spain and, most notably, establishing a "New Carthage" at the strategic point where Spain's eastern coast begins to turn westward. (The site is still an important naval station, with a city that preserves its ancient name barely altered into "Cartagena.")

Even those who have been little interested in the history of ancient Rome will be familiar with Hannibal's invasion of Italy. He had assembled his army in Spain by ferrying his elephants and his native African contingents across from Algeria and drawing on the warlike Iberian tribes of the Spanish interior for his mercenaries. From Spain he marched along the coast into southern France and thence through the Alps into Italy, coming down upon Rome from the north. After a long struggle, in the course of which he very nearly destroyed the military strength of Rome on her own Italian soil, Hannibal was defeated utterly. And this put an end for all time to Carthaginian pretensions to empire and broke for good her closure of the Atlantic gateway. By the peace treaty of 201 B.C., Carthage ceded to Rome all her Spanish territory and surrendered all her remaining ships of war. In consequence, from then on for many centuries, Gadir, under the Latinized name of Gades, marked the western outposts of Roman empire, and the Gibraltar Strait stood open to every ship of Rome's allies. Why, then, did not Massalia, continuing on excellent terms with Rome, seize this opportunity to revive her ancient interest in Atlantic commerce and turn to her own account the Atlantic trade route, the exploration of which was the purpose for which she had equipped Pytheas and sent him out?

Perhaps the answer to this highly pertinent question should be sought in the comment attributed to Pytheas by Strabo and previously cited in this chapter, to the effect that "the portion of Spain that faces north is more readily accessible by way of the Celtic land than by sailing the Ocean." Modern commentators incline to dismiss this remark as too self-evident to merit any further attention. They treat it, therefore, as wholly unimportant. It is true that it may have been a casual comment made in the course of Pytheas' description of the route that he took for his voyage. But at least equally well it might have figured in a concluding summary of his official report to his fellow townsmen as part of a recommendation against inaugurating shipborne traffic with Brittany and Britain by way of the Gibraltar Strait, on the ground that the Atlantic coast could be reached so much more directly and easily by the overland route through southern France. On a rough calculation, the sailing distance from Marseilles via Gibraltar and the Atlantic coast to the head of the Bay of Biscay in the neighborhood of the present frontier between France and Spain is about 1,700 miles; whereas the journey overland to the same destination, measured from Narbonne on the Mediterranean (within easy sailing distance from Marseilles), does not exceed 300 miles. From Narbonne to Bordeaux, somewhat farther up the Atlantic coast of France, the distance overland is even less, while the sailing distance from Marseilles to Bordeaux is proportionately greater. The overland route was an easy one to travel, with no obstacles from the terrain; and there is excellent archeological indication that this "Narbo-Burdigala traverse" was a much traveled road of communication even before Pytheas' lifetime.

It may reasonably be presumed that Pytheas was not intending an elementary lesson in geography so much as giving his fellow citizens a bit of considered advice—to bring tin overland from the French coast instead of by the vastly longer and riskier ocean route. This supposition is borne out by all that is known about the tin traffic in Roman times after Gaul and Britannia (which is to say, France and England) had been annexed to the Roman empire. From the tin mines of Cornwall, native craft that were probably more like leather-lined coracles than wooden ships floated the ore across the channel, ultimately delivering it to the port of Corbilo in southern Brittany at the mouth of the Loire, where the city of Nantes now occupies much the same site. After Caesar's pacification of the whole of Gaul, Corbilo seems to have replaced Bordeaux as the terminal loading point for overland transport, and in consequence Massilia became the immediate goal instead of Narbo. The pertinent passage in Diodorus reads:

> After they have smelted and refined the tin . . . they transport it to an adjoining island named Iktis. . . . There the dealers buy it from the natives and thence convey it across to Gaul. For final stage, proceeding by land through Gaul, in about thirty days they bring their load on horses to the mouth of the Rhone.[47]

In similar avoidance of the long ocean route, amber was carried overland from Denmark to the Mediterranean. Nothing more is heard of Irish gold. Under the empire, seaborne trade was maintained only as far as southern Spain. That traffic, however, was developed on a great scale, to become supremely important to the Roman economy. Strabo speaks of Spain, by then already an integral part of the empire, as the richest in metals of all known lands:

[47] Diodorus, *Historical Library*, V.22.

For neither gold nor silver, nor above all copper, nor yet iron, have ever been discovered hitherto anywhere on earth in such quantities or of such quality.[48]

To this list should also be added lead. And for all of these the Mediterranean ships continued to ply, not only to Cartagena for products of the mines of Murcia, but out beyond Gibraltar at least as far as Huelva and the estuary of the Guadiana and perhaps on occasion to Setúbal in Portugal and to Lisbon on the broad estuary of the Tagus. But this appears to have been the utmost limit of Mediterranean navigation of the northern Atlantic. Britain was reached by crossing the channel from nearest Gaul. No Mediterranean ship ever again reached Thule—even though at the height of the Roman occupation of Britain a Roman flotilla under Agricola, governor of the island, once again passed through the Pentland Firth, where (in the words of Agricola's son-in-law and biographer, the great historian Tacitus) "Thule was sighted!" Most certainly, Agricola was mistaken and made the claim in error, because only the southernmost of the Orkneys around Scapa Flow would have been visible to him. But at least he knew the right direction to look!

Considered literally, therefore, Pytheas' great voyage had accomplished nothing and had been undertaken in vain. The ambitious commercial project contemplated by the merchant city of Massalia was never materialized. Presumably he himself advised against it. But on a different level of intellectual achievement, in adding to the Greeks' knowledge of the northern world outside their own landlocked sea, we can appreciate what Pytheas accomplished if we turn back a couple of hundred years to read what Herodotus wrote about Greek comprehension of the Atlantic north in his day:

Concerning the farthest western parts of Europe I cannot speak with any certainty. For I do not believe that there is any river, called Eridanos by foreign men, that empties into the northern sea and from which amber is reported to come; neither do I know of the existence of any Tin Islands, from which our tin comes. . . . Despite all diligence, I have been unable to hear of anyone who has himself beheld a sea on the other side of Europe. I know only that tin and amber reach us from utmost distance.[49]

[48] Strabo, *Geography*, III.ii.8.
[49] Herodotus, *History*, III.115.

Now at last there was Greek knowledge on all these matters, thanks entirely to Pytheas, whose exploit has survived in history as the most outstanding achievement in the annals of ancient voyaging. To whom else could more fairly be awarded the title of antiquity's Greatest Explorer?

❧ VI ❧

AVIENUS

THE present chapter may be taken as a geographical interlude in the recital of ancient voyages of exploration. But
it is not intended as a mere diversion of the reader's interest,
but as an important postscript to the previous chapter on
Pytheas. Much of the evidence laboriously pieced together there
from scant and scattered references in ancient writers to con-
struct an itinerary for Pytheas' adventurous voyage will here be
found collected into a systematic account of the landmarks on
his journey from Scotland and Brittany to Massilia on the Mediterranean.

This account is to be found in the preserved portion of a very
curious Late Latin poem entitled *Ora Maritima,* the pretentiously literary production of an extremely mediocre versifier
named Rufus Festus Avienus.

It is not likely that my readers have ever heard of Avienus,
much less have ever read the 714 lines of Latin senarian verses
that Time's fitful care has preserved from a much longer poem.
Not that we need rail at Time's cruel whim in this particular
case, for it may well be doubted whether the lost major portion
of the poem would have contained much to excite us, whereas
the part that has survived is precisely that which interests us
most, because it concerns itself with the route of Pytheas'
journey.

Ora Maritima means "Seacoast." If this seems a strange title
for a poetical composition, it should be explained that the
ancient Greeks were addicted to didactic poetry and saw no
reason that a treatise on geography or agriculture or astronomy
or physics or medicine should not be written in meter. In

particular, there was a Greek literary tradition of versified marine handbooks for navigators, listing the landmarks and other features, notably headlands, rivers, harbors, and towns along a given route. Such a set of "sailing directions" (as our Navy's Hydrographic Office calls its pilot manuals) was called in Greek a *periplous* (literally a "sailing past"); and it is known that several such works existed in antiquity. Indeed, some few of them are still extant—notably, a *periplous* of the Black Sea, another of the Red Sea, and fragments of more than one of the Mediterranean coasts. Avienus was only reviving an old Greek tradition when he set out to compile—in compliance with the request of a youthful friend—a Latin metrical *periplous* covering the European Atlantic coast together with the northern shoreline of the Mediterranean all the way to the end of the Black Sea. His ambition was to display his learning and his familiarity with old Greek writers by turning out a *periplous* in the ancient style, a deliberate piece of literary archaism with a minimum regard for contemporary conditions in his own late-imperial Roman era. What Avienus has given us, therefore, is not a picture of the world of his own day, but a rewarmed pot-pourri of Greek sailing books available to him. Unfortunately, he does not acknowledge his debts to these or name his sources for that part of his poem which deals with Pytheas' maritime route. And he nowhere mentions the name of Pytheas.

But what could such an author, writing in the Latin twilight before the onset of the Dark Ages, have known about the Atlantic or the western Mediterranean as they were more than half a thousand years before his time, except what he could discover in surviving ancient manuscripts? And what Greek writer could have supplied a detailed account of the Atlantic and Mediterranean shorelands from Brittany to Marseilles as they were in Greek times, unless it were Pytheas (whose account of his voyage of exploration must have existed in written form, since so many of the later Greek geographers and historians had knowledge of its content)? Whether Avienus actually pos-sessed a copy of Pytheas' documentary report or drew on it from more summary mention and epitomes by others is not of much concern. The important thing is the dependence of Avienus on Pytheas.

Perhaps the reader has remarked that Avienus was nowhere

cited or even mentioned by name in the preceding chapter on
Pytheas. This was a deliberate omission and not an oversight.
For it is not widely recognized—least of all, generally conceded
—that Pytheas was Avienus' source for the surviving portion of
his poem. Consequently, it was important to show that the
details of Pytheas' voyage may be reconstructed without recourse
to Avienus. Once that was done, the striking parallels between
the established course of that voyage and Avienus' recital become corroborative evidence and welcome confirmation of matters already sure.

Avienus himself was anything but a Great Explorer. He had
caught a glimpse of the Atlantic, having visited Gades (and, as
he says, seen nothing notable there!). As an imperial Roman
official of considerable distinction, he must have done a certain
amount of Mediterranean travel; but he had little to add from
firsthand knowledge to the recondite lore that he had dipped
up "out of many an ancient commentary." He never mentions
Rome or the Roman Empire, but refers constantly to the old
Greek names of places and peoples, occasionally warning his
readers that the towns that he mentions stood deserted and
desolate in his own day. Even Gades had been abandoned, he
declares, writing wanly of its ruined state in verses such as these:

> . . . And here is Gadir town
> (For so the Punic tongue was wont to call
> A place fenced-in). Still earlier it was named
> Tartessos—prosperous and peopled state
> In ancient periods, but now forlorn,
> Tiny, deserted, heap of ruined mounds!
> There we ourselves beheld naught notable
> Save for the famous fane of Hercules.[1]

Since Gades continued to be an important shipping center
and a populous city as long as the Roman empire maintained
its greatness, we need not be surprised to learn that Avienus
lived after the imperial capital had been moved to Constantinople and while Spain was being overrun and pillaged by the
Vandals. His *periplous* is accordingly aimed at long-forgotten,
far-off things—and it is precisely this which gives it its great
interest for the modern reader and perhaps its only value, since

---

[1] Avienus, *Ora Maritima*, 267–74.

as literature it is unashamedly feeble and as history it has nothing to say. My turgid and at times bombastic verse translation
is designedly modeled on Avienus' own pretentiously empty
style.

There are seventy-nine lines of introductory matter that need
not be here reproduced. Toward the close of this preliminary
passage, the *periplous* announces its Atlantic theme:

> Where from deep Ocean a great surge sets in
> To spread its waters on our inland sea,[2]

and makes brief mention of Gades and the Gibraltar Strait, as
though these were to be the starting point for the mariner consulting this aid to navigation. But instead of following the
Spanish coast westward toward Cape St. Vincent, Avienus, without further explanation of the sudden shift, begins his voyage
from the other end of the ocean route by dropping down on the
Pointe du Raz in westernmost Brittany.

Rather than commenting on every pertinent point as Avienus
comes to it, I prefer to let the old poet take us where he will,
north and south from Finistère. Thereafter we may turn back
to note how perfectly everything in Avienus corresponds to
what Pytheas must have seen and recorded six hundred years
earlier.

Here, in translation, are the verses that treat of the Atlantic
shores as far as the Spanish frontier at the head of the Bay of
Biscay. (The numerals in the margin refer to the number of the
corresponding verse in the Latin text):

. . . This is the Atlantic Gulf,
And here is Gadir, once Tartessos called,   85
Here too the Pillars of persistent Hercules—
Calpē, the one; the other, on the left
Near unto Afric, Abila by name—
These echo back the northwind, yet hold firm
Their olden place, wherenext uprears its head
A promontory named in former times   90
Oestrymnis, towering mass of rock that veers
Most toward the tepid southwind all its height.
Then next below this jutting ridge there gapes
The gulf Oestrymnian with its native folk;   95

[2] *Ibid., s.v.* 83–4.

And widely scattered isles are stretched along,
Rich with their lodes of lead and metalled tin.
Abundance is there here of proud-willed race
Skilled and adroit, perpetually employed
In trafficking on ships not built, but sewn,   100
Cleaving the stormy strait afar, the surge
Of monster-haunted Ocean. Not from pine
Nor maple know these how to frame a keel,
Nor yet from firwood do they curve a craft,   105
But wondrous fit together skins and hides
On which to cruise across the vasty deep.

Now, from this place 'tis voyage of two suns
Out to the "Holy Isle" (so named of yore).
Wide on the water spreads this out its glebe   110
Where folk Hiernan dwell on it afar:
There too, nearby, spreads out the Albions' isle.
Tartessians to the Oestrymnid islands' bourn
Once used to traffic. Folk from Carthage too
Frequented once these waters, folk that dwelt   115
And strove between the Pillars of Hercules
O'er that expanse which scarce in four months' term
Punic HIMILCO said might be traversed
(As he himself reported, having sailed),
So faltering the winds drive on a ship,   120
So slack and calm the lazy ocean lies.
He adds moreover this: amid the flood
Vast dross there is that oft restrains a ship
As in a thicket caught. Even so (he says)
The ocean's surface drops not into depth   125
But scarcely hides the bottom with scant flood.
On either hand, huge monsters of the deep
Tour round the sluggish, slowly moving bark
And whales float in between.
                            Now, if from thence,
From isles Oestrymnic, anyone should dare   130
To drive his pinnace northward through the sea
To where 'neath polar stars the heavens freeze,
He'd come to land Ligurian, of dwellers void.
Through Celtic violence and constant fights
The fields have long stood empty. Thus expelled,
(As others oft have fared) Ligurians moved   135
To that far land which now they do possess

'Mid thorny thickets. Many a rugged rock
Thrusts skyward peak and mountain's pinnacle
Toward heaven. And here these wretched fugitives
By day keep close between the narrow cliffs   140
In inland hideout, for they fear the sea's
Long-standing peril; but when quiet falls
Thereafter and the hour's security
Strengthens their courage, from their upland lairs
Persuaded to come down, straight they descend   145
To shoreland spots.
                        Again from where we named,
A great expanse of water spreads its gulf
As far as Ophiussa. From its strand
Back to the Inland (or Sardinian) Sea   150
Extends a road of seven days afoot.
                        But farther west   380
Beyond the Pillars, boundless ocean spreads,
The wideswept Main whereof HIMILCO tells.
No one has ever crossed its surge, no one
Set keel upon it; for there are no winds
On high to drive a ship, no breeze or breath   385
Stirring astern. Fog cloaks the sky with mist
And cloud forever holds the sea, to set
A weather denser than the light of day.
. . . .
Beyond, in many parts, the sea is spread   406
So shallow that it scarce conceals the sands
Lying beneath; and clustering growth of weed
O'ertops the sea and checks its flood with wrack,
While crowds of sea-beasts swim athwart the Main   410
And monstrous terror holds the straits in fear.
These things of old upon the ocean stream
Punic HIMILCO said that he had seen,
Bringing back word of trials undergone.

Clearly, whatever is here ascribed to Himilco can have nothing to do with Pytheas. But it is almost equally certain that
all the rest of the long passage, which has nothing to do with
Himilco, closely concerns Pytheas. A certain amount of elucida-
tion may be required; but even without exhaustive, verse-by-
verse study and with only occasional comment on the more
striking points of comparison, the dependence of Avienus on
Pytheas' account of his voyage should be convincingly apparent.

I have already remarked that the opening lines (*vv.* 84–88) have no geographical connection with what immediately follows. By speaking of Calpē (Gibraltar) as on the right, and Abila (Jebel Musa in Morocco) as on the left, Avienus is in imagination headed oceanward through the Straits. But the westward voyage is not pursued farther; so that there is no reason to bring Pytheas in here as yet. Immediately thereafter and with startling abruptness the scene is shifted north to Finistère in Brittany. As the text continues, one would naturally suppose that "they echo back the northwind, yet hold firm" has some reference to Gibraltar and Jebel Musa (even though the mention of a north wind is inappropriate); but the name of Oestrymnis in *v.* 91 disabuses us of any such notion. We have already come across Ostimians in conjunction with Cape Kabaion and the island of Uxantis in Strabo's remarks on Pytheas; and Oestrymnis is known also from other sources to be northwest Brittany. Cape Kabaion has been confidently identified as the Pointe du Raz. Accepting the identification, we may profitably compare Avienus' description of the "promontory named in former times Oestrymnis, towering mass of rock that veers most toward the tepid southwind all its height," where the rocks "echo back the northwind, yet hold firm their olden place," with the following description of the Pointe du Raz paraphrased from a French guidebook for Brittany, which speaks of it as "one of the natural wonders not only of Brittany, but of France:"

> It is a long rocky spur against which the breakers foam, with high overhanging cliffs within whose cavities, when the north-wind blows, the waves resound like the hoarse roar of cannon-shots.[3]

Visitors are warned against being plunged off the high causeway of rock by the force of the wind. (The cliffs, however, "hold firm their ancient place"!)

The "gulf Oestrymnian" that gapes "below this jutting ridge" is the broad Bay of Douarnenez with the adjoining deeply indented roadstead of Brest, "the largest and safest Atlantic harborage of Europe." Avienus' next mention (in *vv.* 96–97) of "widely scattered isles . . . stretched along,/Rich with their lodes of lead and metalled tin" poses an interesting

---

[3] *Les Guides Bleus* (Bretagne. Paris, 1924), p. 647.

problem because the widely spaced string of islands off the
Breton coast, from Ouessant northwest of Brest to Belle-Île almost as far south as the estuary of the Loire, fits Avienus' description geographically but not physically, inasmuch as none
of these islands is endowed with any particular mineral wealth.
Nonetheless, these same islands, together with Saint Michael's
Mount in Cornwall and possibly the Scilly Isles off Cornwall's
westernmost head, must be identified with the fabulous "Tin
Islands" (Greek *Kassiterides*) of the ancients. Pliny even knew
their number, which he set at ten. The crux of the problem
resides in the difficulty of discovering any reason that islands
that could never have been markedly metalliferous should have
been so widely held to be the source of the tin that the Mediterranean world imported for making bronze. The solution to the
puzzle is to be found in the universal role that offshore islands
played in ancient commercial enterprise.

What this role was, is hinted by the Greek historian Thucydides. In describing Sicily he speaks of "Phoenicians . . . who
had occupied promontories upon the seacoast and the adjacent
islets for the purpose of trading with the native Sicels." [4] The
earliest Greek traders in the west had exercised a similar choice.
The firstcomers to the Bay of Naples did not establish themselves
on the mainland there but on the closely offshore island of
Ischia (which, for some reason unknown to us, they dubbed
"Monkey Island") and only later moved to the adjacent coast
to found their famous colony of Cumae. At Syracuse, in Sicily,
the Corinthian traders and settlers originally occupied the tiny
islet of Ortygia with its poetically renowned freshwater spring
Arethusa, and only later, as their city grew, connected this by
a causeway with the closely adjoining land. At the farther
western tip of Sicily, Phoenicians from Carthage similarly
selected a small island in a shallow lagoon for their trading
post of Motya; and this, too, was later connected with the Sicilian mainland by a causeway. Gadir in Cádiz Bay is another
typical instance. We have already seen how St. Michael's Mount
in the Bay of Penzance—island at high tide, peninsula at low—
was the place of exchange for the Cornish tin miners in their,
trade with Atlantic shippers. And Ouessant (Uxantis) is best
interpreted as a similar entrepôt for tin from the Cornish and

4 Thucydides, *History*, VI.3.

the Breton mines. Everywhere the pattern is the same: the seaborne traders, in distrust of mainland native treachery, conducted their business on offshore islands where they would be safe from attack on their persons and from plundering of their cargoes. The "Tin Islands," accordingly, contained only the tin that was brought to them to be bartered on their neutral territory.

To return to Avienus, the "proud-willed race . . . perpetually employed/In trafficking on ships not built, but sewn/Cleaving the stormy strait afar, the surge/Of monster-haunted Ocean" clearly concerns the cross-channel transportation of ingots of tin from Cornwall in the flimsy but buoyant craft known as coracles made of wicker framework covered with hides stitched together and smeared with some substance to make them watertight. Avienus is specific in regard to these "skilled and adroit" mariners that they are Bretons and not Britons—by which I mean that it was not the Cornish miners themselves who transported the tin to Brittany (nor yet Phoenicians from Gadir, nor Celts from Tartessos), but that this was the work of the Oestrymnian folk of Brittany. Diodorus offers much the same picture— one also derived ultimately from Pytheas' account of what he saw.

What became of the tin after it reached Brittany is recounted by Avienus in *vv.* 113–16:

> Tartessians to the Oestrymnid islands' bourn
> Once used to traffic. Folk from Carthage too
> Frequented once these waters, folk that dwelt
> And strove between the Pillars of Hercules."

No word of the overland pack-train transport of Roman days! Avienus is drawing on older times while tin was still being brought in ships from Brittany to Gadir for the Mediterranean market. Who better than Pytheas could have publicized this?

But before Avienus passes this account on to his readers, with his mind still on Channel crossings, he interpolates a brief reference to Ireland and a still briefer one to England, remarking that from Brittany one may cross to Ireland in a couple of days, close to which "Holy Isle" the Albions' isle lies.

Commentators on Avienus have been rather baffled by Avienus' failure to make more than this most cursory and almost slighting mention of Britain. But it must be remembered that

Britain had been a province of the Roman empire from its conquest, begun in A.D. 43, until the withdrawal of the Roman legions in A.D. 411, after Avienus wrote. Britain therefore was abundantly familiar ground to every Latin reader and too fully explored to fit the narrow frame of the antiquarian's *periplous*. Ireland, on the other hand, was never part of the Roman empire and seems to have been almost as little visited in Avienus' time as in the older periods. To Ireland, accordingly, Avienus gives somewhat more attention, calling it the "Holy Isle" through a misunderstanding inherited from the Greek geographers, who had confused the native name *Hi(v)eriyō* with Greek *hiera*, meaning "sacred" or "holy."

But Avienus makes as little out of the Hibernian Isle as Pytheas seems to have done before him, and turns back to Brittany and the Oestrymnic folk with the important remark, just referred to, that Tartessians and Carthaginians from the Gibraltar Strait "frequented once these waters." This reminds him of Punic Himilco, who also had explored the Atlantic—though what his four months' voyage had to do with Brittany is not made clear. In any case, the intrusion is irrelevant and leaves Avienus blankly to pick up his narrative where he digressed from it:

> . . . Now if from thence,
> From isles Oestrymnic, anyone should dare
> To drive his pinnace northward through the sea
> To where 'neath polar stars the heavens freeze . . .

We are back with Pytheas and headed toward his Farthest North!

The significance of this passage of 17 lines (*vv.* 129–46) has escaped the commentators on Avienus, presumably because they were not thinking of Pytheas as the Latin poet's source and therefore did not look far enough afield from Brittany and the coast of France. Yet it should be clear that these temperate regions cannot be fitted to the text. Avienus is very specific in his compass points: we are to venture *due north* from the Oestrymnian islands to the zone of intense cold.

The mention of Ligurians may give us pause until we recognize that, to Avienus' antiquarian thinking, the Ligurians are merely the pre-Celtic population of Europe. These were displaced by the Celts in various sectors and absorbed by them in other localities, according as conditions and the vagaries of chance determined. The Celtic movement overseas into Britain and Ireland had already taken place before Pytheas arrived on the scene; but an aftermath of this invasion still endured. In Ireland the older inhabitants fled westward into the interior of the land, leaving its eastern margin to the Celts, who had landed there from Britain. In Scotland the Celtic penetration would have taken longer and been more arduous, with the original non-Celtic population ("Ligurians" in Avienus' ethnology) taking to the harsh uplands and there holding out for generations. This is the situation that Avienus describes (though it was not in the least applicable to the Caledonia of his own time). Since he could have known nothing of all this directly from recent chronicles or Roman visitors' accounts, he must have derived his knowledge from some much older source. This source could not have been a history of the Roman general Agricola's subjugation of the Caledonian Picts toward the close of the first century after Christ, because in Avienus the conflict is not between Roman and Celt, but between Celt and "Ligurian." Nor would such an interpretation accord with Avienus' ambition to recall the world of remoter times by delving into old Greek authors. Hence, since northern Britain remained unvisited and unexplored after Pytheas' voyage until Agricola sailed through the Pentland Firth, the only possible source for this passage in Avienus is Pytheas' report. That being so, these seventeen lines of mediocre Latin verse deserve the closest attention because they constitute the only surviving ancient account of the conflict of the immigrant Celts with the older neolithic civilization of Britain, descendants of the builders of Stonehenge and the dolmen-folk of a more ancient period. With this in mind, the passage deserves to be reread with fuller understanding of what it means as an historic document of unique interest.

A curiosity of recent scholarship adds a pertinent postscript to this account of the skulking natives with their terror of the Celtic ships and the Celtic occupation of their coasts.

In A. O. Anderson's *Early Sources of Scottish History* reference is made to a Latin manuscript thought to date from the late twelfth century of our era and quite recently discovered in a Scottish library. The manuscript deals with the history of Norway in early times and includes the Orkneys in its survey, stating that, before the coming of the Viking Norsemen (who took these islands over by violence), the Orkneys were inhabited by Picts. Of these there is given the following astonishing account:

> The Picts were scarcely more than dwarves in stature. Evenings and mornings, they were wonderfully active in building their towns; but at middle day they were wholly without strength and lurked in fear in their small underground houses. . . . Whence this people came, we have no knowledge whatever.[5]

There is no difficulty about the Picts' "underground houses" and "towns." Northern Scotland and the islands in the Orkney and Shetland groups are studded with the remains of stone fortress dwellings called *brochs*. A *broch* consisted essentially of a tall round tower, often as much as fifty or sixty feet in diameter at the base and correspondingly high, with an adjoining exterior courtyard surrounded by a deep earth trench or moat. Around the tower, but still inside the encircling trench or trenches, was a scattered collection of tiny stone huts. These huts were the dwelling places of the communal group for which the great tower served as refuge and defense in time of attack.

The date of the *brochs* is difficult to determine with any approach to precision. At the time of Pytheas' visit the Celtish Picts were already installed in these regions, though probably they had not been long in possession of the territory. The original inhabitants (descendants of the first settlers of these islands after the great ice sheet of the last Ice Age had melted away and left the land exposed in the sea) were still unassimilated and had fled inland, venturing only a sporadic appearance down on the shorelands—at least, so we may gather from the account in Avienus. But the *brochs* were not the work of these timid fugitives, but of the Pictish invaders themselves, and seem to have been built many centuries later than Pytheas (or for that matter, Avienus). It is thought that it was not until considerably after Roman times, when the Picts were threatened by new

[5] MSS. *Historia Norvegiæ*, translated by A. O. Anderson, *op. cit.*, and quoted by Hugh Marwick, *Orkney* (London, Robert Hale, Ltd., 1951), p. 34.

seaborne invaders such as the piratical Norsemen, that they constructed the *brochs* for safety from attack.

The *brochs*, then, were not in existence in Pytheas' day, nor yet (apparently) in the time of Avienus. And the weird report in the twelfth-century "history" that the Picts of Orkney were remarkable builders "evenings and mornings" but wholly without strength at middle day, when they lurked in fear in underground houses, is patent nonsense. Cannot its silliness be explained as a mistaken transference from Pytheas' account of the conflict between Celt and pre-Celt, much as Avienus reproduces it, to the *broch* builders of later times? If this is a correct assumption, it helps support the contention that verses 129–46 of the *Ora Maritima* should be localized in the extreme north of Scotland and consequently must have been ultimately derived from Pytheas' narrative of his exploration of that region.

From this far northern digression Avienus returns abruptly to his original starting point in Brittany. After a colorless "again from where we named before," he embarks at last upon the long sea voyage to Massilia. Only the first four verses of this have been translated because there is no proof that only Pytheas could have supplied the geographical information for what follows thereafter.

The great expanse of gulf in verse 147 can signify only the broad Bay of Biscay. The immediately ensuing intrusion of the seven-day journey afoot overland from its shore to the Sardinian Sea (the northern bight of the western Mediterranean) connects directly with Pytheas' reported remark that the Atlantic coast of northern Spain was of easier access overland through Celtic territory than by circumnavigating the Iberian peninsula.

From this stage of the homeward *periplous* to the Mediterranean, because there are no references in other ancient writers that can be traced to Pytheas for the stretch from Bayonne to Cape St. Vincent, Avienus' summary description of landmarks along the northern shore of Spain and the coast of Portugal is of no immediate concern. And after Gadir and the Gibraltar Strait the sudden increase in close and accurate detail for the Mediterranean coast of Iberia and Gaul to the port of Massilia may equally well have been derived from some Massilian sailing book compiled before or after Pytheas' Atlantic exploration.

In view of these considerations, we cannot hope to extract more about Pytheas from the *Ora Maritima* than we have already gleaned.

However, there still remains a topic of outstanding interest in the portion of the text that has been translated. This is to be found in the three passages dealing with "Punic Himilco."

It will be recalled that, while speaking of Brittany, Avienus introduced the remark that "folk from Carthage/Frequented once these waters . . ./O'er that expanse which scarce in four months' term/Punic HIMILCO said might be traversed" and proceeded to list the navigational difficulties that Himilco encountered (*vv.* 119–29), finding occasion later, on reaching the Gibraltar Strait, to repeat these matters twice again with some slight changes and additions (*vv.* 380–88, and 406–14).

Now, in the first place, it may be taken for certain that no navigator would have used 120 days for a trip from Cádiz to Brittany and back. Of course, Himilco might have landed and gone exploring here and there during the voyage; but with equal certainty his experience of doldrum calms, Sargasso-like weedbanks, great shoals and shallows, and cruising sea monsters does not at all correspond to conditions in the Bay of Biscay, either then or now. When these same hindrances to navigation are recounted a second time, dense fog is added and the illimitable open ocean outside the Straits is given as the scene, without suggestion of the North Atlantic seaway.

What are we to conclude about Himilco as an explorer? At any rate, whatever we decide, there is no ground for denying that he undertook and completed some sort of extraordinary Atlantic voyage. But where did he go?

When Avienus asserted (in *vv.* 114–16) that folk from Carthage and the Straits once used to sail to Brittany, and in this context introduces the name of Himilco the Carthaginian, he may have been relying on a remark that he had read in Pliny [6] to the effect that, in the heyday of Carthage, when Hanno circumnavigated Africa, Himilco was at the same time despatched to explore "the parts beyond Europe." There is no reason to doubt Pliny's word; but it is not clear what regions he meant by "the parts beyond Europe" (*extera Europae*). Since Hanno fully merits the title of Great Explorer, his contemporary and fellow

[6] Pliny, *Natural History*, II.169.

countryman Himilco should have been entirely capable of investigating the Atlantic coast of Europe as far as Brittany, if this had been his object. But the list that Avienus gives of marine hindrances encountered by Himilco on his four-month voyage points in a diametrically opposite direction. The completely windless seas of verses 120–21 and 384–86 would lead us to infer that Himilco had been journeying south beyond the trade wind's belt. Even though this belt shifts northward with the sun in summer, the zone of doldrum calms beyond the trades never moves up out of the tropics. But contrary to this assumption of a southward voyage beyond Morocco and Senegal is the mention of thick fog so dense as to hide the light of day—a condition virtually unknown in tropical waters but quite common in the north Atlantic. However, in order to run into heavy fog, Himilco would not have needed to sail as far north as Brittany or the English Channel, since the Atlantic coast of Spain might have given him ample experience. For example, at Corunna on the northwest tip of the Iberian peninsula, eighty-four days in the average year have been reported as foggy, with the main incidence falling in the spring and summer months. The Portuguese coast and the Atlantic coast of southern Spain from Gibraltar westward are beset with dense offshore haze and mist (rather than actual fog) during the summer. And here, between Cádiz and Cape St. Vincent, Himilco could have run upon many a sandy shoal and treacherous bar wherever "the sea is spread/So shallow that it scarce conceals the sands/Lying beneath." But no "clustering growth of weed/[that] O'ertops the sea and checks its flood" has been reported here!

The still more exaggerated version of this untoward obstacle to navigation in verses 123–24, with its "Vast dross there is that oft restrains a ship/As in a thicket caught," has reminded several commentators on Avienus of the Sargasso Sea, the great tract of floating seaweed in mid-Atlantic in which Columbus became involved on his way to the West Indies. But only a few have ventured to suggest that Himilco might ever have sailed so far out on the ocean, even though it cannot be termed completely impossible for him to have reached the Azores.

The only sound conclusion to be drawn from these manifest inconsistencies must be that Avienus' thirdhand knowledge of what "Punic Himilco said that he had seen, bringing back word" of his four months' voyage in the Atlantic, was either extremely fragmentary or has been so arbitrarily and picturesquely edited by the Latin poet as to confuse beyond hope of intelligibility the Carthaginian's accomplishment. This being so, it is idle to do more than speculate on possibilities of what might have been. Thus, we may argue that, if he had been cruising south instead of north from the Straits, Himilco might have sighted the mountainous hills of Lanzarote or Fuerteventura in the Canary Islands, since these lie barely sixty miles off the African coast. Thence he would have sighted and inevitably explored Grand Canary and Tenerife and others of that picturesque group of volcanic isles. Or again, he might have raised the Cape Verde Islands, twelve degrees farther to the south. Indeed, in four months he would have had ample time to visit all the various groups of islands lying west of northern Africa, from Madeira southward; but to suppose that this is what he did, charges Pliny either with having completely misunderstood the scope of the expedition or with having applied his phrase "the parts beyond Europe" in a very loose and even thoroughly misleading sense.

The upshot of the whole matter is that we cannot tell and shall never know where it was that Himilco went exploring. And this is a great pity, for Himilco may well have rated as one of antiquity's Great Explorers. As it is, we can only salute his name in passing and write him off as one more brave navigator of old whom Time has consigned to oblivion.

It is fortunate that we are so much better informed on Himilco's contemporary and rival in exploration, his royal fellow countryman Hanno—as a previous chapter has made abundantly clear!

❦ VII ❦

SEAWAYS TO INDIA

PERHAPS because we are unconsciously reminded of Vasco da Gama and his tremendous voyage from Lisbon to Calicut,[1] we are apt to regard any passage to India as overlong and difficult for a sailing vessel to make. But where the cities on the Tigris or Euphrates were the starting point, the trip to India by way of the Persian Gulf and the Arabian Sea as far as the Indus River represented only about 1,250 miles of seafaring with land in sight all the way. This is no greater than the distance from Suez down the Red Sea to Aden—a voyage that the ancient Egyptians made from the early dynastic period. For the shorter run to India from the head of the Persian Gulf, the archeological evidence indicates sea communication between Sumer in lower Mesopotamia and Mohenjo-Daro on the Indus from almost as early a date. And even the much longer route from Egypt to India—although it necessitated traveling the whole length of the Red Sea and skirting the entire southern coast of Arabia before joining the route from the Persian Gulf —was not very much more of a voyage than a Phoenician ship would have had to make in sailing from Tyre or Sidon to Gadir in Spain. And if advantage was taken of the trade wind down the Red Sea and the monsoon wind across the Arabian Sea, Egypt to India would have been easier going than Phoenicia to outer Spain. Certainly, in comparison with the circumnavigation of Africa, the Indian voyage from Egypt or Persia should have been no great adventure even for an ancient sailing vessel.

However, it must be noted that a continuance of the voyage beyond the mouth of the Indus and around the great triangular peninsula of southern India past Ceylon to the head of the Bay

---

[1] A city west southwest of Madras, on the Malabar Coast.

of Bengal (where Calcutta lies today) was an undertaking of
quite a different order of magnitude, the distance by sea from
Karachi to Calcutta being considerably greater than that from
Aden to Karachi. In discussing ancient Mediterranean voyages
to India it is important to make sure what part of India is
under consideration.

These may be rather elementary findings in Oriental geography. But if they are duly taken into account, they will serve
to clarify various matters that otherwise might remain obscure.
For instance, there should be no difficulty in interpreting the
famous passages in the First Book of Kings that deal with the
greatness and splendor of Solomon—especially if these are kept
in their logical order:

> And King Solomon made a fleet of ships in Ezion-geber,
> which is on the shore of the Red Sea in the land of Edom.
> And Hiram sent to the fleet his servants that were sailors with
> knowledge of the sea, together with the servants of Solomon.
> And they came to Ophir; and they fetched thence four hundred
> and twenty talents of gold and brought them to King Solomon.[2]
> For King Solomon had at sea Tarshish ships along with the
> ships of Hiram: once in three years came the Tarshish ships
> bringing gold and silver and ivory and apes and peacocks.[3]
> And Jehoshaphat built Tarshish ships to go to Ophir for
> gold; but they went not, for the ships were broken at
> Ezion-geber.[4]

At its northern end the Red Sea bifurcates into two long
narrow arms or "horns" on either flank of the mountainous
Sinai Peninsula. The western horn, on the Egyptian side, is
the Gulf of Suez; the other, rather smaller, on the Arabian
side, is the Gulf of Aqaba. At its furthest end was Ezion-geber.
Excavations conducted by Nelson Glueck leave no doubt of its
location or of its importance as a shipping station in biblical
times. Of the size of Solomon's fleet based here there may be
more serious doubt. His people had no experience of the sea,
and his land grew no proper timber for building ships. For this
he had to turn to the Phoenicians living under the heavily
wooded slopes of Lebanon, even as he had to turn to them for
timber to roof his great temple:

[2] I Kings 9:26–28.
[3] *Ibid.*, 10:22.
[4] *Ibid.*, 22:48.

And Solomon sent to Hiram, king of Tyre, saying, . . . "Now
therefore command that they hew me cedar trees out of
Lebanon . . . ; for thou knowest that there is none among
us skilled to hew timber like the Sidonians."

And Hiram sent to Solomon, saying, "I will do thy desire
concerning timber of cedar and timber of fir. My servants shall
bring them down from Lebanon unto the sea, and I will convey
them in floats unto the place that thou shalt appoint." [5]

Similarly when, several centuries after Solomon, the Persian
king Darius built his great palace in his capital city of Susa, he
caused to be recorded on the glazed tiles of his audience
chamber how

The cedar timber was brought from a mountain named
Lebanon: the Assyrian people brought it to Babylon; and from
Babylon the Carians and Ionians [6] brought it to Susa.[7]

So too, for building ships at Ezion-geber, timber from Mount
Lebanon must have been floated to a port in Palestine and
thence conveyed overland to the Gulf of Aqaba. It was to the
interest of the Phoenicians to station their ships there for their
Red Sea commerce and their farther eastern trade; for if they
maintained friendly relations with Canaan, they could convey
their cargoes overland directly to the Phoenician coast and
avoid the ruinous exactions of Egyptian transit toll. What profit
Solomon took for himself from this arrangement does not appear; but if he got gold and silver and ivory (not to mention the
sideline of apes and peacocks) through the Red Sea port of
Ezion-geber, it is reasonable to think that it was the Phoenicians
in Phoenician ships who conveyed these riches to him.

As pointed out in Chapter II, "Tarshish ships" have no special
connection with Spanish Tartessos. As is clear from the passages
cited from the Book of Kings, there were "Tarshish ships" on
the Red Sea making the trip to Ophir for gold. To be sure, it
is not known where or what Ophir was. It may have been the
Nubian coast, since an auriferous belt extends between the Nile
and the Red Sea at about the latitude of the Second Cataract.
(Although the name "Nubia" is not ancient, the fact that *noub*

[5] *Ibid.*, 5:3, 6, 8, 9.
[6] The chief builders of the palace.
[7] R. G. Kent, *Old Persian* (New Haven, 1950), p. 144, item 3g.

is Coptic Egyptian for "gold" suggests that "Nubia" signified "Gold Land"). Alternatively, Ophir may have to be sought on the Arabian side of the Red Sea. But wherever the land of Ophir was, in any case it lay on the way to India. And it was toward India that the longer two-year voyage must have been directed; for no such length of time would have been needed for the trip to Ophir and back, and though the gold and ivory and apes might have been acquired without sailing beyond Africa, the peacocks point surely to southern India and Ceylon, the countries in which these birds were indigenous.

The long absence abroad of the ships from Ezion-geber fits the meteorological conditions governing a sailing vessel's passage to those eastern shores.

During late summer the trade wind funnels down the Red Sea through much of its length, and at this same season the southwest monsoon is still blowing across the Arabian Sea. A sailing vessel departing from the Gulf of Aqaba in midsummer might reach northwest India by late autumn; but unless it turned about almost immediately it would be obliged to spend the rest of the year there, visiting Indian trading ports and exchanging its Mediterranean stock of goods for an Oriental cargo, since the voyage back to Africa could not be made until the reverse northeast monsoon began blowing again during the following autumn. Thereafter, the Gulf of Aden would be reached in time to take advantage of the strong south wind that, in winter, blows into the southern end of the Red Sea. Arrival at Ezion-geber would, in consequence, be predictable for the early spring. If this does not appear to be a three-year absence, it would nonetheless be true that departure during the summer of "Year One" would have been succeeded by return home in the spring of "Year Three," which is all that the writer of the Hebrew text presumably intended by his phrase.

I think that we may safely conclude that Phoenician sailing vessels were making the journey from the head of the Red Sea to India in antiquity. The only difficulty is the date of such voyages. Solomon reigned during the early tenth century B.C.; but since the two Books of Kings bring their chronicle down to the destruction of Jerusalem by Nebuchadnezzar of Babylon in 586 B.C., it is obvious that they need not have been compiled before this latter date, by which time the wisdom, wealth, and earthly power of Solomon had become as much legendary as historically real. Later conditions could readily have been anachronistically ascribed to Solomon's time, so that sea voyages to India, in themselves entirely authentic, may not then have been current.

The use of the maritime station of Ezion-geber by Phoenician ships need not be doubted. At the same time, it is entirely likely that other Phoenician ships were actively engaged in far-eastern trade in the interests of the Egyptian rulers. This would explain how King Necho could have had Phoenician ships and crews at his disposal to be sent out through the Red Sea for the circumnavigation of Africa.

Consequently, if the question is raised as to who it was that first explored the long seaway from Egypt to India and when the event occurred, the answer must be evasive. But if we ask more specifically what *Greek* mariner first explored this route, a specific reply can be offered, with names and date and attendant circumstance to match. The explorer's name was Skylax, and the date of his voyage was the last decade of the sixth century before Christ. All this is known because Herodotus records it. And all this is reasonably certain because there is no clear reason for doubting it. The all too brief notice in Herodotus reads as follows:

> The greater part of Asia had been explored by Darius. He, wishing to learn about the Indus River (which is the second of those known to contain crocodiles) as to where it was that this river emptied into the sea, despatched men whom he could trust to tell the truth; and chief among these was Skylax of Caryanda. [He and his companions] set out by ship from the city of Caspatyrus in the Paktyan country and sailed east toward the sunrise, down the river to the sea, and then through the sea westward until in the thirtieth month of their voyage they reached the port from which the Egyptian king had once sent out the Phoenicians about whom I have already spoken, to circumnavigate Africa. After they had made this voyage, Darius subjugated the Indians and made use of this sea. In this manner all of Asia except its easternmost portion was discovered to be geographically similar to Africa.[8]

Caryanda was a town in Caria, not far from Herodotus' birth-

[8] Herodotus, *History*, IV.44.

place, Halicarnassus. Like this latter it was largely inhabited by
a non-Greek people, the Carians, who spoke a wholly unrelated
language. But to judge from his name, Skylax (like Herodotus)
was of Greek descent. Like other Greeks in this part of the
world, he was a Persian subject; and the Persian king, ruling a
mainly inland realm, found his inborn Greek knowledge of the
sea and of ships serviceable for maritime undertakings. (There
was no Persian navy in the strict sense of the word. Mediterranean shipbuilders and Mediterranean seamen from the coastal
provinces of the empire were requisitioned to make good the
want.)

"The city of Caspatyrus in the Paktyan country," from which
the expedition made its start, is mentioned elsewhere in Herodotus as located in northern India, apparently close to Bactria, and
as inhabited by a most warlike people. This description best
suits the borderland between modern Pakistan and Afghanistan.
The only navigable river flowing thence and leading ultimately
to the Indian Ocean would be the Kabul. And this does indeed
flow "east toward the sunrise"; but it is hardly navigable until
it prepares to quit the wild Afghanistan mountains, not far from
Peshawar. Shortly, after it joins the much larger Indus River.
Here a drastic change of direction, which Herodotus omits to
mention, would have led south to the sea.

What sort of voyage this must have been, through the Punjab
and across the great Thar Desert to the delta of the Indus and
thence at last into the open sea, appears more vividly from the
account of its repetition almost two hundred years later, as it may
be read in the pages of Arrian in which he describes the conveying of Alexander's army down this same long run of river. To
this I shall shortly turn, but meanwhile we are concerned with
Skylax.

The lands through which he passed in descending the Indus
would probably have evinced no hostility and offered no obstruction to his ship's passage with its (to Indian eyes) weirdly
foreign crew. In Herodotus' listing of the tribute-paying provinces of the vast Persian Empire under Darius' rule, Bactria
and Paktya are included. As final item are set "the Indians, by
far the most populous of all known nations: these paid the
largest tribute of all." [9] In Iran, on the face of a high cliff

[9] *Ibid.*, III.94.

located on the main caravan route from Baghdad to Teheran, at a height of about 225 feet above the road, there are still legible panels of long inscriptions. These are accompanied by relief sculptures carved in the natural rock and representing the Persian god Ahuramazda floating above the standing figure of Darius, who is shown with two attendants and a string of nine captive rebels personifying the nations brought under his rule.[10] This, the trilingual inscription of Behistan, may rank with the record of the *Res Gestae* (or acts and deeds) of the first Roman emperor, Augustus, on the wall of his temple in the heart of the modern capital of Turkey, as one of the two most remarkable of all ancient historical inscriptions. At Behistan, in proud and lordly phrases, Darius sets forth how he came to the throne of Persia by slaying the pretender and proceeded to remove all rebellious competition to his rule. As there is no mention of India or adjoining lands, it may well be that these were not yet part of his empire.

But the accuracy of Herodotus' listing of the provinces is fully substantiated by other, less extensive inscriptions that Darius caused to be carved on the retaining wall of the magnificent palace that he erected at Persepolis later in his reign, and again on the exterior of his own tomb, a few miles north of Persepolis. In these he announces "the countries which I seized outside of Persia: I ruled over them: my law held them firm." [11] In the long list are included northern and southern Afghanistan and the eastern portion of Beluchistan—all more or less closely bordering on northwest India—and finally Gandhara and Sind.

This sets the scene for Skylax; for it was from Gandhara that he set out and it was through Sind that he sailed downriver to the sea. But did he ever actually complete his assignment and sail "through the sea westward until in the thirtieth month . . . [he] reached the port from which the Egyptian king had once sent out the Phoenicians" to circumnavigate Africa? Many in modern times have doubted the truth of the story, objecting that the expedition should not have taken more than a year at the most and that, in any case, the magnitude of the exploit made it very unlikely of accomplishment by a Mediterranean Greek without any previous knowledge of the great Indian rivers

[10] Cf. R. G. Kent, *op. cit.*, p. 107, item DB.
[11] *Ibid.*, p. 136, item 2; p. 138, item 3.

or the even greater Indian Ocean and Arabian Sea, and with nothing to steer by except a conviction that, if he held to the coast, he must ultimately reach Egypt.

Yet here Darius himself rises from the dead to bring testimony for the man he sent exploring.

Through the centuries and until quite recent times there stood, not far from the present canal (it is now more safely stored in the garden of the tiny museum at Ismailia on the Suez Canal), a granite stele with an inscription in Egyptian hieroglyphic on one face and on the other a series of cuneiform inscriptions in the ancient languages of Elam, Babylon, and Persia. Of these, the version in Old Persian, after a grandiloquent preamble, reads in translation as follows:

> I am Darius the Great King, king of kings, king of countries of all kinds of men, king of this great earth, far and wide. . . .
>
> Says Darius the King: I am a Persian, son of a Persian, an Achaemenian. From Persia I seized Egypt. I gave command to dig this canal from the river named Nile, that flows through Egypt, to the sea which extends from Persia. After this canal was dug even as I had ordered, ships went from Egypt through this canal to Persia, as was my desire.[12]

There is, of course, no mention here of Skylax. But inasmuch as the stele stood about where the Phoenicians who circumnavigated Africa had set out on their voyage, and as it is not likely that there was ever any frequent communication between Egypt and Persia by sea in the time of King Darius, it is at least arguable that (even though we hear nothing of Skylax returning from Egypt to Persia to report to his royal master the results of his great voyage of exploration) it was Skylax on whom the Persian king's bombastic self-glorification relied to make true his boast that in his reign "ships went from Egypt to Persia," as was his desire. In any case and however we judge this matter, in view of the Suez stele it cannot be maintained that a voyage such as Skylax is said to have made would have been impossible in the days of Darius.

Much more detail has come down to us out of antiquity about a repetition of Skylax's exploit nearly two centuries later, performed under identical circumstances of royal command to satisfy imperial curiosity. On this occasion it was Alexander the

[12] Paraphrased from *ibid.*, p. 147, item 3.

Great who, having acquired by conquest the whole vast Persian empire, found himself in much the same situation as Darius before him, being (like Darius) interested to define the boundaries of his realm and explore its commercial and political potential. So, precisely as Darius had done, Alexander dispatched ships under a tried navigator to make their way down the Indus River and trace the ocean margin of his newly acquired continental possessions.

But where Herodotus could devote only a paragraph of summary notice to Skylax because he had only oral and unofficial report to go on, the late-Roman historian Arrian, in compiling his chronicle of Alexander's conquest of the Persian empire, excerpted page after page of the published account that had been written by the explorer himself in such ample detail as to make Arrian's *Indica* the best authenticated eyewitness narrative of any exploratory expedition that has survived from classical antiquity.

The voyage here in question was under command of a well-trusted aide to Alexander, named Nearchus. Since he was an important figure in Alexander's entourage, a good deal is known about him. He was born on the island of Crete, but moved to Amphipolis in eastern Macedonia, perhaps as a soldier of fortune. There he came under the notice and into the friendship of the crown prince of that northern half-Greek land, the youthful Alexander. For reasons not recorded, Alexander's father Philip, the Macedonian king, sent him into exile. But when Philip died and Alexander succeeded to power, the fortunes of Nearchus took a decided turn for the better. Not long after his accession, Alexander commenced his great career of conquest directed against the Persian empire. As, one after another, Alexander deposed and expelled the Persian governors (the so-called satraps) of the various regions of Asia Minor, he replaced them with members of his own staff or other associates. In this way Nearchus came to be appointed satrap of Lycia, a seaboard Mediterranean province where his familiarity with ships and knowledge of naval matters could have been turned to account. But his administrative post seems to have stranded him temporarily in Alexander's wake, so that he probably had no part in the overthrow of the Persian monarch, Darius III (also titled Codomannos). It is some time before we hear of Nearchus again.

But after Babylon had been occupied, and the Persian capital of Susa taken and the great palace at Persepolis burned, and Alexander had marched to the Caspian Sea in pursuit of the fugitive Darius and, after that king's murder by a treacherous subject monarch, had captured and put to death this latest pretender to the Persian throne—after all these stirring events, when Alexander was wintering in northern Afghanistan with an army depleted by battle and long marches and the vicissitudes of campaigning in wild mountainous lands, he sent back word to Nearchus and a neighboring Greek satrap to recruit reinforcements in Asia Minor and march them out to him in Bactria.

Apart from a minor operation in which Nearchus was sent in command of light troops to scout the country, to capture natives for questioning, and in particular to discover whether the rumor was true that the enemy ruler's brother was hiding in the hills with his elephants, there is no record of the part that Nearchus took in Alexander's campaigns on the Indian front. But after Alexander had succeeded in crossing the Indus River and most of its sizable tributaries in the Punjab, but hesitated to march farther beyond the Persian empire's long-established frontiers (he never reached the Ganges or, for that matter, ever penetrated any distance at all into the country that is now India as distinct from Pakistan!), it is then that Nearchus suddenly comes to the forefront of attention.

The invading Greeks were greatly surprised and somewhat appalled at the number and huge size of the Indian rivers, in comparison with which their own short rivers, and even the Nile and the Danube, seemed very minor streams. Now, to the Greek way of thinking, large rivers constituted natural boundaries for countries and continents. Herodotus records a current notion that the Nile was the dividing line between Asia and Africa. Although he objected to this as unrealistic, he agreed that the Russian river Don was the boundary between Asia and Europe. In Roman thought, the Rhine and the Danube were territorial demarcations imposed by Nature on man—and this not merely because they were inconvenient to cross and convenient to defend. Similarly, Darius seems to have accepted the Indus River as defining the eastward limit to his empire. Alexander, however, was unwilling to admit any limitation to conquest, short of the all-confining Ocean. But when his troops to-

gether with their commanders resisted his ambition to penetrate
farther the vast Indian plainland, he was forced reluctantly to
accept the rivers of the Punjab for his boundaries of empire.
Aware that the time had come for turning back to his Persian
capital, he planned to complete the trace of his newly acquired
domains by following their bounding rivers to their ending in
the sea and thence to track the coast which that sea confined,
until sea and land together led back to his starting point of
Susa and Persepolis. To conduct this nautical survey by commanding and guiding a flotilla down the Punjab rivers and the
Indus to the Arabian Sea and thence coasting through that sea
westward into the Persian Gulf—this was the difficult task for
which Nearchus volunteered. Alexander had by this time
thought better of his idea (recorded below) that the Indus must
be the upper Nile and would lead him around to Nubia and so
to Egypt and the Mediterranean. But more correct information
about the nature and career of the Indian rivers must have left
him even more uncertain how one could sail from the Punjab
to Persepolis. Not so (we may guess) felt Nearchus, if he had
read and remembered the famous *History* of Herodotus. As a
recent writer remarks:

> If Nearchus, on the strength of what he had read in Herod-
> otus, believed the voyage of Skylax to be an historical fact, his
> readiness to accept command of this enterprise is easier to
> understand. It appears from his narrative that Alexander and
> almost everybody else regarded the expedition by sea as a
> desperate venture; but if Nearchus believed Skylax had ac-
> complished his task, he might well think himself able to do what
> Alexander wanted—which was not to repeat the voyage of
> Skylax but to do something different and easier; not to sail
> from India to Egypt, but from India into the Persian Gulf.[13]

Alexander decided to take his army in company with Nearchus' flotilla down the Indus valley to the coast and thence to
return to Persia by keeping as close to the sea as might be practicable, while Nearchus sailed a parallel course to the same distant goal. Far up on one of the main tributaries of the Indus
(known to Arrian as the Hydaspes and in modern parlance as
the Jhelum),

[13] Lionel Pearson, *The Lost Histories of Alexander the Great* ("Philological
Monograph," No. 20) (N. Y.: American Philological Association, 1960), pp. 140–1.

Alexander had already equipped himself with many thirty-oared and one-and-a-half-banked vessels, as well as transports for horses and other craft useful for moving an army by river. With these he determined to sail down the Hydaspes to the Great Sea.

Now, he had earlier seen crocodiles in the Indus but in no other river except the Nile; and on the banks of the Acesines [14] he saw beans [15] growing like those which the Egyptian land produces; and on hearing that the Acesines runs into the Indus, he thought that he had discovered the sources of the Nile! . . . And indeed, in a letter to his mother, Olympias, describing the country of India, he wrote among other things that he had found the springs of the Nile. However, when he had more accurately informed himself about the Indus River and learned from the natives that the Hydaspes joins its waters with the Acesines and this in turn with the Indus (to which both of these relinquish their names) and that the Indus actually empties into the ocean through two mouths and has no connection whatever with Egypt, he canceled that part of his letter to his mother concerning the Nile.

So then, with intent of navigating these rivers all the way to the ocean, he gave orders for the ships to be made ready. And the crews for the ships were recruited from the Phoenicians, Cyprians, Carians, and Egyptians accompanying his army. . . .

He appointed Nearchus admiral of the entire fleet. The total number of ships was eighty thirty-oar vessels and, with the transports and light galleys and whatever other rivercraft had been plying the rivers or been then constructed, was not far short of two thousand.[16]

Arrian quotes from Nearchus' published account a stirring picture of the setting forth of the great fleet on its long journey to the sea:

When everything had been made ready, the army began at dawn to embark on the ships, while Alexander made sacrifice to the gods as was his wont, and to the river Hydaspes as the soothsayers instructed him. Then, himself going aboard, he poured from the ship's bow a libation from a golden bowl into the river, calling by name upon the Acesines along with the Hydaspes . . . and upon the Indus into which these flow. Then

[14] Modern Chenab.
[15] I.e., lotus?
[16] Arrian, *Anabasis of Alexander*, VI.i.1–6; ii.3–4.

he poured a libation to Heracles, his own ancestor, and to Ammon, and to the customary gods, and gave order for the bugle to sound departure.

Never was there a sound like that of the fleet rowing all together, with the coxswains crying the strokes and the oarsmen chanting as they struck the swirling water in unison. . . . The horses caused amazement in the natives who beheld them aboard the transports (for no horses had ever been seen on ships in India); so that the natives who had been present at the embarcation followed a long way, while those whom the shouts of the rowers and the beat of the oars attracted, came running down to the riverbank and followed along, singing their native strains.[17]

Needless to say, Alexander's two hundred elephants followed afoot by land; and it appears from Arrian's account that the bulk of the army similarly made its way down either bank of the Jhelum. No doubt, the going was easier for those embarked on the ships; but even for these the voyage was not without its excitements and perils. The confluence of the Jhelum with the even greater stream of the Chenab made a great impression on all concerned:

Where these two rivers join, there results a single stream with swift currents through a narrows and terrific whirlpools where the water surges and boils mightily. So great was the roar of the rapids that when the army drew near the junction of the rivers the oarsmen stopped rowing, not by command but because the coxswains were struck dumb with amazement and the rowers were overwhelmed by the noise. But when they were close, the steersmen bade them lay to their oars with full strength so that the ships might not be caught and upset in the whirlpools. The barges that were whirled around by the current suffered no damage in turning about, though their passengers were greatly alarmed. But the long ships did not come off equally unscathed because they did not ride as high over the swirling waves. Those with two banks of oars had difficulty in keeping the lower bank clear of the water, and their oars were snapped as the boats turned broadside on the stream. Many ships were in trouble, and two actually collided and were wrecked, with the loss of many of their crews.[18]

[17] *Ibid.*, VI.iii.1–2; 3; 4–5.
[18] *Ibid.*, VI.iv.4–v.3.

After laying up for repairs and overhauling, the fleet continued down the combined Jhelum and Chenab toward their junction with the Ravi River. As the army advanced, much of it on shipboard but more along the riverbanks on foot, on horse, and on elephant, Alexander

> sent Nearchos on ahead with the fleet, bidding him keep three days in advance of the main force in the descent of the river.[19]

Such a disposition might seem to presage a speedy culmination for the long journey to the sea. But the sea was still distant five hundred miles or more; and Alexander, with his usual restless energy, found opportunity to engage in punitive expeditions and campaigns of subjugation and destruction in the surrounding countryside. On one of these, with foolhardy courage, he scaled a city wall and leapt ahead and alone into the midst of its defenders, very nearly at the loss of his life; for he was grievously wounded and carried away unconscious. So it transpires that, many chapters later in Arrian's history of Alexander, we find Nearchus and the fleet no farther along than the junction of the Chenab and the Ravi rivers, where a sort of general headquarters camp and gathering place had been constructed.

Thither Alexander was conveyed by ship down the Ravi River, preceded by the alarming rumor that he had been killed in battle. Grief and despair swept through the camp

> as one told the report to another. They despaired how to get back safely to their own lands, shut in as they were by so many warlike nations and believing that they were in between impassable rivers; so that every prospect seemed to them helpless and hopeless if they were bereft of Alexander. . . .
>
> As the ship on which the king lay drew near the camp where Nearchus had his fleet, the troops even then continued to believe that it was Alexander's dead body that was being brought; but at length, when the ship touched shore, Alexander held up his hand toward the crowd, which shouted aloud, holding up its hands to heaven. Some of his bodyguard brought a litter as he was being lifted ashore; but he bade them lead him his horse. When he had mounted, such a tumult of clapping and shouting arose that the very banks and the nearby copses reechoed the uproar.[20]

[19] *Ibid.,* VI.v.5.
[20] *Ibid.,* VI.xii.1–2; xiii.1–3.

During all these adventures and misadventures Nearchus had been doing little more than biding his time at the river station. But now,

> when all had been set in order and a large number of additional craft had been constructed during the term of Alexander's recovery from his wound, he embarked seventeen hundred cavalry of his companions together with the previous number of light-armed troops and up to ten thousand footsoldiers, and with these sailed down the Hydraotes [21] the short distance to its junction with the Acesines and so to the junction where the four great navigable rivers pour their combined waters into the Indus. . . .
>
> At this point there joined Alexander some additional thirty-oar ships and transports that had been built for him among the Xathrians, another Indian tribe that had come over to him. . . .
>
> Then Alexander had Craterus, with the main part of the army and all the elephants, ferried over to the left bank of the Indus . . . and he himself sailed down toward the royal city of the Sogdians. There he built and fortified a new city and built more dockyards for refitting whatever of his ships had suffered damage.[22]

And so, after still more incidents of the familiar heroic and destructive sort, the great expedition came at last to the peak of the great delta where the Indus divided and sent two great branches to the sea.

Alexander himself was eager to look upon the Indian Ocean, which Nature had set as his empire's southern boundary; and so,

> taking the swiftest sailing ships and those of one-and-a-half banks of oars and all the thirty-oar ships and some of the light boats, he sailed down the right-hand branch of the river. But as he had no pilot, all the Indians of those parts having decamped, the voyage proved to be full of difficulties. On the day after they set out, a storm arose and the wind blew contrary to the river current, making troughs wherein the craft were shaken, so that most of the ships were damaged and some of the thirty-oar vessels completely came asunder.[23]

Replacements were built and the trip to the sea was again

[21] Today known as the Ravi.
[22] Arrian, *Anabasis of Alexander,* VI.xiv.4–5; xv.1; xv.4.
[23] *Ibid.,* VI.xviii.3–4.

attempted, with captured natives for pilots and no repetition of
disaster, except that the southwest monsoon was still blowing
strong. The flotilla took refuge in a side channel away from the
open sea, and there

> they anchored; whereupon there ensued the usual event in the
> Great Sea, the ebbing of the tide, with the result that the
> entire fleet was left stranded. Now this was something of which
> Alexander's company had no previous knowledge, so that it
> caused them great bewilderment. But they were yet more sur-
> prised when after the normal interval the sea advanced again
> and the ships were floated. As the tide rushed in all at once,
> those of the ships that lay keeled over on harder bottom were
> knocked together or hurled against the land and staved in.
> These Alexander repaired as best he could.[24]

In time, Alexander succeeded in passing through the several
mouths of the river as he sought to discover the readiest channels
to the sea and satisfy his ambition "to have sailed on the Great
Ocean outside the Indies."

It was now Nearchus' turn to take command and set out with
his task force of the great fleet for the long journey from India
to Persia. But before he was given the word to put out to the
open sea, Alexander sent a force on foot along the coast westward "to dig wells, that there might be water for the fleet as they
sailed past," [25] and gave instructions for provisions to be stored
at convenient points ashore.

But, all being now ready, Nearchus could not set sail because
the southwest monsoon was still blowing contrary from the open
sea. Not until late autumn does its counter wind, the northeast
monsoon, descend from the Himalayas to blow across the Indian
plains and the Arabian Sea to the East African coast. Meanwhile
Alexander had begun his homeward march through the arid
wilds of southern Baluchistan, a retreat (to my thinking) more
terrible than Napoleon's from Moscow, with intense heat and
drought and hunger in place of heavy cold and snow and
famine. But it is not with this ordeal (which, perhaps, deserves
to be included in this volume as exploration of a sort, whatever
its immediate motive) but with Nearchus' reopening of the

[24] *Ibid.*, VI.xix.1–2.
[25] *Ibid.*, VI.xx.4.

waterway between the Indian Orient and the West that the present chapter is concerned.

Nearchus' expedition was not intended merely as a convenient method of shipping troops and military supplies and booty back to Persia. It was to be also a serious geographical enterprise. Arrian specifically defines its purposes as Alexander formulated them to Nearchus:

> To explore the coasts en route for their harbors and islets and inlets and whatever towns were along them, and to note which regions were fertile and which were uncultivated.[26]

Nearchus therefore rates not only as a naval commander but as a true Explorer.

To trace his itinerary in detail, as Arrian records it, would not be profitable. The headlands and bays and beaches and other features of the coast, as listed and described, have almost all been successfully identified on modern charts of the Arabian Sea's borderlands in Baluchistan and southern Iran; but the modern names would scarcely be more significant to the Western reader than the ancient ones in the Greek text. (Nearchus has greatly exaggerated point-to-point distances, but otherwise seems to have kept an accurate log.) Fortunately for what might otherwise have been only a topographical gazetteer of unattractive and wholly unfamiliar country, Nearchus possessed a lively sense for *incidents de voyage* with sufficient literary talent to work them up attractively. The most picturesque of these excursive interludes are herewith assembled, divorced from the bleak background of desolate and savage countryside against which they are sketched:

1. Nearchus' men, inured to the notion that boats are propelled by oars pivoted on fixed tholes, get their first sight of a native dugout being paddled by the Fisheaters:

> Here there dwelt fishermen, and their boats were small and wretched. They did not row them with oars against an oarlock in the Greek manner, but as though scooping up water in a river, this way and that, like men shoveling earth.[27]

2. Whales are sighted blowing—startling and very frightening behavior of swimming monsters:

[26] Arrian, *Indica*, 32.11; and in much the same terms, *Anabasis of Alexander*, VII.xx.10.
[27] *Ibid.*, 27.5.

On leaving Cyiza about daybreak, water was seen being blown upward from the sea as though from bellows. In amazement the men inquired of the pilots of the fleet what this might be and what was its cause. These replied that they were whales floating about on the sea and blowing the water aloft. But the sailors were so startled that the oars fell from their hands.

Nearchus, however, moved through the fleet, exhorting it to be of good courage; and as he passed a vessel he gave order to turn the ship bow on, as in a naval engagement, and row at the monsters with rapid stroke, all shouting together. At this they took heart and rowed in unison, and, as they approached the monsters, they shouted their heads off and splashed their utmost with their oars, while the bugles blared. At that the whales, visible now beneath the very bows of the ships, took fright and dove to the bottom, only to come to the surface not long afterward astern and again blow high their spouting. At this there was applause among the sailors at their unlooked-for salvation, and great praise of Nearchus for his courage and intelligence.

Occasionally whales are stranded on various parts of the coast by being caught in the shallows at ebb tide, while others are cast up on dry land by heavy storms. As a result they perish and rot and their flesh falls away, leaving their bones for men to use for their houses. The larger ribs make the beams for their dwellings; the smaller ones, the rafters; while the jawbones serve as doorframes. For many of these whales are as much as a 150 feet long.[28]

All this refers to the open sea. Considerably later in the voyage, well up toward the head of the Persian Gulf,

a whale was sighted stranded on the beach. Some of the sailors worked their way up to it and measured it. They said it was 135 feet long.[29]

3. Earlier in the voyage, folklore superstition created a weird adventure. About midway between the mouth of the Indus and the entrance to the Persian Gulf, rumor reached the fleet

about an island lying some ten miles offshore and uninhabited. The natives said it was sacred to the sun and that no human being was willing to put in at it, since whoever in ignorance did so, vanished utterly. One of the lighter vessels in the fleet,

28 *Ibid.*, 30.2–9.
29 *Ibid.*, 39.4.

carrying an Egyptian crew, disappeared while close to the island; whereupon the native pilots insisted that it had unwittingly touched the shore and thereby been made to vanish. Hereupon Nearchus despatched a thirty-oar ship around the island, with orders not to land but to have the sailors, on approaching as near as they dared, call out the name of the steersman [of the lost vessel] and of anyone of the crew known to them. No one replied. Then Nearchus himself sailed up to the island and compelled his crew against their will to put in. He himself went ashore, thereby proving the story about the island to be empty fairytale.[30]

No doubt the other members of the expedition should properly have reasoned that the Egyptian boat must have struck a reef and foundered with all hands lost. But superstition is not so easily dispelled or so cavalierly dismissed from human minds. An alternative story about the island was promptly circulated, to the effect that men *used* to disappear on landing. This was due to the guile of a certain mermaid who once abode there:

> Her name was unknown; but she was quick to consort with any sailor who neared the isle; after which she transformed him into a fish and threw him into the sea. The Sun grew annoyed at the mermaid's doings and ordered her to quit the isle. To this she agreed, on condition that he heal her of her tendencies. The Sun consented and taking pity on the men she had turned into fishes, turned them back into men. It is from these men (they said) that the present native race of the Fisheaters is descended.[31]

Monotonous desert aridity, with its attendant discouragements to mind and body, suddenly gave way to joy at the sight of shorelands green with trees and bushes and vines as the fleet sailed from the broad Gulf of Oman into the narrowing Strait of Ormuz, which bends around an enormous peninsula of Arabia into the long Persian Gulf. Conditions do not seem to have changed much through the centuries. In the year 325 B.C. Nearchus moored his fleet by the mouth of a river called Anamis in a district known as Harmozia.

> Pleasant it was, with fruits of every kind, save that olive trees did not grow there. Then they went ashore from the ships and

30 *Ibid.*, 31.1–5.
31 *Ibid.*, 31.6–8.

rested gladly from their many tribulations, recalling to mind how many ills they had suffered at sea and along the Fish-eaters' coast, how desolate the land, how barbarous its inhabitants, thus to one another recounting their past miseries.[32]

Near at hand lay a small, wild, and uninhabited island and, within a day's sail, another much larger one, on which men dwelt. One thousand six hundred and fifty years after Nearchus' brief sojourn there, this region was still to bear its ancient name, barely altered into Hormuz. The little wild island had become the site of a fabulous trading center, likewise known as Hormuz (or Ormuz), frequented by Portuguese and English merchants as a great marketplace for exchange of the rich products of India and Persia. Today its glory is gone, its seawalls crumbled, its stout fort in ruin. A late-nineteenth-century visitor noted, "five rusty old iron guns lying on the roof; six others on the strand before the modern village are used for fastening boats, and another serves as socket for a flagstaff." Nearchus' men saw even less of human enterprise in these parts when they landed and roamed about, rejoicing in the fertility of a friendly land.

Here there befell them an incident that—at least as Nearchus wrote it up and Arrian transmitted it—is one of the most vividly and picturesquely recounted stories preserved from classical literature. Since it is not only celebrated but eminently readable, it follows here in full:

> Some of the men went inland from the sea, scattering from camp in search of this and that. Here there appeared to them a man wearing a Greek cloak and otherwise arrayed in Greek manner. Those who first caught sight of him said that they broke into tears, so unexpected did it seem to them after so many ills to see a Greek and hear the Greek tongue. They asked him who he was and whence he came. He said that he had wandered away from Alexander's encampment and that this was not far away and Alexander himself was at it. Shouting and clapping their hands they led him to Nearchus; and he told Nearchus everything—that the camp and the king were distant five days' journey from the sea and that he would show Nearchus the local governor of the region. This he did; and Nearchus consulted with him how he should go inland to the king.
>
> Then they returned to the ships; and these he caused on the

next day at dawn to be drawn up on the beach for overhauling of those which had suffered damage on the trip, and also because he had decided to leave most of his force there [while he went in search of Alexander]. So he constructed a double stockade around the ships' emplacement consisting of a mud wall and a deep trench beginning from the riverbank and continuing to the beach where the ships had been drawn ashore.

While Nearchus was arranging all this, the governor of the district, being aware that Alexander entertained the greatest concern about the expedition, presumed that he himself would get some great reward from Alexander if he were the first to announce the safety of Nearchus and his fleet and bring him word that he would shortly arrive in the king's presence. So he rides off by the shortest road and announces to Alexander that "Nearchus is here, on his way from the ships." Although Alexander did not altogether believe the report, he was naturally pleased at the news. But when day after day passed and calculation of the time since receipt of the message suggested that its content could not be true, and from the relays sent out to bring in Nearchus some went only a short distance on the road and came back without having encountered anyone, while others, although advancing farther, failed to meet Nearchus and his party and so also returned empty-handed—then Alexander orders the man arrested for bringing false report and making evil matters worse with vain encouragement. He himself showed in his countenance and his conversation how deeply he was distressed.

Now in the meantime some of those who had been sent in search of Nearchus with horses and wagons for conveying him did actually come upon Nearchus himself and Archias and five or six companions on the road; but they failed to recognize either Nearchus or Archias, so altered were their looks, what with their long hair, their filthy garments coated with brine, their shrunken limbs, their countenances sallow from sleeplessness and suffering. So, when these inquired where Alexander might be found, the search party made answer and started on. But a thought struck Archias and he says to Nearchus, "Nearchus, I opine that these men here are traveling the same desert road as we for no other purpose than because they have been sent out in search of us! I am not surprised that they did not recognize us, since we are in such a state that no one would know who we are. Let us tell them; and let us ask them for what reason they are traveling." This seemed reasonable to Nearchus, so they asked them whither they were bound. And they replied, "In search of Nearchus and his fleet." "But," says he, "*I* am Nearchus! and this is Archias. Come, show us the way and we shall give Alexander our report on the expeditionary force."

So they took them on their wagons and drove back. But some of their number, wishing to be beforehand with the news, ran ahead and told Alexander, "Nearchus is here! And Archias is with him, and five others are being brought to you." About the rest of the fleet, however, they were unable to make reply. At this Alexander conceived the idea that these few had been unaccountably preserved, but all the rest of the expeditionary force had perished. In consequence he was not so much rejoiced at the salvation of Nearchus and Archias as he was grieved at the loss of all his forces. But hardly had all this been said when Nearchus and Archias came up. It was only with the greatest difficulty that Alexander recognized them; and because he beheld them unshorn and ill arrayed, he was all the more convinced in his grief for the entire navy. Clasping Nearchus' right hand, he led him aside from his royal companions and his bodyguard, and for a long time he wept. At length recovering himself, "But that you at least and Archias here are come back safe to us is some assuagement of the whole disaster. But the ships and the army, in what manner were they lost?" But he replied saying, "O king, the ships are safe and the army too. We whom you see are come to announce their salvation." At this Alexander wept even more, inasmuch as the saving of the entire force was so unexpected.

"And where," he asked, "are the ships?"

"They are at the mouth of the river Anamis," he replied, "beached for refitting."

Thereupon Alexander called upon Zeus of the Greeks and Ammon of the Africans, swearing by these that he had more joy of this announcement than of his own return with all Asia conquered.

But the district governor whom Alexander had arrested for bringing false tidings, when he beheld Nearchus in the king's presence, fell at his feet, saying, "I am he who reported to Alexander your safe arrival. See now how I have fared!" On this, Nearchus besought Alexander to release the man; and he was let go.

Then Alexander made sacrificial thank-offerings for the preservation of his force, to Zeus the Preserver and to Heracles and Apollo, Averter-of-Evil, and Poseidon and all the other divinities of the sea, and held athletic games and lyric contests and a triumphal procession, with Nearchus in the front rank, showered by the army with ribbons and flowers.[33]

Alexander was inclined to call Nearchus' task accomplished and to send someone else to bring the fleet the rest of the way through the Persian Gulf to Susa. But Nearchus begged to be permitted to complete what he had begun and not be required to relinquish to another the easy ending of a difficult task. To this Alexander agreed. So Nearchus, not without trouble from unfriendly natives along the way, returned to the fleet and there made due sacrifice to Zeus the Preserver.

There was still before him the five-hundred-mile voyage along the Persian coast to the head of the Gulf. But this was accomplished without noteworthy event or untoward incident. The shoreland proved to be abundantly supplied with provisions for the fleet, and its inhabitants had become amenable to Alexander's rule. When at length the expedition reached the mouth of the Euphrates, Nearchus learned that Alexander had not yet advanced as far as Susa. Accordingly he did not continue upriver to Babylon, but crossed the head of the Gulf to a lesser but readily navigable river with the picturesque name of Pasitigris, now known as the Karun, on which the fleet was able to ascend until it reached the pontoon bridge prepared for the crossing of Alexander and his land army to the royal capital of Susa.

So ends the story of Nearchus.

There was to have been an epilogue in the shape of a supplementary naval expedition planned by Alexander to explore the entire seacoast of the Arabian peninsula, from the head of the Persian Gulf to the head of the Red Sea. Some preliminary reconnaissance seems to have already been made of the western shore of the Persian Gulf. Nearchus, it will be remembered, had followed its *eastern* or Persian shore and barely caught glimpse of its Arabian counterpart while passing through the narrows of the Straits of Ormuz. At that time an argument had arisen between the admiral and his head pilot:

> They sighted a great headland projecting far out into the sea, perhaps a day's journey distant from them. Those conversant with the region said that the headland was part of

[33] *Ibid.*, 33.4–36.3.

Arabia. . . . Now, when they sighted this promontory, Onesicritus [the pilot] ordered the course to be laid toward it, in order
to avoid the trouble of circumnavigating the entire circuit of
the gulf. But Nearchus replied that Onesicritus was silly in
thus misunderstanding the purpose for which the expedition
had been sent out by Alexander, which was to reconnoitre the
coast en route with its roadsteads and isles and follow around
every inlet or gulf, to ascertain what seaboard towns there might
be and whether the land was fertile or desert.[34]

This is the clearest statement of Alexander's interest in geographical exploration. It is beside the point that Arrian, in
reporting it, seems to have missed the point of the debate between Nearchus and his head steersman. A glance at the map
will show that the Strait of Ormuz swings in a great half-circle
around the jutting Arabian promontory, which Arrian called
Maketa and the modern charts Cape Musandan. Onesicritus'
suggestion was that it would be much shorter to cut directly
across past this cape than to hug the Persian shore around the
great loop (on the simple geometrical proposition that the diameter is less than the perimeter). Arrian seems to have misunderstood the issue, imagining that Onesicritus was suddenly
agog to explore Arabia instead of confining himself to Persia.
And perhaps Nearchus suffered under the same misapprehen-
sion. In any event, the report of the mysterious Arabian headland—sighted in the distance but left unexplored—seems to have
fired Alexander's imagination and incited him to plan a new
expedition to probe its Arabian setting.

Graphically, the Arabian peninsula is shaped somewhat like a
broken isosceles triangle, with its apex at Aden and the side
fronting the Arabian Sea of equal length with that on the Red
Sea. Neither Alexander nor any of his advisers had any correct
notion of the vastness of its dimensions, but seem to have
thought that, once the headland of Maketa had been rounded,
the entrance to the Red Sea would not be far away. Strangely,
although Arrian composed his history in an age when the
southern coast of Arabia had become abundantly familiar to
shipmasters trading with India and farther east, he reproduced
without comment or correction Nearchus' confession of ignorance about this region, saying,

[34] *Ibid.*, 32.8–11.

From the Arabian Gulf along Egypt [35] men have set out intending to circumnavigate the bulk of Arabia in order to reach
the sea opposite Susa and the Persian land; and it is true that
these have succeeded in voyaging along the Arabian coast as
far as the supply of fresh water aboard their ships held out. But
then they always turned back. [In the opposite direction] those
whom Alexander sent out from Babylon to explore the right-
hand [36] shore of the Persian Gulf as far as they could sail,
sighted various islands lying on their course and touched here
and there on the mainland. But no one ever succeeded in
doubling the cape which Nearchus saw jutting out opposite
Carmania.[37]

There were several attempts made at Alexander's bidding:

Archias was sent out with a thirty-oar ship to explore the coast
of the gulf on the Arabian side. He got as far as the island of
Tylus; [38] but he ventured no farther. Next, Androsthenes was
dispatched, also with a thirty-oar ship; and he skirted somewhat
[more] of the peninsula of Arabia. But of all those who were
sent out, the pilot Hiero from Soli went the farthest. He
too had been assigned a thirty-oar ship by Alexander, with orders
to circumnavigate the entire Arabian peninsula as far as the
Egyptian Gulf at Heropolis.[39] Even so, although he passed
along most of the Arabian shore [of the Persian Gulf], he had
not the courage to continue, but turned back and reported to
Alexander that the peninsula was enormous—not much smaller,
indeed, than India!—and that a headland of it jutted far out
into the ocean. This was, of course, the same that Nearchus'
fleet on its way from India had sighted close at hand as they
turned into the Persian Gulf.[40]

But when Alexander died of fever in Babylon, all plans for
further explorations were abandoned. For the better part of two
centuries thereafter the outer shore of Arabia remained an
unknown land, until the expansion of Egyptian foreign trade
under the Greek Ptolemies and the reuse of the Nile–Red Sea
canal brought India within range of Mediterranean shipping.

[35] I.e., from the Red Sea.
[36] I.e., western.
[37] Present-day Kerman.
[38] Today, under the name of Bahrein, familiar to all who traffic in oil.
[39] The terminus of the canal from Bubastis on the Nile.
[40] Arrian, *Anabasis of Alexander*, VII.20.7–9.

But if Strabo's account may be trusted, actual connection between Orient and Occident was first made more by accident than design. Eudoxus of Cyzicus has already appeared in these pages in connection with the exploration of the West African coast, where he and his ship met an unknown fate. But previous to his ill-starred final venture in the west, Eudoxus had made two successful voyages in the east. Strabo (drawing on Posidonius, who ought to have been correctly informed on this) tells the story as follows:

> Eudoxus came to Egypt during the reign of [Ptolemy] Euergetes II,[41] having been recommended to the king and his court, particularly in connection with expeditions up the Nile (for he was an educated man and greatly interested in local geography). Now it so happened that an Indian was brought before the king by the Egyptian frontier guards of the Arabian Gulf, who said that they had come upon him half-dead and stranded alone on his ship, but did not know who he was or whence he came, since they could not understand his language. The king gave him over into the charge of men who were to teach him Greek; and when he had learned the language, he told them about his voyage, how on his journey from India he had strayed from the proper course and only reached Egypt after losing all his shipmates through starvation. His tale being disbelieved, he agreed to act as pilot to India for any party appointed by the king; and Eudoxus was made one of the company.
>
> So Eudoxus sailed off with a cargo of presents and returned, bringing back spices and precious stones; but he was cheated of his hopes when Euergetes took away the entire cargo.
>
> On the death of Euergetes his widow Cleopatra succeeded to the throne; and by her Eudoxus was again sent out, this time with even greater equipment. On his return journey from India the winds carried him off course beyond Ethiopia and brought him to a region where, by sharing his bread and wine and dried fruit with the natives (who had none of these commodities), he won them over to supplying him with drinking water and pilots to guide him on his way. Incidentally, he made a list of some of the words of their speech.
>
> Now, he had come upon the wooden figurehead of a wrecked vessel, carved as a horse. Being informed that this was a bit of flotsam from a sea voyage undertaken from the west, he took

---

[41] This is Ptolemy VII, who reigned from 145 to 116 B.C.

it with him when he turned home. He arrived safely in Egypt; but with Cleopatra no longer ruling, but her son reigning in her stead, everything was again taken from him, on the ground that he had dishonestly appropriated to himself much of the cargo. But he kept the figurehead and showed it to the ship-masters in the marketplace and learned from these that it came from Gades. For (he was told) whereas the merchants there equip large vessels, the poorer classes fit out small ones, called "horses" from the devices at their prows. With these they sail on fishing trips along the Moroccan coast as far as the Lixus river. And some of the shipowners even pretended that they recognized that particular figurehead as belonging to a certain vessel that had ventured too far beyond the Lixus river and never returned! Eudoxus concluded from this that the circumnavigation of Africa must be possible. So he went home,[42] put all his property into the venture, and set out. He sailed first to Dicaearchia,[43] next to Massilia, and thence along the coast to Gades, every-where crying abroad his project and amassing funds.[44]

The rest of the story, as Strabo recounts it, has already been told in Chapter III. There it was related how, on his second attempt to reach India by the western passage that was to take him direct to the Arabian Sea without Egyptian interference, he and his ship vanished without trace—"though perhaps (added Posidonius) those at Gades and in Spain may know something about him!"

It was not Egypt under the Ptolemies nor Hellenistic Greece under its kings, but imperial Rome that occasioned the full and final opening up of the Orient to shipborne commerce. The situation is so well summarized by Cary and Warmington that it would be idle to rewrite here what they have so well written elsewhere:

> The new conditions of peace and security which rose under the monarchy of Augustus fostered a fresh spirit of enterprise. The compelling motive of exploration was an unmixed love of gain [arising] from the rapid growth of wealth in Rome and the western provinces, which led to a demand for oriental luxuries on a scale unknown before. The Romans did not participate directly in the eastern trade, which they left in

[42] To Cyzicus, on the Black Sea.
[43] In the Bay of Naples.
[44] Strabo, *Geography*, II.3.4.

the hands of Greeks and others, but they backed the Greek merchants with their prestige and eventually also with their capital. Greek seafarers therefore showed a new readiness to make long journeys into the unknown East.

Clear evidence of this renewed enterprise is furnished by Strabo, who informs us that in the reign of Augustus as many as 120 ships would put out in a single year from [the Red Sea ports of] Myos Hormos and Berenice for North-East Africa and India and that some even sailed as far as the Ganges. In the reign of the same emperor we find the first embassies passing between India and Rome. . . . The evidence of literature and archaeology alike records a large inflow into the Mediterranean of Arabian, African and Indian products—spices, perfumes, gums, pearls, ivory, woods, precious stones, and so on. The second emperor Tiberius was worried over the fact that Roman money was beginning to leave the empire in quantities in order to pay for the gems and silks beloved by girls and women and even by men.[45] The increased trade with the East under the early Roman emperors was essentially an overseas traffic.[46]

By and large, there was a steady growth in nautical enterprise and expansion of commerce, stepping up the frequency of voyages to the Orient and extending their scope. But for this very reason, because advance was gradual and consecutive, few individual names stand out in the record of Roman expeditions to the Far East. There may have been occasional penetrations of hitherto unvisited regions; yet—with a single exception—we hear of no Great Explorers. The exception was Hippalos.

In the early years of the reign of the emperor Tiberius (which is to say, somewhere about A.D. 20) a Greek merchant-captain of this name Hippalos performed an important voyage of exploration, not in search of any hitherto unknown country, but of a shorter passage across the hitherto untraversed open sea.

It has several times been remarked in earlier chapters that sea voyages in antiquity were nearly always coastal expeditions. For lack of properly oriented and correctly scaled charts based on compass readings, courses laid across open water to distant landmarks could not fail to be uncertain and precarious, whereas

[45] One is reminded of contemporary American worries over the outflow of the nation's gold supply into foreign lands.
[46] M. Cary and E. H. Warmington, *The Ancient Explorers* (Baltimore, Md.: Penguin Books, Inc., 1963), pp. 73–4.

the shoreland was an infallible guide that needed only to be followed to insure attainment of the desired goal. Besides, the cramped facilities of shipboard deterred the ancient navigator from staying out of sight of land: drinkable water, cooked food, and comfortable sleep were all to be sought ashore.

Yet even without correct survey maps to put geographic relations into intelligible and computable form, it must often have been thoroughly apparent to the steersman on a long voyage that the endless ins and outs and changes of sailing direction incident to a coastal journey added needlessly to a distance that might be drastically curtailed by laying a direct course from point to point across the open sea. Nowhere would this consideration have had more force than for the run from the Gulf of Aden to India. In whichever direction the prevailing monsoon might be blowing, it would carry a sailing vessel across the 1,500 or more miles of landless ocean with the certainty of striking the coast of India when heading east, and, if headed west, the continent of Africa. For a ship aiming to visit Ceylon or the Bay of Bengal, the distance of a direct crossing of the Arabian Sea is roughly 2,200 miles; whereas the roundabout coastal route by way of Arabia, Iran, Beluchistan and western India is about 1,000 miles longer—an enormous difference in time, provisions, and human energy.

Hippalos does not seem ever to have attempted the direct sea route to southernmost India, but contented himself with crossing to the vicinity of modern Bombay. Nevertheless, he at least introduced the idea of taking to the high seas beyond the Gulf of Aden and steering eastward thence without further sight of land. Our source of information about him is a remarkable Greek document called *The Periplous of the Erythraean Sea*, whose authorship and date of composition are alike unknown, though the latter is very generally held to have been around A.D. 60 or 70. About the person who compiled it, a modern commentator has remarked:

> That he was not a highly educated man is evident from his frequent confusion of Greek and Latin words and his clumsy and sometimes ungrammatical constructions. The value of his work consists, not in its literary merits, but in its trustworthy account of the trade of the Indian Ocean and of the settlements

around its shores; concerning which, until his time, we possess almost nothing of an intelligent and comprehensive nature.[47]

In the course of a highly detailed description of the coastal route to India and beyond, combined with a listing of an astonishing variety of articles of export thence for the Roman market, the author of the *Periplous* has this to say about Hippalos:

> The entire voyage that I have thus far described used to be made in small vessels following the sinuosities of the land. But the navigator Hippalos, having observed the location of the ports and the configuration of the sea, discovered the course through the open ocean. That is why in the Indian Ocean the trade wind that blows from the high seas about the same time of year as in our regions—but from the southwest—is known as the *hippalos,* taking its name from the original discoverer of the crossing. And from his time until the present day, navigators [bound for India] take off, some from Kanē,[48] others from the Cape of Spices.[49] Those bound for Dimyrica[50] sail more across the wind [?], while those bound for Barygaza and the Scythian land[51] hold the coast for two or three days and then steer much the same course out over the high seas, past the aforementioned gulfs.[52]

From the foregoing passage it is clear that in Imperial Roman times the sea voyage to India was quite a commonplace event. While the political power of Rome extended no farther than the mouth of the Red Sea, Mediterranean commerce had outstripped the march of the Roman legions. With the entire western world at peace under the Antonine emperors of the second century of our era, Mediterranean traders—mainly of Greek and Syro-Phoenician nationality—sailed unmolested across the Arabian Sea to the ancient ports that served commerce in place of modern Karachi, Bombay, Goa, and Calicut, and trafficked freely from the mouth of the Indus (beyond which neither Alexander nor Nearchus had sailed) south to Malabar, Cape Comorin, and Ceylon.

[47] *The Periplous of the Erythraean Sea,* edited and with an introduction by Wilfred H. Schoff (New York: Longmans Green & Co., 1912), p. 16.
[48] On the Arabian Coast, east of Aden.
[49] Now known as Cape Guardafui.
[50] I.e., southwest India.
[51] I.e., northwest India.
[52] *The Periplous of the Erythraean Sea,* Chapter 57.

In connection with the presence of Greek traders in India a passage from Cary and Warmington (partly derived from a source unfamiliar to most scholars) deserves to be quoted here:

> The Greeks, and also Syrian traders in growing numbers, came to know the western coast of India better than ever. Not only did they reside at the ports, but they penetrated inland and visited most of the native rulers at their courts. . . . The Greeks also explored extensively the districts of the Indus with its tributaries and divarications, and inland regions of northern India, whose capital towns were known by name if not visited. . . . We have some interesting details about the visits of Greek merchants to South India in Tamil poems of the second century. We are told that to Muziris the Yavana, that is, the Greeks, brought gold in large ships which beat the water into foam, and exchanged it for pepper which was carried away in large sacks, and for other rare things of the mountains and of the sea. A Pandya prince is asked by a poet to drink in peace the fragrant cool wine brought by the Greeks. Yavana of stern looks served as guards in the king's tent on the field of battle and at the gates of the Pandya capital. Again, Greeks had their own quarter in Kaviripadinnam of the Chola kingdom, and Greek carpenters helped to build a Chola king's palace. Ptolemy shows that nearly forty inland towns of the Tamils were known to Greek traders, who thus learnt, among other things, of the important beryl mines of India. Large quantities of Roman coins have been found near the mines of the Coimbatore district and in the marts from Cannanore to Pudukkottai.[53]

With the seaway to India thus known and open to all, it was only a matter of time before western ships were venturing still farther east, to Burma, Malay, and Indonesia. Now as before, it was mainly the Greeks and not the Latin-speaking races of Roman Italy who sailed these far waters. As an indication of Mediterranean penetration of Oriental regions lying nearly a third of the way around the world, there is reasonably reliable evidence that a Greek sea captain bearing the familiar name of Alexander rounded the tip of the Malay Peninsula, crossed the Gulf of Siam to Laos and Vietnam, and finally reached the southernmost border of China. But just who Alexander was, whence he hailed, in what period he lived, and even to any

[53] M. Cary and E. H. Warmington, *op. cit.*, p. 81.

degree of certainty whether he actually came into touch with the Chinese, are all unknown. An explorer who is little more than a free-floating name in the annals of human history is hardly enough of a personality to find more than passing mention here. It should suffice to say that, by and large, the Great Explorers of the ancient Orient have been lost in the stream of time.

❧ VIII ❧

EXPLORATION BY
LAND

IT will not have escaped the reader's notice that all the voyages
of exploration by Greeks, Phoenicians, and Carthaginians
recounted in previous chapters were nautical expeditions that
seldom touched more than the thinnest fringe of the territories behind the coast. Except as the Nile led into it, the heart
of Africa remained unvisited by other than native Africans.
Until Alexander had opened up Hither Asia by force of arms,
the Mediterranean peoples had no fuller knowledge of its vast
extent and variety than they could casually acquire from conversations with Persian officials. Europe north of the Alps and behind the Balkans was by no means steeped in utter barbarism;
yet so widely traveled and otherwise so well informed an investigator as Herodotus, writing at a time when all the coastal
world of the Mediterranean together with the immediately
nearer East and the Nileland were in mutual contact, could say
without apology or apparent embarrassment:

> While the foregoing are the known limits in Asia and Africa,
> I am unable to give any exact information about the limits
> to the West, in Europe. I do not allow that there is any natively
> named river Eridanos emptying into the northern sea . . . nor
> have I ever succeeded in getting firsthand word from anyone
> who has seen such a sea on the margin of Europe. . . . There
> appear to be quantities of gold in northern Europe; but I
> cannot say for certain that this is so. There is a story that one-
> eyed men called Arimaspi seize it from the griffins. But I do
> not believe this either, that there exist one-eyed men in other
> respects like the rest of humankind.[1]

[1] Herodotus, *History*, III.115–16.

Because no navigable seaway led from the Mediterranean into central Europe, neither Greek nor Carthaginian ever undertook to explore that continent. It is typical that, although Herodotus passed a number of years in southern Italy, he never learned anything about the land back of the long narrow peninsula's shoreland cities. The rest of Europe, as he admitted, was a closed book to him. One would have thought that the Greek merchants of Massalia, who lived close to the mouth of the Rhone and were much occupied with Celtic trade, would have traveled upriver into central France and founded trading posts among the Gallic towns. Yet there is no evidence that they did so. There is much wisdom in the oft-quoted remark that neither the ancient Greek nor his beloved olive tree ever flourished far from the sea. If a line is drawn on the map of Europe, keeping everywhere about a hundred miles inland from the nearest salt water, the world known to the Greeks, and dwelt in by them, will lie within that boundary.

Yet there is one slight exception to the rule that the Greek never went except where salt water led him.

If the sea may be called the "highway" of Greek travel and exploration, the larger rivers were its byroads and spurs, penetrating the continental interior but otherwise leading no farther. The rivers emptying into the Black Sea are the prime example. By navigating the Danube and the Black Sea rivers of Russia as far upstream as local conditions favored, the Greeks may have become familiar with narrow riverine stretches of country in Bulgaria and Rumania, in the Ukraine as far north as Kiev, and in the lowlands of the Don. But there is no indication that they took advantage of these paths of penetration to go ashore and explore on foot the regions to which their ships had brought them. There was no attempt at colonization or even at establishing trading settlements. A dominating instinct to hold to the sea explains the course of Greek history better than all the political chronicles of the textbooks. It also throws much light on the peculiar limitations and self-imposed restrictions in ancient Greek exploration.

Occasionally, prompted by the mass of archeological material accumulated in recent decades, students of Greek commerce and trade routes have imagined that Greek trade greatly outstripped Greek military and political expansion and, whether by concerted enterprise or individual effort, brought Greek merchants with their wares far inland in Europe and Asia. Had this been the case, these traders would have been explorers, and their inland journeys would have precisely paralleled those of their shipborne countrymen on the sea. But no such inference from archeological discoveries is valid. Obviously, the fact that objects of Greek manufacture (chiefly pottery, including wine jars, but also bronze work and gold and silver coinage) have been unearthed in significant quantities in most of the countries of central Europe from the Ukraine westward through Hungary, Austria, Germany, northern France, and the Lowlands does not in any way prove or even suggest that these objects were brought there by Greek traders in person. Commerce through the hands of middlemen has always characterized the Asiatic caravan trade from the earliest times almost to the present; and similarly the ancient trade routes that can be traced through the length and breadth of Europe illuminate only the mechanism of exchange for the distribution of Mediterranean products through other lands.

Just as the sea was the great highway of exploration and commerce, so the land was the highway of conquest. Only as exploration attended on military penetration of the interior of the continents and commercial expansion followed behind it, did the mountains and plains, the river valleys and the upland gorges, the lowland basins and upland plateaus, in all their complex physical variety, begin to equal the seas as passageways by which the Mediterranean habitants gained firsthand knowledge of the hitherto unknown lands around them.

Throughout the length and breadth of the European continent human beings have been existing ever since the retreating ice cap of the last Ice Age made all the land accessible and inhabitable 10,000 years ago. These dwellers in the European hills and valleys must have explored the forests and mountains and lake basins amidst which they built their huts and villages, a great many centuries before any Greek trader or Roman soldier set foot on their territory. But history—because it must depend on written record and cannot cope with the distant illiterate past of mankind—can tell us nothing about this primal exploration of Europe. What archeology is able to report on this subject goes much deeper in time; but it is necessarily fragmentary, fortuitous, and impersonal, so that no chronicle of specific exploration can be constructed from its findings. Not until armies from the Mediterranean literate world moved in, and historians showed interest in chronicling their campaigns, was anything accurately known about the geographical structure of the continental interior.

How little of the European interior had been even cursorily explored before the advent of the Roman armies united all but its northeastern quadrant to the Mediterranean world under the Roman emperor, may be deduced from the extreme ignorance of the Greek geographers about the origin of the Danube, a topic that remained almost as obscure to them as the sources of the Nile.

In the fifth century B.C., Herodotus held that the Danube "began from among the Celts and from the town of Pyrene, cleaving mid-Europe in its course." (Apparently he was thinking of Spain, because he elsewhere repeats this remark about the river, adding the information that "the Celts are outside the Pillars of Heracles, and border on the Cynesians, who live the farthest west of all the inhabitants of Europe"; and the "town of Pyrene" cannot be connected with anything unless it be the Pyrenees range). In the fourth century, Ephorus talked vaguely of the Danube as rising in the "Pillar of the North" (by which he may have meant the Swiss Alps), while Timaeus placed its origin in the Hercynian Forest (which might have had something to be said for it, had Timaeus had any notion of what he meant by "Hercynia"). An early-third-century source, passing as Timogenes, is reported as making the Danube issue from "a Celtic lake" (perhaps referring to Lake Constance, through which flows the Rhine and not the Danube, or the Lake of Geneva, through which the Rhone flows: the Danube itself is lakeless). At the opening of the second century B.C., the poet Apollonius of Rhodes had acquired no more exact information, since he set the source of the Danube in the "Rhipaean Mountains" (a "northern" range in which all the earlier Greek geographers firmly believed, without having any definite idea of what they meant by the term).

Still, some of this seeming ignorance is more a matter of imprecision in geographical nomenclature than of utter absence of correct information. There are instances in which the accuracy of the ancient geographers about matters where they could not possibly have had any firsthand knowledge is disconcerting. Thus, there was a widespread belief, persisting into advanced Roman times, that an arm of the Danube connected with the Adriatic Sea. This has often been cited by modern writers as a conspicuous example of ignorance and even gullibility in ancient geographical thinking. Of course, if the proposition is interpreted as meaning that a ship could pass from the Black Sea to the Adriatic by ascending a tributary of the Danube, it is completely false and even nonsensical. Yet, on a more lenient viewing, the ancient "delusion" proves to be essentially correct. One of the Danube's major tributaries is the Drave (or Drau), which joins the main riverstream about halfway between Budapest and Belgrade. If one follows the Drave upstream westward to its source, one reaches at last a marshy meadow high in the Italian Dolomites, so nearly level that the eye cannot detect the watershed that it forms. Yet, while water draining from its eastern edge starts the Drave on its long career, only a few hundred paces away the surface tilts imperceptibly toward the west to initiate a watercourse that finds its way to the Isarco and so to the Adige and thus empties at last into the Adriatic not far from the mouths of the Po. It is true that the passage from the Drave to the Adige is not navigable; but it is also true that there is unbroken connection by river valley between the Black Sea and the Adriatic by way of an "arm" of the Danube.

If this incidental detail proves anything, it shows that the Greeks took sufficient interest in European geography to cross-question non-Greek native informants, who passed on to them what they had learned from others still farther inland. To this extent, Europe was not a totally mysterious land of unknown empty spaces. But it also indicates that the Greeks themselves never journeyed there and made no attempt to explore its un-Mediterranean fastnesses. To them it was cold and wet and thoroughly unattractive.

Neither the Greeks nor their fellow Mediterraneans were in any way better informed about inland European Russia or its Asiatic steppeland.

There is a strange story in Herodotus about a Greek named Aristeas, inhabiting an island in the midst of the Sea of Marmora (about halfway between Troy and Constantinople). He

vanished from his native town under extremely mysterious circumstances, only to reappear after an absence of six years, asserting that during all that time he had been traveling inland
beyond the Black Sea among Scythian tribes and a people whom
he called the "Issidones." After composing an epic poem about
his experiences in these regions—the poem "which the Greeks
nowadays know as *The Arimaspea*," says Herodotus, who knew
its contents, though it seems to have been lost to the later Greek
and Roman public—Aristeas disappeared a second time, never
to be seen again except as some sort of ghostly apparition that
turned up in far-away southern Italy, claiming to be a companion and confidant of the god Apollo. The story, as Herodotus
recounts it, is too engagingly told to be omitted here:

> Aristeas, son of Kaystrobios, a man of Proconnesus,[2] writing
> poetry, says that under Apollo's inspiration he reached the land
> of the Issidones and that beyond these there dwelt one-eyed men,
> Arimaspi, and beyond these there were gold-guarding griffins,
> and yet beyond these the People-behind-the-Northwind, extend-
> ing to the seaboard. . . . I have just said whence the writer of
> this poetry came, and shall proceed to tell the tale about him
> that I heard in Proconnesus and in Cyzicus.[3]
>
> The story runs that Aristeas, who was one of the leading citi-
> zens, entered a cleaner's shop in Proconnesus and died there.
> The cleaner locked up his workplace and went to inform the
> dead man's next of kin. Now, the rumor had barely been spread
> through town that Aristeas was dead when a man of Cyzicus
> arriving from Artakē disputed the report, asserting that he had
> just met Aristeas on the road to Cyzicus and had words with
> him. While this man continued obstinately disputing the issue,
> the dead man's relatives turned up at the cleaner's shop with
> the gear for carrying away the corpse. Yet when the room was
> unlocked there was no sign of Aristeas, dead or alive!
>
> Six years later he reappeared in Proconnesus and proceeded
> to compose the poem which the Greeks nowadays know as *The
> Arimaspea,* on completion of which he disappeared a second
> time.
>
> Now, this is the tale as they tell it in the two towns; but the
> following is something I learned from chance encounter with
> inhabitants of Metapontum in [southern] Italy two hundred
> and forty years after Aristeas' second disappearance (as calcu-

[2] Today known as Marmora, an island in the Sea of Marmora.
[3] An ancient city on the isthmus leading to a peninsula on the Sea of Marmora.

lated by me in Proconnesus and in Metapontum). The Metapontines say that Aristeas showed up in their country in very
person and bade them establish an altar of Apollo and set up
beside it a statue bearing the name of Aristeas the Proconnesian.
He told them that Apollo was come only to them among all
the Greek communities of Italy and that he himself accompanied the god, even he that was Aristeas. At the time, however,
he had taken the shape of a raven. Having so said, he vanished.

The Metapontines say that they thereupon sent an embassy to
Delphi to inquire of the god what this apparition might mean.
The priestess enjoined them to do as the apparition said, for it
would be better for them if they obeyed. Accepting this advice,
they carried out the prescribed injunction. Accordingly there
stands to this day beside the image of Apollo a statue bearing
the name of Aristeas, with laurel bushes planted about it. The
image stands in the marketplace of Metapontum.

So much for Aristeas. But as for the country which I have
been discussing, no one knows for certain what lies beyond it;
for I have been unable to find anyone who says that he has himself seen it. Not even Aristeas made this claim, since in his poem
he did not say that he got any farther than the Issidones but was
recounting only by hearsay what there was beyond, the Issidones
being his informants.[4]

If Aristeas really made the journey claimed, he must have
taken ship through the Sea of Marmora and crossed the Black
Sea to the southern shore of Russia, proceeding inland thence,
at first perhaps by boat from the Sea of Azov up the river Don,
but in any case on foot thereafter. Such an expedition could
hardly have been attempted much earlier than the close of the
seventh century B.C. because—as already pointed out—it was not
until the early seventh century that Greek ships even began to
explore the Black Sea; and it was not until the end of that century that the violent inroads of Cimmerians and Scythians had
ceased and peaceful conditions had been established in the
Crimea and the adjacent Scythian land. Even at that time it
might not have been possible for a lone Greek traveler to wander
very far into Asia. We know little or nothing about a people or
tribe of Issidones, and can hardly fail to concur with Herodotus
in disbelieving in the existence of men with only one eye or
griffins that hoard gold. In consequence we might well be in-

[4] Herodotus, *History*, IV.13–16.

clined to dismiss Aristeas' poetic autobiography as Apolline moonshine and literary imposture, were it not that certain details in his poem suggest knowledge scarcely accessible to the Greek colonists and merchants of the Black Sea littoral in early times.

Modern critics have expressed an astonishing variety of opinions about Aristeas' performance. For some of them, the ruse of a mysterious disappearance from his native isle and the attendant claim to have wandered into Asia "possessed by Apollo" were a purely literary device to enhance the poem with pretense of divine inspiration and guidance and attach persuasion to a wholly fictitious exploit.

For others, despite these transparent tricks and idle pretenses, Aristeas' journey to the otherwise unknown Issidones actually took place. His six-year absence from his native land gave opportunity for a sojourn among inland Asiatic tribes sufficiently prolonged for him to acquire their language and learn their myths and legends about a race of men who had only one eye and stole the gold that griffins tried to guard. But in that case, his "north wind" must have been blowing from the east (there are numerous parallels among ancient writers for such a cardinal confusion of the compass points) and his gentle and civilized folk "behind the north wind" could actually have been the Chinese, of whose more fortunate existence the dwellers of the steppes might have had some distant knowledge. To subscribe to this hypothesis would be to make Aristeas the first great overland explorer among the ancient Greeks—hardly another Marco Polo, to be sure, yet almost that on a lesser scale!

As for his subsequent eerie manifestation in an opposite quarter of the ancient world in ghostly seance with citizens of Metapontum, we need not give this any credence in order to maintain our faith in Aristeas as a flesh-and-blood traveler.

Aristeas, with his strange behavior, his supernatural claims, his lost epic poem, his apparent knowledge of inner Asia, sets such insoluble problems, leading to such tenuous and indecisive conclusions, that he would not rate so much space here in a history of the ancient explorers were it not that our estimate of the man vacillates uneasily between two completely opposite verdicts as we ask ourselves, Was Aristeas a Great Explorer or a great humbug? To this query, unfortunately, there seems to be no ascertainable answer.

Aristeas apart, a genuine and indubitable exploration of southwestern Asia may be credited to the kings of ancient Persia, if political penetration backed by armed invasion is taken as a form of territorial exploration. Two among these kings were preeminent as military leaders. Cyrus the Great, by taking over the ruling power of the Medes, became the founder of the Persian empire, which he elevated to hitherto unrivaled greatness. Cyrus was succeeded by his son, Cambyses, whose ill-starred attempt to invade Nubia and to send an expeditionary force to the oasis of Ammon have been recounted in an earlier chapter. Cambyses was succeeded briefly by a pretender to the throne, who was slain by a group of more legitimate aspirants. From among these, Darius emerged as sole ruler, extending and consolidating his power through all the neighboring lands until he had created the greatest empire that the world had seen, reaching some three thousand miles from west to east and (on an average) more than one thousand miles from north to south, over a territory vaster even than Rome ever succeeded in dominating.

If these Persian kings in their role of commander in chief of their armed forces may be claimed as Ancient Explorers by virtue of their invasion of hitherto unfamiliar regions, the occasional glimpses that history affords of their expeditions must be added to the present record.

In the case of Cyrus, we can hardly reckon as exploration his march through Asia Minor to take Croesus captive and annex Lydia to the Persian realm, since his road led through abundantly familiar country. But when he turned his attention east to middle Asia, he was passing through regions of which the western world knew virtually nothing—only to come to grief near the northern border of Afghanistan, whither he had led his army in the vain expectation of subduing the wild Massagetae on the open arid plains of southern Turkestan. The tale as Herodotus tells it bulks too large to be repeated here in full. But no one who has read the *History* will have forgotten the bloodthirsty Massagetan queen Tomyris, how she made a sporting offer to Cyrus to fight him on either side of the great river Araxes, at his choice, how Cyrus tricked his adversaries by laying out for them an abundant meal "with bowls of undiluted wine in liberal measure," and how, after Cyrus had taken the queen's son prisoner by this ruse and the unfortunate youth had killed himself in chagrin, there ensued the grisly denouement, which (at least, as Herodotus tells it) is one of the most dramatically vivid incidents in all ancient history:

> So then Tomyris gathered together all her remaining forces and engaged Cyrus in a battle that in my estimation was the fiercest ever fought by a barbarian people. . . . But in the end the Massagetae gained the upper hand and destroyed the greater part of the Persian soldiery. And Cyrus himself was killed. Then Tomyris filled a leather bag with human blood and searched among the slain for the body of Cyrus, which having found, she did it great outrage, dipping his severed head into the bag and saying, "You took my son by trickery while I alive was getting the better of you in battle. Now—even as I warned you then—I shall give you your fill of blood!" Such was Cyrus' end.[5]

What Cyrus failed to accomplish, Darius succeeded in doing. He pushed the frontier of empire east of Afghanistan into India as far as the Indus river; and northward he added the great stretch of desert and arid plain between the Caspian Sea and Samarkand. How thoroughly this region had been explored by the close of Darius' reign may be judged from the remarkably exact information that Herodotus was able to gather from Persian officials and others with whom he came into conversation when he visited Babylon and Susa early in the fifth century B.C. As a specimen of the accuracy of geographical knowledge that the Persians possessed about the remoter regions of their empire, a passage in Herodotus may serve, in which he describes the country around the great body of inland water already known in his day as the Caspian Sea:

> The river Araxes flows from the land of the Matieni and discharges itself through forty channels, all but one of which empty into swamp and marshland reportedly inhabited by men who live on raw fish and dress in sealskins. The single remaining channel runs out unobstructed into the Caspian Sea. Now, the Caspian is an independent body of water without connection with the other sea. For the sea which the Greeks navigate, and that outside the Pillars of Heracles called the Atlantic, and the

[5] *Ibid.,* I.214.

Erythraean, are all one and the same; [6] but the Caspian is distinct unto itself. In length it is fifteen days' rowing, and in width eight days' rowing where it is widest. The Caucasus extends along its western shore. This is of all mountain ranges the most complex and the highest, containing many races of every sort, most of them living from wild forest land. . . . The Caucasus, then, shuts off the western borders of this Caspian Sea, while on its east there stretches an immense plain as far as the eye can reach. Most of this great steppeland is inhabited by the Massagetae, whom Cyrus tried to attack.[7]

This is all quite accurate and considerably better geography than Alexander the Great acquired two hundred years later, when (as Arrian reported)

he dispatched Heracleides, son of Argeios, into Hyrcania [8] taking shipwrights along with him under orders to hew timber on the Hyrcanian mountainsides and build longboats, some without deck and others decked over in the Greek fashion. For a desire had seized him to explore this sea also—to wit, the Caspian, which is also called the Hyrcanian Sea—in order to discover with what sea it was united, whether with the Black Sea or whether the Ocean spread around from India in the east and poured its water into this Hyrcanian Gulf—even as he had discovered that the Persian Gulf, known also as the Erythraean Sea, is an inlet of the Ocean. No one had hitherto discovered the sources of the Caspian Sea, despite the fact that numerous races dwell about it and navigable rivers empty into it. Thus, from Bactria the river Oxus, second greatest of Asia's rivers after the Indus, debouches into this sea, as does also the Iaxartes through Scythian territory; and most people hold that the Armenian Araxes flows into it. These are the chief; but there are a great many others, either tributary to these or reaching the sea independently. Of all these, some were known to Alexander's company as they advanced among the various tribes, whereas the rest, on the farther side of the Gulf among the nomad Scythians, were of course entirely unknown.[9]

Alexander's expedition to investigate the Caspian seems never to have got under way, so that this corner of the ancient world remained unexplored. Thus it was that Arrian (presumably

[6] He means they are all connected, while the Caspian is landlocked.
[7] Herodotus, *History,* I.202–4.
[8] The southeastern shoreland of the Caspian.
[9] Arrian, *Anabasis of Alexander,* VII.16.1–4.

quoting one or more of Alexander's chroniclers) could write
that "the Hyrcanian Sea too is a bight of the Ocean." Even in
advanced Roman times Strabo, and after him Arrian, believed
that the river Don (which empties into the Sea of Azov and thus
feeds the Black Sea) flowed "also into the Caspian" (perhaps
they confused the Tanais-Don with its immediate neighbor, the
Volga). Herodotus, long before, had already known better.

Alexander's invasion of Hither Asia through Iran, Afghanistan, and parts of Turkestan into northwest India—like Julius
Caesar's later military expeditions into northwest Europe—
should perhaps be included among ancient exploits of exploration. Certainly it may be claimed that neither Alexander nor
Caesar had any previous firsthand knowledge of the lands
through which they were obliged to find passage for their armies,
and in this sense they were conducting geographical exploration. On the other hand, Alexander was taking over, by default
to his superior military might, a largely civilized and adminis-
tratively well organized empire that had already been adequately
explored and was locally familiar to the Persian civil servants
controlling its revenues. And while Caesar wrote a commentary
about Gaul as a land strange to his Latin readers and displayed
genuine interest in its geographical and racial characteristics;
his campaigns in France, Flanders, and Britain were in no sense
undertaken for the furtherance of knowledge that might put
their leader in the ranks of the Great Explorers. On this reason-
ing, neither Alexander nor Caesar is a prominent figure in the
present volume.

However, certain other expeditions under Greek and Roman
generals into neighboring or more distant lands partook very
definitely of the nature of true exploration. Such was the retreat
of the Ten Thousand under the leadership of Xenophon (who
later published the vivid account of it known as *The Anabasis*).

The "Ten Thousand" were Greek mercenary soldiers whom
Cyrus the Younger had hired for an attempt to wrest the Persian
empire from its reigning monarch, his brother Artaxerxes II. All
went well on the long march inland (the "up-journey" from
which the book takes its title) from western Asia Minor to the
vicinity of Babylon, where the King's forces were encountered
and battle was joined. But then Cyrus was slain on the field
and the Greek commanding officers were treacherously mur-

dered by the Persian satrap Tissaphernes while they were negotiating with him for an armistice and safe-conduct back to Greece. In a desperate quandary, with the route by which they had come cut off by hostile Persian forces, the Greek survivors of the battle saw no avenue of escape except by retiring northward into the deep, wild mountainland from which the Mesopotamian river Tigris issues onto the desert plain. Kurdistan is still today a rude and remote country, whose inhabitants are jealous in defense of their right to keep their own laws and live their own way of life. No railroad has ever been built across its intricate network of harsh, high ridges and deep intervening river valleys, through which even passable highroads seldom lead. Through this terrible terrain in the depth of winter, safe from Persian pursuit but constantly harassed by hostile mountain tribes, the staffless mercenary army tried to break its way after electing new officers from the ranks. Chief among these makeshift captains was Xenophon, a well-educated Athenian who quickly showed that he had a gift for command and was later to prove that he possessed an equally great gift for vivid prose narrative. It took the hard-beset and starving band five months to find a way through the rugged uplands of Armenia, to sight at long last the shimmering Black Sea and to greet it with that famous shout of *"Thalassa! Thalassa!!"* [10] that has resounded down through the centuries wherever *The Anabasis* has been read.

This was true exploration, even though its compelling motive was not geographical curiosity but mere physical survival and desperate escape from calamity.

Another instance of inland military exploration through unknown country is the expedition to Arabia sent out by the emperor Augustus in the year 25 B.C. under command of the Roman prefect of Egypt, Aelius Gallus. The immediate object seems to have been either to add Arabia to the Roman empire (in which case Augustus could have had no notion of the huge size of this new "province") or, more probably, to put an end to Arabian molestation of the sea traffic with India by compelling the coastal tribes on either side of Aden to acknowledge Roman overlordship. On either score, the expedition was a failure except insofar as Rome acquired some geographical information

[10] "The sea! The sea!!"

about a part of the world of which she had hitherto been totally ignorant.

Strabo makes profession of close personal friendship with Aelius Gallus, claiming to have once accompanied him on an official journey up the Nile as far as the First Cataract. His account of the expedition against Arabia may therefore be accepted as adequately informed, though perhaps prejudiced toward accepting its leader's excuses for his own incompetence by laying the blame elsewhere. Here is Strabo's version:

> The recent expedition of the Romans against the Arabians, that took place in my own time under the leadership of Aelius Gallus, whom Caesar Augustus sent out to explore their tribes and their settlements . . . with intent either to win them over to Rome or subjugate them by force. . . . For he expected either to treat with prosperous friends or to overpower wealthy enemies. The hope encouraged him also that the Nabataeans, being friendly disposed, would keep their promises of cooperation.
>
> So, with all this in view, Gallus organized the expedition; but Syllaeus, who was administrator of the Nabataeans, deceived him. Although promising to act as guide on the march, to supply all necessities, and to make all arrangements, he behaved treacherously throughout. He failed to show them a safe route either by sea or on land, but led them astray on trackless and circuitous marches through regions utterly destitute or along rocky coasts without harbors, full of shoals and underwater reefs, where flood tide and ebb tide worked them woe.[11]
>
> Gallus' initial mistake was to construct warships when no naval war was either on or imminent; for the Arabians are merchants and traders without recourse to the sea. Yet Gallus constructed no less than eighty vessels, both two-banked and three-banked, at Suez where the old canal comes from the Nile. Then, when he realized his mistake, he proceeded to build a hundred and thirty transports. On these he set sail, carrying some ten thousand infantry of Romans and allied people of Egypt, including five hundred Judaeans and a thousand Nabataeans under Syllaeus. After fourteen days of untoward incidents he reached Leukē-Komē in the Nabataean land, a considerable trading port. He had lost many of his ships, some of them with

[11] Incidentally, it might be remarked that it was hardly Syllaeus' fault that Arabia was that sort of a land!

all men aboard, through poor seamanship, not war. This was due to Syllaeus' evil devices in asserting that Leukē-Komē could not be reached overland, in spite of the fact that traders' caravans make the journey thither from Petra and back to Petra in perfect safety and in such numbers as to differ little from an army on the march!

The truth of the matter was that the local king, Obodas, paid no heed to public affairs, especially where war was concerned (a common trait of all the Arabian rulers), but relied entirely on the provincial administrator, who was Syllaeus; and Syllaeus was a treacherous commander whose aim (in my opinion) was to explore the region in order to destroy various cities and tribes with Roman assistance and then make himself sole ruler of them all, once the Romans had been wiped out by hunger and weariness and sickness and whatever else he had treacherously contrived for them.

So Gallus put ashore at Leukē-Komē with his forces already plagued with scurvy of the mouth and paralysis of the legs, local ailments due to the drinking water and the plant food. In consequence he was obliged to spend the summer and ensuing winter there restoring the sick to health.

When Gallus at length got his army under way from Leukē-Komē, he had to march through such desolate country that even water had to be brought on camelback—but this was due to the baseness of his guides—so that it was only after many days that he reached the land of Obodas' kinsman Aretas. Now, Aretas welcomed him hospitably and gave him presents; but his country too was made difficult of passage by Syllaeus with his treacherous schemes. At any rate, he got through it in thirty days, even though it was trackless and offered only low-grade wheat and occasional palm trees and butter in lieu of olive oil. The next country through which he marched was inhabited by nomads and in very truth almost entirely desert. It was called Ararēnē; its king was Sabos; and Gallus consumed fifty days in getting through its roadless waste before he reached the city of the Negrani in a peaceable and fertile land. Here the local king took to flight, and the city was taken over by direct assault. Thence he marched in six days to the river.[12]

The same climatic factors that are responsible for the Sahara's desert condition—notably the year-round return of the trade wind to the equatorial zone—have rendered the heart of the

[12] Strabo, *Geography*, XVI.4.22–24.

great Arabian peninsula equally desolate. In contrast to this interior aridity, the coastal district adjoining the ocean waters of the Persian Gulf, the Gulf of Oman, the Arabian Sea, the Gulf of Aden, and the Red Sea—a circuit of nearly four thousand miles—is in general more amenable to settled life, though only the southernmost belt in Yemen and Hadramaut deserves the ancient epithet of *Arabia Felix*.[13] In the preceding account from Strabo, after the landing on the Arabian coast about a quarter of the way down the Red Sea (about level with the present city of Medina), Gallus has been keeping to the relatively livable inland strip near the sea, past the site of Mecca, and has finally reached the more fertile district of Yemen after taking between three and four months to cover a distance that, in direct line, measures little more than six hundred miles!

Strabo next mentions an encounter with the Negrani at "the river," in the course of which an incredibly large number of them was slaughtered without appreciable Roman losses. Thereafter two more "cities" were captured; whereas an attempt against a seemingly well fortified town called Marsiaba (which might be Marib near Sana on the modern map) was completely unsuccessful. But then, after having almost attained his objective on the coast of Aden, with the worst of his difficulties now behind him, Gallus suddenly abandoned all attempt at farther advance and turned back whence he had come:

> As he was informed by captured natives, he was now but two days' march from the spice lands. But he had already used up six months on his undertaking by reason of improper guidance— as he realized when he marched back by a different route and discovered how he had been plotted against. For on the way back he accomplished in sixty days the entire journey that had previously taken six months!
>
> So he shipped his forces across [the Red Sea] to Myos Hormos,[14] proceeded overland to Coptos,[15] and disembarked at Alexandria all who had managed to survive. Only seven men had perished in engagements; the rest were lost, not to the enemy, but to disease and exhaustion and starvation and the wretched roads. Because of these, the expedition did not add

[13] "Fertile Arabia."
[14] At the mouth of the Gulf of Suez.
[15] On the Nile.

much to geographical knowledge. Nevertheless it made some slight contributions.[16]

Strabo closes his account with the remark that Syllaeus, who had been chief cause of the expedition's troubles, was subsequently beheaded (without doubt to the entire satisfaction of Aelius Gallus).

All in all, it is a dreary tale of ignorance and ineptitude heightened by lack of that chance stroke of good fortune which sometimes crowns the unworthy with success and fame. No further attempt was made to explore Arabia overland by any Roman emperor, with the result that all inner Arabia remained an unknown land for European geographers until quite recent times. But the Roman ships (under Greek and Syrio-Phoenician captains) continued to sail to India. For the seas were open and the ocean was the highway of commerce, even as it had been the highway of the ancient explorers.

[16] Strabo, *Geography*, XVI.4.24.

INDEX